# The
# Good Beach Guide

**A guide to over 450 of Britain's best beaches**

*Updated by*
**Jenny Norman**

*From work done by*
**Dr. Anne Scott**
**and**
**Richard Caines**

*Marine Conservation Society*

EBURY PRESS 🙶 LONDON

The editor would like to acknowledge the huge amount of work done by Anne Scott and Richard Caines in setting up the Good Beach Guide, and to thank the following people for providing information and help in producing this edition: Lyn Tomlinson and other MCS staff, district and local councils, the National Trust, tourist authorities, coastal wardens and members of the Marine Conservation Society.

Published by Ebury Press
an imprint of the Random Century Group
Random Century House 20 Vauxhall Bridge Road London SW1V 2SA

First impression 1988
Reprinted twice 1988
Revised and updated 1989
Revised and updated 1990
Revised and updated 1991

Illustration by Kate Simunek
Front cover by Trevor Wood © Image Bank
**British Library Cataloguing in Publication Data**
The good beach guide. – New ed.
  1. Great Britain. Beaches
  I. Norman, Jenny (Editor) II. Marine Conservation Society
  551.4'57'0941

  ISBN 0-71264-703-1

Typeset in Souvenir by Textype Typesetters, Cambridge
Printed and bound in Great Britain at The Bath Press, Avon

# Contents

All information received from local authorities, the National Rivers Authority and water companies up to 1 January 1991 has been included in this revised edition. Marine Conservation Society and Ebury Press take no responsibility for data that has been altered and amended after *The Good Beach Guide 1991* has been compiled.

**MARINE CONSERVATION
SOCIETY**

# Foreword
## by David Bellamy

A day trip or holiday at the seaside is a traditional summertime activity for many British families and visitors to our country. Weather permitting, a paddle or swim in the sea can be an additional treat and add to the fun.

Sadly, however, a visit to the seaside nowadays is not always the pleasure it should be. Instead of golden sands and a clear blue sea, you may well be confronted with beach and waters spoilt by oil, rubbish, and even raw sewage. All too often the sea is used as an outlet for the waste products of our society which means that many of our beaches fall far below the standard established by the EC for safe bathing.

**Q** Why, in 1991, should we be faced with the problem of bathing in our own, and other peoples', diluted sewage?

**A** We shouldn't, and money *must* be found to alleviate the problem. Simply dumping further out to sea is not the answer.

**Q** Why should we throw away multi millions of tonnes of potential energy and potential organic fertiliser and cause massive pollution of the sea at the same time?

**A** We shouldn't. We should be using our rubbish and our sewage in the cogeneration of energy and the manufacture of organic soil conditioners.

By buying this book you will be supporting the very important work of the Marine Conservation Society who are coming up with the right answers, thus protecting the marine world for us all to enjoy.

HAPPY HOLIDAY

7

**The Marine Conservation Society** is a rapidly expanding national conservation organisation formed to protect Britain's seashore and coastal waters by campaigning and lobbying on issues which threaten the seas. It also undertakes research and education to help develop a better understanding of the marine environment. Already the Society can be proud of its achievements. It forced a ban on competitive spearfishing which threatened to decimate fish stocks in inshore areas. It successfully fought to have marine nature reserves included in the Wildlife and Countryside Act and has already seen the first statutory reserves declared – Lundy Island and Skomer Island. It has actively promoted the creation of voluntary marine conservation areas, the most recent being the Seven Sisters in Sussex. The Society has achieved a major victory in the fight against pollution by getting the Government to ban the use of anti-fouling paint containing the poisonous chemical TBT. Joining forces with the Coastal Anti-Pollution League, it has forced the authorities to increase the amount of money spent on cleaning up our bathing waters.

The Society is currently tackling the pollution problems of the North Sea, quality of our beaches, the threats to sharks, the trade in corals and shells and the impact of fish farming on our coastal waters.

Membership is £12.00 a year (see page 207) and you will receive the quarterly magazine 'Marine Conservation'.

Help make the proper protection of our seas, their resources and their wildlife a reality. Join the Society now.

**Heinz** is a major sponsor of British conservation programmes and has been closely involved with The Good Beach Guide since its initial launch in 1988.

For many years Heinz has recognised the environmental responsibilities of its factories and offices. As a company it is committed to protecting the environment and this is very much part of its overall drive towards a cleaner, safer and healthier world. In 1986, its centenary year, Heinz launched a major conservation programme entitled Guardians of the Countryside. Its objective has been to protect those wildlife species and habitats in danger.

The programme has supported many conservation projects including funding of coastal wardening at several sites; sponsorship of a marine conservation officer to co-ordinate national campaigns and the Marine Conservation Society's Coastal Directory.

Through the programme protection of a number of important marine sites has been achieved, including the Helford River and sites in Devon, Dorset and Northumberland as well as the purchase of Cape Cornwall (including Priest's Cove) for the National Trust.

8

# Introduction

Everyone's expectations of a day at the seaside are different. Some people look for quiet and solitude, an escape from the hustle and bustle. Others look for just the opposite – amusements and bright lights, sun-bathing by day and dancing by night.

Britain has more than 7,000 miles (11,000km) of coastline, with literally thousands of beaches, varying from long, sweeping sandy bays gently lapped by sparkling clear water to tiny rocky coves. There are banks of groyne-ribbed shingle, flat golden sands pounded by Atlantic rollers, and secluded coves ringed by cliffs with rocky outcrops and pools waiting to be explored. In addition, there are the resort beaches, traditional promenades with their Victorian piers, pavilions, bandstands, fun-fairs and amusements.

### 'Why is my favourite beach not included in the guide?'

We have not attempted to describe every British beach; the beauty of many is the very fact that they remain undiscovered. The guide is a selection, a mere 156 of Britain's beaches, a mixture of popular holiday resorts, quieter secluded bays and some faraway places – hopefully a beach to suit every taste. Use the guide as a starting point for exploring the delights of our beautiful coastline. Part of the fun is searching out your own personal favourite.

For beaches which are not featured, the Golden List within each regional chapter may be of help too, but again, this is a mere starting point. However, some very good beaches *are* missing from the guide because water quality monitoring by the water authorities or River Purification Boards found that they did not meet the minimum European Community standard for clean bathing water. Details of all the monitored beaches are given in the Golden List within each regional section.

Any beaches where there have been reports of significant pollution of the shore, whether industrial or domestic, are also excluded. We have not included beaches where there is major industrial development on the shore, beaches which are shadowed by power stations,

9

construction yards, refineries, or gas and oil terminals. If a beach is used for military purposes, there are times when it is dangerous, with restricted access and therefore cannot be considered as a good beach.

In choosing good beaches we also felt that they had to be reasonably accessible; having to scramble down wet cliffs is probably not the ideal way to start a relaxing day on the beach. Beaches should also have reasonable parking facilities for beach users. Parking on narrow roads and verges should be avoided; it is not only very damaging, but also causes problems for the local people, rescue services and other visitors.

### The Blue Flag Award

The Blue Flag Award is part of the programme of awards for good beaches run by the Foundation for Environmental Education in Europe. The Blue Flag is awarded to beaches which have a high standard of water quality, are cleaned daily during the bathing season and have good facilities, toilets, life-saving equipment, first aid etc. On these beaches there is strict control of domestic animals, and driving or racing on the beach are prohibited. Provision is also made for environmental education, public information and safety.

Twenty-nine British beaches received the Blue Flag award in 1990. The next annual Blue Flag Awards will be announced in June 1991. Look out for the latest winners.

### Visiting Beaches

There is intense pressure at many beauty spots where the number of people visiting the beach and surrounding area leads to damage, particularly when cars are parked close to the beach. Sand dunes are particularly vulnerable; their protective covering of marram grass is easily damaged and, once lost, the wind blows the sand away, destroying the dunes. Only by taking care of what is often a fragile environment will we be able to continue to enjoy the unspoilt beauty of our coastline. So please remember to follow the seashore code:

TAKE NOTHING BUT PICTURES
WASTE NOTHING BUT TIME
LEAVE NOTHING BUT FOOTPRINTS.

### Help us to help you

If, on a visit to any of these beaches, you find pollution problems or changes in facilities, please write to the Society and let us know.

# Marine Pollution

Over the past few years the deaths of thousands of common seals, massive blooms of algae, and the deaths and breeding failure in seabird colonies on Orkney and Shetland, have highlighted the problems of our seas as never before. The causes have been the subject of fierce debate but few would deny that pollution is a major threat to the health of our seas and wildlife, and that something must be done to clean them up.

Pollution occurs when we introduce any substance into the sea which is harmful to wildlife, threatens human health or reduces marine activities and amenities. An enormous range of such substances enters our seas – deliberately, accidentally, or through sheer negligence – often creating pollution problems far from their source.

Golden sands littered with rubbish, raw sewage at the water's edge, oil on the rocks and lumps of tar on your flip-flops. These are the highly visible signs for the holiday maker. But there are other pollutants which remain unseen – for example, poisonous chemicals, pesticides and radioactivity. Such pollutants themselves may be invisible but their effects are not, and they can be equally, or more, damaging. The sea has no fences and therefore the effect of a pollutant never occurs in isolation – it spreads through the environment, combining with other pollutants to create a highly poisonous cocktail.

### Types of Marine Pollution

Waste can be classed under three main types: domestic, industrial and agricultural. *Domestic waste* includes sewage, silt, oil, lead, tar and de-icing chemicals which are used on the roads. *Industrial waste* includes, for example, radioactive waste, toxic chemicals, thermal discharges, refuse and oil from ships, as well as degradable organic waste from the paper, pulp and food processing industries. *Agricultural waste* – fertilisers, herbicides, and organic matter – is all potentially dangerous. Other pollutants that must also be considered are discarded pyrotechnics (e.g. ships' flares and distress rockets),

11

drugs, and chemicals leaked from the hulls of ships.

For years the sea has been used as a cheap and easy waste disposal system on a vast scale. Nine million tonnes of sewage sludge (the by-product of sewage treatment works), 42 million tonnes of dredged spoil – the silt removed from harbours and estuaries to keep them clear for shipping – and over 2 million tonnes of industrial waste, including coal waste and fly ash, are dumped off the UK shore each year. The wastes also contain high levels of chemical contamination with the result that the North Sea, for example, receives over 10 tonnes of mercury, 12 tonnes of cadmium, 1250 tonnes of lead and 200 tonnes of copper each year.

## Sources of Pollution

The source of a pollutant may be easy to identify – an outfall pipe or dump ship deliberately discharging waste into the sea. Waste also enters the sea via rivers, from ships, in land run-off, and from the atmosphere. Some of the sources are easy to locate, others are less easy to define and hence control. An estimated 5 million tonnes of oil enter the sea each year, but only 4% comes from major tanker accidents. The majority is released during routine shipping and oil refining operations. In many cases individual pollution incidents are neither obvious nor devastating to the local area. However, their cumulative effect means that all the trade routes and ocean currents abound with tar balls, many of which will eventually end up on beaches.

The sources of pesticides and other agricultural chemicals which find their way into streams, rivers and eventually the sea are difficult to locate accurately. These chemicals, particularly the organochlorines like aldrin and dieldrin, are extremely stable and persistent. They accumulate in the sea and have been found in virtually all marine mammals and in humans.

## The Effects of Pollution

In some cases the effects of pollution are easy to identify and link to specific causes. Plastics discarded overboard entangle wildlife causing death by drowning or strangulation. It has been estimated that 2 million seabirds and 100,000 marine mammals are killed each year due to marine debris, either by eating it or becoming entangled in it. The death of a marine animal may not be as easily attributed to marine litter if the animal has eaten the refuse and died either because of some poisonous chemical in the waste or starvation due to a permanently full stomach. On the shoreline, where much refuse ends up, it remains a hazard for wildlife and the holiday-maker.

The consequences of oil pollution are not only the obvious oiled seabird or oil-spotted sands; there are also toxic effects. Water-soluble chemicals in oil are poisonous to animals and plants. The dumping of solid wastes also causes direct physical damage to marine life, smothering animals and plants, but as with many pollution problems there are combined effects. For example, dredged spoil is highly contaminated with chemicals. Dumping wastes offshore not only does physical damage to the environment but the chemicals are released and may poison wildlife, or affect their growth and reproduction.

Thousands of chemicals like mercury (used in the paper and pulp industry), lead from petrol, titanium dioxide (a whitener in the paint industry), polychlorinated biphenols (found in electrical components), pesticides like organochlorines (eg DDT) are released into the sea and have been found in all marine life. They have been linked to fish diseases, the disappearance of species and breeding failure.

In very low concentrations the chemicals may have minimal effect but the danger increases as they become concentrated up the food chain. A single shrimp may have a tolerable amount of a chemical in its body but when a fish eats lots of shrimps it absorbs all the chemicals from each shrimp and the result can be lethal. For example, around Minamata Bay in Japan, 46 people died and 2,000 people suffered from crippling mental and physical deformities. The tragedy was the result of eating shellfish from the bay which had accumulated methyl mercury released to the waters from a local factory.

Sewage is a particular problem that has direct effects on beaches and bathers. Over 300 million gallons (1350 million litres) of sewage are disposed of in our coastal waters each day; most is untreated or receives only primary treatment. It is frequently discharged close to the shore and the raw sewage, often including toilet paper, fat balls and other nuisance solids, is washed back on to the beach with each incoming tide. This is not only very unsightly but also harmful to health. The sewage contains bacteria and viruses that can cause a number of infections so that an upset stomach or bad throat suffered on holiday might have been caused by swimming in polluted water or eating shellfish that had accumulated the bacteria as they filtered the sea water to feed.

The discharge of sewage also has effects on marine life. The decomposition of the sewage requires oxygen, and the reduction in oxygen that occurs as the sewage is broken down can lead to a decline in the number and variety of plants and animals. This can also result from the high nutrient input from sewage, when plankton and vegetation bloom at the expense of less tolerant species. As the algal colonies die, they break up and create foam which is frequently washed up on to the shore.

There has been much debate about the final fate and the effect of the many pollutants that find their way to our seas. Much, however, remains largely unknown. Are the problems we are seeing now the result of pollution? Are the algal blooms caused by the high nutrient inputs from sewage and agriculture? Where did the seal virus originate? We need more information about marine pollution problems and a better understanding to help us answer these questions and protect the sea.

## Pollution Control

There are several international and national agreements which aim to control pollution. The problem with many of these agreements is achieving their successful implementation. For example, the International Agreement on the Prevention of Marine Pollution from Land (the Paris Commission, 1974) lists a series of chemicals that must only be discharged in 'trace amounts'. It is the interpretation of this definition that has caused problems in its implementation. The International Convention for the Prevention of Pollution from Ships (MARPOL 73/78) and its five annexes were originally drawn up in 1973. But they were only to come into force when enough countries, representing 50% of the world's shipping tonnage, signed each part of the agreement. Until then it could be effectively ignored even by those that had signed. The convention and Annexes 1 and 2 were agreed and became law in 1978. It was not until the end of 1987, ten years later, that the United States signed Annex 5, concerning dumping of refuse from ships. This took the tonnage over the 50% mark, making the annex law 12 months later in December 1988.

As of 1st January 1989 it became illegal to dispose of any plastic from ships at sea. Added to this, other forms of garbage, biodegradable food waste etc, can only be discharged at sea under strictly controlled conditions. The refuse now has to be deposited at special reception facilities which should have been set up at ports and harbours. It is hoped this will improve the colossal problem of marine litter. Unfortunately the law only applies to the countries who have signed the annex (approximately 75% of the world fleet). How the regulations are to be enforced remains to be seen. Annexes 3 and 4 of the convention are not yet ratified by sufficient countries.

The European Community too has introduced legislation to control pollution, but there have been problems with the implementation of these regulations also. The Directive on Discharges into the Aquatic Environment, which attempted to stop dumping, was never introduced because of a UK veto. The EC Bathing Water Directive was introduced in 1976 when, after three years and much persuasion, Britain designated its 'bathing beaches'. It designated only 27. France designated 1498, Italy 3308, and even Luxembourg, with no coastline, came up with more bathing sites than Britain – 34. Resorts such as Brighton and Blackpool (without a doubt one of the largest bathing resorts in Europe) did not feature within the 27, indicating a lack of commitment to the spirit of the Directive. It was not until 1987, after much criticism, that the Government yielded to pressure and the number was increased to 391.

By 1990 this had risen to 446, but this should not encourage complacency – the Marine Conservation Society has more than three times this many 'bathing beaches' on record. The problem is that of defining and agreeing on terms and such dogma has plagued the EC Bathing Water Directive throughout its existence. Even now, there is no standard European interpretation of the directive and thus the results from each EC country are not comparable.

In the past, pollution control has very much been the implementation of regulations to solve problems when they have been proved to be damaging the environment.

If we are to solve the problems of our seas, however, we must adopt a precautionary approach. This acknowledges that we do not know the effects of all substances that are discharged and that we should therefore err on the side of caution and not discharge these materials, even if there is no scientific evidence that they actually cause damage. Widely accepted throughout Europe, this concept is only just beginning to be given consideration in the UK.

Governments are beginning to realise that the sea is not infinite and we cannot continue to use it as a huge dustbin. International agreements are being reached, often due to the pressure from people like you and me. Industry, bowing to opinion and legal enforcement, is slowly cleaning up its act. As 1992 and the Single European Market approaches, legislation from Brussels will have increasing influence in the UK and this too may bring environmental gain. However, there is still a long way to go, and if we are to enter the 21st century with cleaner seas it is up to everyone who goes down to the shore to keep an eye out for any pollution and to report it to the water authority, environmental health department, local council, MP and the Marine Conservation Society.

15

# Where Land Meets Sea

## S. GUBBAY

*Senior Conservation Officer at the Marine Conservation Society*

The best time for exploring a beach is when the tide is out. It is especially interesting then to walk down to the water's edge, where you can get a glimpse of the plants and animals which live permanently submerged by the sea.

## At the Edge of the Sea

At the edge of rocky shores you may be able to see the tops of kelp plants bobbing on the surface of the water. These are large brown seaweeds which form underwater forests just beyond the level of the lowest tide down to a depth of 50 feet (15m). Just like an oak tree in a forest on land, kelp plants provide shelter and food for animals. They also provide a firm surface on which a variety of seaweeds and animals will attach themselves. The leafy parts of the kelp plant are known as fronds and a close look at these will usually reveal an encrusting layer of delicate grey-coloured 'sea mats'. These are colonies of very small animals which are an important source of food, particularly for the many snails which wander over the surface of the kelp. The multi-coloured top shells also take advantage of this food so these can be found in large numbers on the kelp. Another species which can be seen on the fronds is the attractive Blue-rayed Limpet. It may only be half an inch (1cm) long but is quite distinctive because of the iridescent blue stripes along the length of its shell.

Kelps do not have true roots like land plants. Instead they attach themselves to the rock surfaces by means of a 'holdfast'. This provides an ideal shelter for small animals which can live amongst its branches. A closer look will reveal brittle-stars, sponges, and even small shrimp-like animals.

Underneath the kelp plants, where less light penetrates, red seaweeds are common. Many have delicate branches and resemble land plants but often the most common, although least obvious, are the encrusting red seaweeds. These species form a thin covering over rock surfaces, making them appear pink. They can be widespread, particularly where there are many sea urchins, as the urchins are

16

efficient at grazing away most other species of seaweed.

The Common Sea Urchin is one of the most distinctive animals you might find under the kelp and amongst the red seaweeds. It can be as large as 6 inches (15cm) in diameter, which makes it one of the world's largest urchins. The spiky surface is very obvious and some of the spikes have small pincers at the ends to act as additional discouragement for predators. Because of their efficient grazing powers sea urchins have a considerable influence on the type of kelp forest that develops, so it is particularly important not to collect them.

The water's edge is also a good place to look for fish. One species that comes close inshore to lay its eggs during the summer months is the Lumpsucker. This is a large, round-bodied fish with rows of lumps along its side. The male, which has a distinctive bright orange belly during the breeding season, guards the eggs until they hatch, even if they were laid near low water. If you are lucky you might find one on the lower shore. Another fish you are likely to find is the Butterfish. It has an eel-like body, up to 8 inches (20cm) long, with distinctive dark spots along the body. These fish depend on camouflage for protection so usually lie very still on the surface of a rock.

## The Shore Between the Tides

Further up the beach is the area uncovered by every tide. Animals and plants that live here have to survive extreme conditions. They have to contend with the full force of storm waves breaking on the beach, and the danger of drying out on hot sunny days while the tide is out. To cope with the latter many of the animals of the intertidal zone are likely to be hiding or tightly closed at low tide. The best places to find them are the damp areas between rocks, under overhangs and beneath stones and boulders. The shore crab in particular likes to hide in these places, but you might also find starfish, small shrimp-like animals and snails. Remember these animals are in shaded places to stop them drying out so, after having a look, return them to the same area so that they can survive until the tide comes in. Overhangs are the place to look for sponges but don't expect to find them the size of a bath-sponge! They are usually spread like a mat over the rock surface, although you can see the pores through which they circulate seawater to feed.

One conspicuous animal you are likely to find on a rocky shore is the Beadlet Anemone. It comes in a variety of colours ranging from red to green and yellowy-brown. Its surface is covered with a slimy film to prevent drying out during low tide. The anemone feeds by extending its tentacles and catching small animals.

17

The animals on the open rock are better able to withstand drying out. Limpets, for example, clamp themselves down tightly against the rock face while the tide is out; whereas barnacles, which are permanently attached to the rock, close the valves at the top of their shells. When they are covered with water these valves slide apart and the barnacle, which looks like a shrimp lying on its back, sticks its legs out of the top to catch food. Amongst the barnacles you will probably find Dog Whelks. These are smaller versions of the Edible Whelk and measure up to 1 inch (2.5cm) in height. Dog Whelks feed on barnacles and mussels by boring a hole through their shells and sucking out the contents. Their diet is thought to influence shell colour, so Dog Whelks feeding on barnacles tend to have a light coloured shell, and those feeding mainly on mussels can have a shell with dark bands. Clusters of pale yellow egg cases of the Dog Whelk are easy to find if you look beneath overhangs or in damp crevices.

## Rock Pools

In some rocky intertidal areas pools of sea water remain after the tide has dropped. These rock pools are some of the most interesting places to look for marine life. They not only contain typical rock pool species but also offshore animals that have been stranded until the next tide.

The variety of life in a rock pool depends on its size. Deep, large pools can be a suitable habitat for some of the kelps but perhaps the seaweed most frequently seen in rock pools is the Coralweed. This small, tufty red seaweed has a chalky skeleton and grows around the edge of the rock pool along with encrusting red seaweeds that make the rock surface appear pink. Rock pools are well-known haunts of shrimps but you can also find small fish like the Blenny and Goby, along with starfish, mussels and sea anemones.

## Sandy Beaches

The sandy shores we head for when looking for a good beach can be very hostile areas for marine life. Areas where the sand is coarse dry out quickly and do not contain much organic material for food. As the sand grains get finer the sandy shores become more hospitable to marine life. These conditions limit the variety of animals which live on sandy beaches and those that do usually bury themselves into the sand while the tide is out. Despite this it is possible to find the hiding places of the animals by the clues they leave behind.

The Sand Mason Worm is a frequent inhabitant of many sandy

beaches and can be found near the low water mark. It lives in a tube which it builds from coarse sand and fragments of shells. This projects above the beach surface as a ragged-edged tube. On some beaches large areas of the lower shore are covered by these tubes with perhaps more than 25 in a square yard (metre). The Lug Worm also provides a clue of its whereabouts on the surface of the sand. These worms live in burrows, leaving a conspicuous cast on the surface around the hole. A more obvious worm which can be found on sandy beaches where there are outcrops of rock is the Honeycomb Worm, found on southern and western coasts of Britain. Each worm forms a tube of coarse sand on the surface of the rock and in this way 'reefs' many yards across are built up.

One of the larger animals that lives buried in the sand is the Sea Potato or Heart Urchin. This hairy looking, sandy coloured ball is a sea urchin but unlike the Common Sea Urchin of rocky areas it has a distinctive head and tail end. The Sea Potato tunnels its way through the sand, feeding on small particles of organic matter. At the same time it maintains a channel to the surface through which water is drawn for respiration. The Masked Crab has a somewhat similar life style. It also lives buried in the sand and uses its two long antennae to form a tube to the surface, bringing down sea water from which it can extract oxygen.

Some of the more muddy beaches are colonised by 'beds' of Sea Grasses. These are flowering plants just like those found on land, and are able to survive when totally submerged by the tide. They produce small flowers during spring and summer, and it is also possible to find the seeds attached. Sea Grass beds provide shelter for a variety of juvenile fish and it is possible to find Cuttlefish eggs and small Stalked Jellyfish attached to the leaves. These areas can be damaged by trampling so do try and walk around the edges of any Sea Grass beds.

## The Strand Line

The strand line is a popular haunt for beachcombers because there is always something new brought in with every high tide. It is a particularly interesting area to explore after stormy weather because seaweeds and animals found in deeper waters are washed ashore. Among the more common types of animals you will find in this area are jellyfish. Often swarms are washed up on the beach, where, without the support of the seawater, they lose all shape and look like a lump of jelly. Some jellyfish can still sting so don't touch them with bare hands. Along with other dead animals, they are soon cleaned away by gulls, crabs and even small snails.

**19**

The Sand Hopper is a common animal to be found near the strand line. It lives in burrows or under seaweeds and emerges at night to feed on any debris which has been brought in with the tide. It gets its name from its habit of springing away when disturbed.

## Nature Conservation on the Coast

The coast around the British Isles is under continual pressure from urban, industrial and recreational uses. The sea and shore are also a source of food and minerals and are often used for waste disposal. These competing demands have made it necessary to ensure that areas which have special features are not lost or damaged. This can only be achieved by management of the coastal zone, and there is a network of protected and designated areas to help achieve this.

There are 38 stretches of undeveloped coastline of high scenic quality in England and Wales, totalling 785 miles (1263km), which have been designated as Heritage Coasts by the Countryside Commission. The Scottish Development Department has defined 22 Preferred Conservation Zones, areas considered to be of environmental, scenic or ecological importance. Often these areas are also designated as Areas of Outstanding Natural Beauty in England, Wales and Northern Ireland or National Scenic Areas in Scotland. These various designations do not give specific protection but there are management plans drawn up which are referred to when local developments are being considered.

In addition, several thousand Sites of Special Scientific Interest have been identified because of their flora, fauna, geology or physiography. They are not managed reserves but any development by the private landowner should be reported to the Nature Conservancy Council and potentially damaging operations can be restricted. There are also a wide range of reserves with coastal sections that are managed to protect their environment – for example National Nature Reserves, County Conservation Trust, Royal Society for the Protection of Birds and local authority reserves.

However, all these designated conservation sites are for the management and protection of features above the tide line. The area below high water mark is owned by the Crown and managed by the Crown Estates Commission. Until recently even the most outstanding sites for marine life had no legal protection.

One method being used to afford some protection to the marine environment is the establishment of Voluntary Marine Conservation Areas. These are areas where some form of consultative/management group has been set up to bring together organisations and individuals involved with the sea, whether for work or recreation. Their aim is to promote harmonious use of the area, while preventing deterioration of the quality of the marine environment and the life it supports. There are nine of these Voluntary Marine Conservation Areas; five in England – Helford River, Roseland, Wembury, Purbeck and the Seven Sisters; two in Wales – Bardsey Island, Skomer Island; one in Scotland – St Abb's Head; and one in Northern Ireland – Strangford Lough.

Since 1981, it has been possible to set up legally protected Marine Nature Reserves. The first one was declared in November 1986, around the island of Lundy which lies off the coast of Devon, an area which is particularly rich and varied in its marine life. In 1990 the second Marine Nature Reserve around Skomer Island off the Pembrokeshire coast was designated and at least five more Marine Nature Reserves are planned around the country. These are likely to be at the special places along our coast but we still have a responsibility to be thoughtful when we explore the beach wherever we are. The Marine Conservation Society's 'Seashore Code' is a useful guide to help you enjoy exploring the coast while keeping it intact for those who follow you.

# *Seashore Code*

* SHOW RESPECT FOR SEA CREATURES
* TAKE YOUR RUBBISH HOME WITH YOU
* TAKE PHOTOS, NOT LIVING ANIMALS
* DRIVE ON ROADS, NOT BEACHES
* BE CAREFUL NEAR CLIFFS
* AVOID DISTURBING WILDLIFE

# Coastal Paths

### DR CAROLYN HEEPS

*Conservation Officer*

Walking is the best way to appreciate the seascape and rich diversity of plant and animal life around the coastline of the British Isles. Parts of Britain's 7,000 miles (11,000km) of coastline are owned or managed by conservation bodies such as the National Trust, RSPB and County Wildlife Trusts while other areas, although in private ownership, are within designated National Parks, Areas of Outstanding Natural Beauty and Heritage Coasts; most allow access via a network of public footpaths and bridleways, many of which follow long stretches of the coastline. It is worth getting away from the hustle and bustle of the main tourist resorts in order to explore and appreciate breath-takingly beautiful scenery and the rich and varied wildlife – linger a while on a prominent headland, look out to sea, and you may be rewarded with a glimpse of dolphins or basking sharks.

### Planning and Preparation

Footwear is vitally important. Don't be tempted to walk any distance in beach sandals; a good pair of trainers may be adequate for a stroll along a well-used path but for more serious walking over more rugged terrain a pair of well-fitting comfortable walking boots is essential.

Invest in a map of the area; the Ordnance Survey produces a range of maps suitable for recreational and leisure purposes with footpaths and bridleways clearly marked. Alternatively, purchase a good local guidebook which details walks of varying distance over a range of terrains. Other essentials include a small rucksack for carrying food and drink, a First Aid kit and lightweight waterproofs – we all know how unpredictable the British weather can be! A pair of binoculars and a camera are useful if you have them – they enable you to get a good view of animal wildlife without disturbing them and photographs are a good reminder of an enjoyable walk. It is wise to plan your walk in advance – the local Tourist Board, National Trust office or any nearby nature reserve information centre will be able to give advice and details of local walks. They may also advertise guided walks in the company of an expert; guided walks are a good way of learning a lot about a specific site in a limited amount of time.

For those who enjoy walking holidays many long distance footpaths have coastal sections – indeed, some of Britain's finest footpaths are completely coastal.\* These paths are clearly marked on Ordnance Survey maps and are well signposted on the ground.

Above all enjoy your walk, whether it is a short, leisurely amble along a deserted beach or a hike along the rocky slopes of our wildest stretches of coastline. Remember the Seashore and the Country Codes and take time to enjoy the wonders of the marine environment.

\* The major coastal paths of the British Isles are marked on the maps in the regional sections.

# *Naturist Beaches*

This list contains all the information we have at present. There will be other beaches used by naturists which are not in the guide, and we should be glad to hear about them so that they may be included in future editions.

SOUTH-WEST – Wild Pear Beach, near Combe Martin, Devon.
Polgaver Bay, Carlyon Bay, Cornwall.
Pilchard Cove, Slapton Sands, Devon.
Labrador Bay, Shaldon, Devon.
Studland Beach (middle section), Dorset.

SOUTH-EAST – Brighton East Beach, Brighton, East Sussex.
Fairlight Cove, Hastings, East Sussex.
Long Rock Beach, Swalecliffe, Whitstable, Kent.
Shellness, near Leysdown, Isle of Sheppey, Kent.
St Osyth, Essex.
Corton Sands, near Lowestoft, Suffolk.
Holkham, Norfolk.

EAST COAST – Fraisthorpe Sands, Bridlington, North Humberside.

SCOTLAND – Ardeer Beach, Stevenston, Ayrshire.
Cleat's Shore, Lagg, Isle of Arran.

**23**

# Key to the Entries

## The Golden List

*The Golden List* gives at-a-glance information on any beach which is designated by the EC as a bathing water, any undesignated beach which is monitored by the local NRA unit, or any beach where there is a sewage outfall. Where an outfall is present, details of the treatment method, the population that the outfall serves and the location of the pipe itself is listed. *The Golden List* for each area is given at the beginning of the relevant section.

## Water Quality

The 1976 EC Bathing Water Directive specifies that designated bathing beaches in each EC country must be monitored throughout the bathing season (usually taken to be May – September) and their compliance to the Directive published. The UK government has chosen to base compliance of beaches on the levels of total coliform bacteria and faecal coliform bacteria found in the samples. These bacterial levels give a good indication of the level of human sewage in the water. For a beach to pass, the imperative (I) (or minimum standards) must be met. Guideline (G) standards also exist which are twenty times stricter than the (I) values.

When the government releases the annual bathing water results for the UK, each beach is simply listed as pass or fail. This will tell you whether a beach met minimum standards during the season, but will not tell you just *how* well (or how badly) a beach passed or failed. We have therefore devised a grading system to help further distinguish the quality of bathing water.

There are many criteria listed in the directive (such as viral levels and the presence of salmonella) which the Marine Conservation Society would like to see considered in the monitoring of beaches, but as the government only bases its results on two sets of criteria we can only do the same. However, we have decided to make more use of the guideline (G) values for total/faecal coliform bacteria and grade beaches in relation to these values too. This has been done by

24

allocating star ratings to each monitored beach where:

★★★★     has met *all* (I) and (G) values. These waters are of a very high quality.

★★★     has met all (I) values but not all (G) values. These waters are of good quality.

★★     has not met either all (I) or (G) values. ★★ is the border area for pass or fail and so some will be marked f★★ if they failed in 1990.
The ★★ band is a very broad one: it runs from generally clean beaches where one exceptional sample has not met the (I) values to others where the (I) values have been exceeded in several samples. Certainly beaches which passed but only have a ★★ value should not be considered a cause for great concern.

★     beaches *are* a cause for concern. All fail the minimum EC standard for clean bathing water, have exceeded the (I) values in more than a third of the samples taken and have failed.

Star gradings divided by a line are those where there was insufficient data to distinguish water quality further.

### Sewage Treatment

Details of sewage discharge are given in both *The Golden List* at the start of each regional chapter and with the entries in the guide itself. Entries in the text show the type of treatment given and these are explained below.

#### Raw sewage

Sewage that goes straight from the toilet or sink to the sea.

#### Screening

A wire mesh (usually with a pore size of less than 6mm) sieves out any large non-biodegradable solids such as plastics or rock.

#### Maceration

The sewage is mashed (or comminuted) to aid the breakdown of the organic material after sea disposal. Its value is now under question:

not only may its acceleratory effect be overestimated but other wastes, such as plastic strips from sanitary towels, tend to be chopped up too and land up as plastic 'confetti' on the beach. (If people stopped putting plastics down the toilet altogether this would be a great help).

### Tidal tank

If the waters off a beach are shallow a tidal tank may be used. The sewage, treated or untreated, is stored in a tank and is only released as the tide is going out. The aim is to achieve maximum dilution and prevent the sewage washing back on to the beach.

### Primary treatment

Sewage is passed through settlement tanks. Large solids settle out and are disposed of as a sludge, either by dumping on land or at sea.

### Secondary treatment

After primary settlement, the sewage passes to an activated sludge plant where it is mixed to increase the oxygen content and hence increase bacterial activity which breaks it down. The effluent is then passed slowly through a final treatment pond, where the bacterial numbers fall before the treated effluent is discharged. Alternatively, after initial treatment the sewage is trickled through a gravel bed before disposal through a pond. There is bacterial growth on the large surface area of the gravel and this ensures the breakdown of the sewage.

### Other treatments

A large number of different chemical treatments can be used to disinfect and sterilise sewage effluent before discharge; for example, hydrogen peroxide, chlorine or ozone. An alternative to disinfection is flocculation – a process in which a lime-based chemical slurry is combined with the sewage in a single stage upward flow treatment tank. This makes the suspended solids combine with the slurry to form a sludge that can be removed from the tank.

## KEY TO GOLDEN LIST

Beaches in **bold** are EC designated beaches which have been monitored between May and September. Beaches in light type are not EC designated beaches.

LSO    Long Sea Outfall
SSO    Storm Sewer Overflow
STW    Sewage Treatment Works

LWM    Low Water Mark
HWM    High Water Mark

### Other entries

### Litter

Where possible, we have tried to include details of any significant litter problems reported and any cleaning undertaken on a regular basis.

### Dogs

We have tried to indicate where dogs are not permitted on beaches. In most cases local bye-laws have been introduced to restrict access of dogs to the beach, with provisions for their control on the surrounding land – promenades, paths, gardens etc. In some areas laws regarding the removal of canine faeces have also been applied and owners are required to clean up any mess their pet makes on the beach or surrounding area. At some beaches 'poop scoops' are available.

### Bathing safety

Reported conditions that make bathing dangerous are indicated, but always remember to take great care wherever you enter the water.

# South-West England

**f** = failed to meet EC standard for clean bathing water in 1990.
Numbered beaches are included in the following chapter.

**Long distance coastal paths**
South West Coast Path
562 miles (904km), but made up of four main sections:
(1) Minehead to Padstow 131 miles (211km).
(2) Padstow to Famouth 158 miles (254km).
(3) Falmouth to Exmouth 174 miles (280km).
(4) Exmouth to Poole 99 miles (159km).

Isle of Wight Coastal Path
A circuit of the island 60 miles (97km).

Solent Way
Milford on Sea to Portsmouth 60 miles (97km).

## South-West England

There are hundreds of miles of glorious coastline along the south-west peninsula. Long sweeping bays and small secluded coves are separated by rugged headlands. There are spectacular rocky cliffs to contrast with smooth turfed slopes where wild flowers abound. Some of Britain's loveliest unspoilt scenery is to be found along this coast.

But the area is not completely free of problems. Various forms of pollution affect the beaches; untreated sewage discharged close inshore is washed back on to the sands at several places. A number of beaches are affected by industrial pollution. The china clay industry has covered some sands with a film of white dust and the Cornish tin mining industry discharges waste either directly into the sea or into rivers flowing to the sea; for instance one of the beautiful beaches on the eastern side of St Ives Bay is affected by a 'red' river. The river, containing suspended mining waste, flows across the sand, turns the waves pink and the waste is washed back on to the shore.

Large numbers of tourists flocking to the beaches during the summer can cause problems. Long queues of traffic develop on the narrow lanes and the picturesque Cornish fishing villages become congested. The beaches become crowded and this can lead to damage; for example, the erosion of dunes is a particular problem. Careless visitors leaving rubbish can ruin an otherwise lovely beach. To avoid some of these problems a visit in the spring or autumn is recommended, and in winter you can have miles of golden sands to yourself.

### Beaches receiving the European Blue Flag in 1990:

Porthmeor – St Ives, Sennen Cove, Crinnis (Carlyon Bay), Paignton, Torre Abbey Sands (Corbyn), Meadfoot Beach, Ansteys Cove, Oddicombe, Teignmouth, Dawlish Warren, Exmouth, Budleigh Salterton, Sidmouth, Jacob's Ladder (Sidmouth), Weymouth (Central), Swanage, Poole Shore Road, Bournemouth Pier.

## The Golden List    *See page 25 for further details*

| Beach No on Map | Rating. The more stars the better. f=failed | Resort | Sewage outlets | Population discharging from outlet | Type of treatment | Discharge point relative to low water mark. unless otherwise stated. Distance given in metres | Remarks |
|---|---|---|---|---|---|---|---|
| **AVON** | | | | | | | |
| | ★★ | **Clevedon** | 1 | 60,000 | Fine screening, filtration, settlement | At HWM | Rocks and mud. Crude discharges now removed. All flow to STW at Kingston Seymour. |
| | ★★ ★★ ★★★ | **Weston-Super-Mare** | 1 | 75,000 | Fine screening, disinfection | 400m below LWM | Improvement scheme completed 1990. |
| **SOMERSET** | | | | | | | |
| | | **Berrow** | | | | | Sandy. |
| | ★★★ | **North** | | | | | |
| | ★★ | **South** | | | | | |
| | ★★★ | **Brean** | | | | | Sandy. |
| | ★★ ★★★ | **Burnham-on-Sea** | 1 | 36,000 | Fine screening, filtration, settlement | At HWM | All flow to West Huntspill STW. |
| | | East Quantoxhead | 1 | 800 | Maceration | At LWM | Rocks and sand. |
| | | Doniford | 1 | 5,000 | Fine screened | 100 above LWM | Sand and mud. |
| | | Watchet | 1 | 4,500 | Raw | 100 above LWM | Sand and mud. |
| | ★★★ | **Blue Anchor** | | | | | Sand and shingle. Flows to Minehead headworks. |
| | ★★★ | **Dunster** | | | | | Sand and shingle. Flows to Minehead headworks. |
| | ★★★ | **Minehead** | 1 | 35,000 | Screening, long outfall & tidal discharge | 750m below LWM | Sandy. Headworks and outfall completed 1989. |
| | ★★★ | **Porlock Bay** | 3 | 850 1,200 450 | Raw Raw Raw | At LWM At LWM At LWM | Pebbles. |
| | f ★★ | **Lynmouth** | 1 | 4,349 | Raw | 110 below | Pebbles. New LSO planned. |

31

| Beach No on Map | Rating. The more stars the better. f=failed | Resort | Sewage outlets | Population discharging from outlet | Type of treatment | Discharge point relative to low water mark, unless otherwise stated. Distance given in metres | Remarks |
|---|---|---|---|---|---|---|---|
| | ★★ | **Combe Martin** | 1 | 3,522 | Raw | 65 below | Pebbles and sand. New LSO planned. |
| | ★★★ | **Ilfracombe: Hele Beach** | 2 | 22,022 | Raw | 235 below | Sandy. Bathing safe. |
| | f ★★ | **Capstone Beach** | | 744 | Raw | 30 below | |
| 1 | ★★★★ ★★★ | **Woolacombe: Putsborough Village** | 1 | 11,000 | Secondary | 100 below | Sandy. New plant gives full treatment. |
| 2 | ★★★ | **Croyde Bay** | 1 | 6,431 | Maceration | At LWM | Sandy. Surf bathing. Strong undertow at all times. Lifeguards. |
| | ★★★ | **Saunton Sands** | | | | | Sand. Safe bathing except near river mouth. Lifeguards. |
| | f ★★ | **Instow** | | | | | Polluted by River Taw and Torridge. £62.4m LSO and STW scheme. |
| | ★★ | **Westward Ho!** | 1 | 8,521 | Raw | 10 below | Sand and pebbles. Surf bathing. |
| | | Clovelly | 1 | 259 | Raw | At LWM | Sand at low tide only. |
| 3 | | Shipload Bay | | | | | Pebbles, sand at low tide. |
| | ★★★ | **Hartland Quay** | | | | | Rocks and pebbles. |

### CORNWALL

| Beach No on Map | Rating. | Resort | Sewage outlets | Population discharging from outlet | Type of treatment | Discharge point | Remarks |
|---|---|---|---|---|---|---|---|
| | ★★★ | **Sandy Mouth** | | | | | Sandy. Swimming dangerous at low tide. Surf bathing. Lifeguards. |
| | ★★ | **Bude Crooklets** | | | | | Sandy. Surf bathing. |
| | ★★ | **Bude Summerleaze** | 1 | 13,143 | Tidal tank | 75 below | Scheme to resite outfall and screen sewage. |
| 4 | ★★★ | **Widemouth Sand** | | | | | Sandy. Bathing dangerous at low tide. Lifeguards. |

| Beach No on Map | Rating. The more stars the better. f=failed | Resort | Sewage outlets | Population discharging from outlet | Type of treatment | Discharge point relative to low water mark, unless otherwise stated. Distance given in metres | Remarks |
|---|---|---|---|---|---|---|---|
| 5 | ★★★ | Crackington Haven | | | | | Sandy. Safe bathing in centre of bay. Lifeguards. |
| | | Boscastle | 1 | 1,285 | Raw | At LWM | Harbour outfall inaccessible. |
| | | Tintagel | 1 | 1,724 | Raw | At LWM | Shingle. |
| 6 | | Trebarwith Strand | | | | | Sand and rocks. Swimming can be dangerous. Lifeguards. |
| | | Port Isaac | 1 | 1,910 | Secondary | At LWM | Fishing port. |
| | ★★★ | **Polzeath** | 1 | 656 | Primary | At LWM | Sandy. Bathing can be dangerous at low water. Lifeguards. |
| | ★★★ | **Daymer Bay** | | | | | Sandy, Safe swimming. |
| | ★★ | **Rock** | | | | | Sandy. Good sailing. Swimmers beware currents. |
| | | Padstow | 1 | 3,874 | Raw | | Small harbour. No swimming. |
| | ★★ | **Trevone Bay** | 1 | 1,104 | Raw | At LWM | Sandy. Bathing can be dangerous. Lifeguards. |
| 7 | ★★★ | **Harlyn Bay** | 1 | 3,202 | Secondary (summer) | At LWM | Sandy. Safe bathing. Lifeguards. |
| | ★★★ | **Mother Ivey's Bay** | | | | | Sandy. Safe bathing. Pedestrian access. |
| 8 | ★★★★ | **Constantine Bay** | | | | | Sandy. Bathing dangerous. |
| | ★★★ | **Treyarnon Beach** | | | | | Sandy. Surfing dangerous at low tide. |
| | f ★★ | **Magwan Porth** | | | | | Sandy. Surfing dangerous at low tide. |
| 9 | | Bedruthan Steps | | | | | Sand and rocks. Bathing dangerous. |
| | ★★★ | **Watergate Bay** | | | | | Sandy. |

| Beach No on Map | Rating. The more stars the better. f=failed | Resort | Sewage outlets | Population discharging from outlet | Type of treatment | Discharge point relative to low water mark, unless otherwise stated. Distance given in metres | Remarks |
|---|---|---|---|---|---|---|---|
| | ★★<br>f ★★ | **Newquay Bay**<br>Towan Beach<br>Porth Beach | 1 | 50,078 | Maceration/<br>screens | 75 below | Sandy. Surfing.<br>Lifeguards. |
| 10 ★★★ | | **Fistral Bay** | | | | | Sandy. Strong currents when rough. |
| 11 ★★★ | | **Crantock** | | | | | Sandy. Surfing. Swimming dangerous at low water and near Gannel estuary. |
| 12 ★★★ | | **Holywell Bay** | | | | | Sandy. Surfing dangerous at low tide. Lifeguards. |
| | ★★★<br>★★★ | **Perranporth:**<br>Penhale Village<br>Perran Beach | 1 | 11,872 | Maceration | At LWM | Sandy. Good surfing. Dangerous at low tide. Lifeguards. |
| | ★★ | **Trevaunance Cove** | 1 | 4,140 | Maceration | At LWM | Sandy. Powerful surf. New £2.3 million improvement scheme. |
| | ★★★ | **Porthtowan** | | | | | Sandy. Surfing dangerous at low water. Lifeguards. |
| | ★★★ | **Portreath** | 1 | 24,143 | Raw | At LWM | Sandy. Surfing. Swimming dangerous near pier. Lifeguards. |
| | | Deadman's Cove | 1 | 25,000 | Raw | At LWM | Sand and rocks. |
| 13 ★★★ | ★★ | **The Towans –<br>Hayle**<br>**The Towans –<br>Godrevy** | | | | | Sandy. Surfing. Swimming dangerous at low water. Lifeguards. |
| | ★★<br>★★★ | **Carbis Bay**<br>Porth Kidney<br>Sands<br>Station Beach | | | | | Sandy and sheltered. |
| | ★★★ | **St Ives**<br>**Porthminster** | 1 | 50 | Raw | At LWM | Sandy. Sheltered. Safe swimming. Overflow only. |
| | f ★★ | **Porthgwidden** | 1 | 42,000 | Raw | 20 below | Sandy beach. Outfall to be linked to the new £48.7m Marazion sewage scheme. |
| 14 ★★★ | | **St Ives**<br>**Porthmeor** | 1 | 50 | Fine screened | 150 from harbour wall | Sandy. Surfing. |

| Beach No on Map | Rating. The more stars the better. f=failed | Resort | Sewage outlets | Population discharging from outlet | Type of treatment | Discharge point relative to low water mark, unless otherwise stated. Distance given in metres | Remarks |
|---|---|---|---|---|---|---|---|
| 15 | | St Just Priest's Cove | | | | | Shingle. |
| 16 | ★★★ | Sennen Cove | 1 | 1,489 | Maceration | 130 from sea wall | Sandy. Surfing north of beach is dangerous. Lifeguards. |
| | | Porthgwarra | 2 | 32 500 | Tidal tank Tidal tank | At LWM At LWM | Sandy at low tide. |
| | ★★★ | Porthcurno | 1 | 211 | Maceration | At LWM | Sandy. |
| | | Lamorna Cove | 1 | | Tidal tank | At LWM | Sand and rocks. |
| | | Mousehole | 1 | 2,100 | Raw | At LWM | Fishing port |
| | f ★★ f ★★ f ★★ f ★★ ★★★ | Penzance Marazion and Mounts Bay | 12 | 37,585 | Raw | 11 at LWM 1 at 50 below | Sand and shingle. New £48.7m sewage disposal scheme proposed for Newlyn and Penzance for completion in 1995. |
| | ★★★ | Perran Sands | 1 | 1,615 | Raw | At LWM | Sandy. Good swimming. |
| 17 | ★★ ★★★ | Praa Sands: West East | | | | | Sandy. Surfing. Lifeguards. |
| | f ★★ | Porthleven West | 1 | 3,852 | Raw | At HWM | Flint and pebbles. Bathing dangerous. £3.2 million improvement scheme. |
| | ★★★ | Gunwalloe Cove | | | | | Swimming dangerous in rough weather. Lifeguards. |
| 18 | ★★ | Poldhu Cove | | | | | Sandy. Bathing dangerous at low tide. Lifeguards. |
| | ★★★ | Polurrian Cove | 1 | 2,000 | Macerated | At LWM | Sandy. Weekend lifeguards. |
| 19 | | Kynance Cove | | | | | Sandy. Safe bathing. |
| 20 | | Polpeor Cove | | | | | Rock and shingle. Safe bathing. |
| | | Church Cove | 1 | 4,375 | Maceration | 500 below | Rocky fishing cove. |
| 21 | ★★★★ | Kennack Sands | | | | | Silver sands. Safe swimming in calm weather. |

35

| Beach No on Map | Rating. The more stars the better. f=failed | Resort | Sewage outlets | Population discharging from outlet | Type of treatment | Discharge point relative to low water mark, unless otherwise stated. Distance given in metres | Remarks |
|---|---|---|---|---|---|---|---|
| | ★★ | **Coverack** | | | | | Sand and shingle. |
| | ★★★★ | **Porthoustock** | | | | | Shingle with sand at low tide. |
| | ★★ | **Porthallow** | | | | | Grey stones. |
| | ★★★ | **Maen Porth** | | | | | Sand and shingle. Safe swimming except when rough. Lifeguards. |
| | ★★★ | **Swanpool Beach** | 1 | 31,156 | Maceration | At LWM | Sand and shingle. £14.5m improvement scheme planned. |
| | ★★★ | **Gyllyngvase (Falmouth)** | | | | | Sandy. Safe swimming. Lifeguards. |
| | ★★★ | Loe Beach Feock | | | | | Sand and shingle. Boating beach. |
| | | St Mawes | 1 | 1,551 | Other | | Sandy. Safe swimming. |
| **22** | | Portscatho | 2 | 1,988 52 | Raw Raw | At LWM At LWM | Sand and rock. |
| **23** | ★★★ | **Pendower Beach** | | | | | Sand and rock. Safe bathing. |
| | | Portloe | 1 | 431 | Maceration/ screens | At LWM | Sand and rock. Fishing village. |
| | ★★★ | **Porthluney Cove** | | | | | Sandy. Safe swimming. |
| **24** | ★★★ ★★ f ★★ | **Gorran Haven:** Bow or Vault Little Perhaver | 1 | 2,487 | Raw | At LWM | Sandy. Safe swimming. Improvement scheme planned for completion in 1997. |
| | ★★★ | **Portmellon** | | | | | Sand and shingle. |
| | | Mevagissey | 1 | 5,865 | Raw | At LWM | Fishing harbour. No beach. |
| | ★★★ | **Polstreath** | | | | | Contaminated by the Mevagissey sewage outfall – improvements planned. |
| | ★★★ | **Pentewan** | | | | | Sandy. STW planned. |
| | ★★★ | **Porthpean** | 1 | 34 | Raw | At LWM | Sandy. |

| Beach No on Map | Rating. The more stars the better. f=failed | Resort | Sewage outlets | Population discharging from outlet | Type of treatment | Discharge point relative to low water mark, unless otherwise stated. Distance given in metres | Remarks |
|---|---|---|---|---|---|---|---|
| | ★★★ <br> f ★★ | **Charlestown** <br> **Duporth** | 1 | 3,248 | Raw | At LWM | Sandy. Leisure complex. |
| | <br> ★★ <br> ★★★ | **Crinnis Beach:** <br> Golf Links <br> Leisure Centre | | | | | Sandy. Swimming dangerous near stream. |
| | ★★★ <br> f ★★ | **Par Sands** <br> Spit Beach | 1 | 23,263 | Primary | 60 below | Sandy. Dominated by china clay factory. |
| | ★★★ | **Polkerris** | 1 | 57 | Raw | 5 below | Sandy. |
| | ★★ | **Readymoney Cove (Fowey)** | 1 | 3,448 | Raw | At LWM | Sandy. |
| 25 | | Lantic Bay | | | | | Sand and shingle. Strong under tow. |
| 26 | | Lansallos Bay | | | | | Sand. Safe bathing. |
| | | Polperro | 1 | 3,466 | Maceration | At LWM | Pebbles. |
| | ★★★ | **East Looe** | | | | | Sandy. Safe bathing. |
| | ★★★ | **Millendreath** | | | | | Sandy. |
| | ★★ | **Seaton Beach** | 1 | 1,337 | Raw | At LWM | Grey sand and pebbles. Improvement scheme planned. |
| | ★★★ | **Downderry** | 1 | 938 | Raw | At LWM | Silvery sand. |
| 27 | ★★★ | **Portwrinkle** | 1 | 768 | Maceration | At LWM | Grey sand. |
| 28 | | Cawsand Bay | 2 | 188 <br> 301 | Raw <br> Raw | At LWM <br> 50 below | Pebbles and rocks. |

### DEVONSHIRE SOUTH

| Beach No on Map | Rating. The more stars the better. f=failed | Resort | Sewage outlets | Population discharging from outlet | Type of treatment | Discharge point relative to low water mark, unless otherwise stated. Distance given in metres | Remarks |
|---|---|---|---|---|---|---|---|
| | | Kingsands Bay | 2 | 157 <br> 665 | Raw | 5 & 12 below | Sand and shingle. |
| | f ★★ | **Plymouth Hoe** | 3 | 49,000 <br> 368 <br> 2,300 | Primary <br> Raw <br> Raw | | £37.6 million improvement scheme. |
| | ★★★ | **Bovisand Bay** | | | | | Sand and rocks. Polluted by untreated sewage from Plymouth outfalls. |

| Beach No on Map | Rating. The more stars the better. f=failed | Resort | Sewage outlets | Population discharging from outlet | Type of treatment | Discharge point relative to low water mark, unless otherwise stated. Distance given in metres | Remarks |
|---|---|---|---|---|---|---|---|
| 29 | ** | **Wembury** | 1 | 4,383 | Primary | 100 below | Silvery sand and rocks. |
| | *** | **Mothecombe** | | | | | Sandy. Bathing safe only on incoming tide. |
| | *** | **Challaborough** | | | | | Sandy and rocky. Bathing dangerous at low tide. |
| 30 | | **Bigbury-on-Sea:** | 1 | 1,286 | Primary/other | At LWM | Sandy. Swimming dangerous near river mouth. |
| | **** | North | | | | | |
| | *** | South | | | | | |
| | ** | **Bantham** | | | | | Sand and mud. Bathing dangerous. |
| | | **Thurlestone:** | | | | | |
| | f ** | **North** | 1 | 1,161 | Raw | At LWM | Red sand. Sheltered swimming. Improvement scheme. |
| | *** | **South** | | | | | |
| | *** | **Hope Cove** | 1 | 1,152 | Primary | At LWM | Sandy. |
| | | **Salcombe:** | | | | | |
| | ** | **North** | 1 | 2,226 | Raw | 50 below | Sandy. |
| | ** | **South** | 1 | 21 | Raw | 7 below | Improvement scheme. |
| | *** | **Mill Bay** | | | | | Sandy. |
| | *** | Torcross | 1 | 693 | Raw | At LWM | Fishing port. |
| 31 | *** | **Slapton Sands** | 1 | 889 | Raw | 30 below | Tiny red pebbles. |
| 32 | *** | **Blackpool Sands** | | | | | White sand. Shelves steeply. |
| | | Leonard's Cove | 2 | 1,051 | Raw | At LWM | Shingle. |
| | | | | 1,044 | Raw | At LWM | |
| | *** | **Dartmouth Castle & Sugary Cove** | | | | | Shingle. |
| | *** | **St Mary's Bay** | 1 | 90,000 | Screened | 220 below | Sand and pebbles. Improvement scheme. |
| | *** | **Shoalstone Beach** | | | | | Pebbles. |
| 33 | | **Torbay (Broadsands to Watcombe)** | | | | | |

| Beach No on Map | Rating. The more stars the better. f=failed | Resort | Sewage outlets | Population discharging from outlet | Type of treatment | Discharge point relative to low water mark. unless otherwise stated. Distance given in metres | Remarks |
|---|---|---|---|---|---|---|---|
| | ★★★ | **Broadsands Beach** | | | | | Muddy sand and pebbles. |
| | ★★★ | **Goodrington Sands** | 1 | | Screened | At LWM | Sand and pebbles. Storm water overflow. |
| | ★★ | **Paignton Sands** | 1 | | Screened | 200 below | Red sands. |
| | ★★★ | **Preston Sands** | 1 | | Screened | At LWM | Red sands. Stormwater overflows. |
| | ★★★ | **Hollicombe** | | | | | |
| | ★★★ | **Torre Abbey Sands** | | | | | Safe bathing. |
| | ★★★ | **Beacon Cove** | | | | | |
| | ★★★ | **Meadfoot Beach** | | | | | Sandy at low tide. |
| | ★★★ | **Anstey's Cove/ Redgate Beach** | 1 | 89,000 | Screened | At LWM | Shingle. Sand and shingle. Outfall off Hope's Nose. Improvements planned. |
| | ★★★ | **Babbacombe** | 1 | 1,000 | Raw | 5 below | Shingle. |
| | ★★★ | **Oddicombe** | | | | | Shingle. |
| | ★★★ | **Watcombe Beach** | | | | | Sand. |
| | ★★★ | **Maidencombe** | | | | | Red sand. |
| | ★★★ | **Ness Cove** | | | | | Sandy. |
| | ★★★ | **Shaldon** | 1 | 1,869 | Raw | At LWM | Sandy. |
| 34 | ★★★ | **Teignmouth** | 2 | 17,400 | Screens/tidal tank | At LWM | Sandy. |
| | ★★ | **Holcombe** | 1 | 1,639 | Raw | At LWM | Rocky. |
| | ★★★ | **Dawlish** | 2 | 22,301 | Maceration | At LWM/ 330 below | Red sand/shingle. |
| 35 | ★★★ | **Dawlish Warren** | | | | | Sand and dunes. Bathing dangerous near river. |
| 36 | ★★★ | **Exmouth** | 1 | 43,009 | Primary | 166 below | Sandy. Improvement scheme. |
| | ★★★ | **Sandy Bay** | | | | | Red sand. |

**39**

| Beach No on Map | Rating. The more stars the better. f=failed | Resort | Sewage outlets | Population discharging from outlet | Type of treatment | Discharge point relative to low water mark, unless otherwise stated. Distance given in metres | Remarks |
|---|---|---|---|---|---|---|---|
| 37 | ** | **Budleigh Salterton** | 1 | 5,066 | Raw | 50 below HWM | Pebbles sloping steeply. |
| | *** | **Ladram Bay** | 1 | 3,055 | Primary | At LWM | Pebbles. |
| 38 | *** | **Sidmouth** | 1 | 15,880 | Maceration/ screens | 400 below | Pebbles with sand. |
| | *** | **Sidmouth: Jacob's Ladder** | | | | | |
| 39 | | Branscombe | | | | | Pebbles. |
| | *** | **Beer** | 1 | 3,016 | Raw | At LWM | Pebbles. Steep beach. |
| | *** | **Seaton** | | | | | Pebbles. Steep beach. Improvement scheme. |

**DORSET**

| | | | | | | | |
|---|---|---|---|---|---|---|---|
| | f ** ** | **Lyme Regis** | 2 | 32 9,519 | Raw Raw | 10 below 15 below | Sandy. £8.7 million improvement scheme. |
| | *** | **Charmouth** | | | | | Sand and shingle. £2.7 mllion improvement scheme. |
| 40 | *** | **Seatown** | | | | | Pebbles. |
| | *** | **Eypemouth** | | | | | Pebbles. |
| | *** | **West Bay** | 1 | 30,000 | Maceration/ screens | 1500 below | Shingle; steep beach. |
| 41 | **** | Burton Bradstock | | | | | Shingle. |
| | | Chesil Beach | 1 | 86,000 | Maceration/ screens | 1300 below | Pebbles. Swimming very dangerous. |
| | **** | **Church Ope Cove** | | | | | Shingle. |
| | ** *** | **Portland Harbour: Sandsfoot Castle Cove** | | | | | Sandy. Sandy. |
| 42 | *** **** | **Weymouth** Lodmoor | | | | | Sandy. |
| | *** | **Bowleaze** | | | | | Fine shingle and sand. |

| Beach No on Map | Rating. The more stars the better. f=failed | Resort | Sewage outlets | Population discharging from outlet | Type of treatment | Discharge point relative to low water mark, unless otherwise stated. Distance given in metres | Remarks |
|---|---|---|---|---|---|---|---|
| 43 | ★★★ | **Ringstead Bay** | | | | | Shingle and pebbles. |
| 44 | ★★★★ | **Durdle Door** | | | | | Sand and pebbles. |
| 45 | ★★ | **Lulworth Cove** | 1 | 2,000 | Maceration/ screens | below LWM | Shingle. Discharge is outside the cove. Improvements planned. |
| 46 | ★★★ | **Kimmeridge Bay** | | | | | Rocky. |
| 47 | ★★ | **Swanage** | 1 | 20,000 | Maceration | 100 below | Sandy. Outfall off headland. |
| 48 | ★★★ | **Studland Bay** | | | | | White sand. |
| | ★★★ | **Shell Bay** | | | | | Sandy. Strong currents. |
| | | **Poole:** | | | | | |
| | ★★★ | **Rockley Sands** | | | | | Sand and shingle. |
| | ★★ | **Lake** | | | | | Muddy at low tide. |
| | ★★★ | **Harbour** | | | | | Sand and mud. |
| 49 | ★★★ | **Sandbanks/ Shore Road** | | | | | Sand. |
| | ★★★ | Branksome Chine | | | | | |
| 50 | ★★★ ★★★ | **Bournemouth** | | | | | Sandy. |
| | | **Christchurch:** | | | | | Sailing harbour. Shingle and mud. Rivers Avon and Stour contain treated sewage giving a high bacterial count in the harbour. |
| | ★★ | Mudeford Quay | | | | | |
| | ★★★ | Avon Beach | | | | | |
| | ★★★ | Friars Cliff | | | | | |
| 51 | ★★★ | **Highcliffe** | | | | | Shingle. |

### ISLE OF WIGHT

| | Rating | Resort | Sewage outlets | Population | Type of treatment | Discharge point | Remarks |
|---|---|---|---|---|---|---|---|
| | ★★★ | **Totland** | 1 | 2,000 | Maceration | 300 below | Shingle. |
| | ★★ | **Colwell Bay** | | | | | Shingle. |
| | | Yarmouth | 2 | 15,000 | Raw | 170 below | Sailing harbour. Shingle beach. |
| | | | | | Maceration | 230 below | Sandy. |
| | f ★★ | **Gurnard Bay** | 2 | 1,500 | Maceration | 250 below | Shingle. Safe bathing. |
| | | | 2 | 4,300 | Raw | 150 below | |

**41**

| Beach No on Map | Rating. The more stars the better. f=failed | Resort | Sewage outlets | Population discharging from outlet | Type of treatment | Discharge point relative to low water mark, unless otherwise stated. Distance given in metres | Remarks |
|---|---|---|---|---|---|---|---|
| | | **Cowes** | 15 | 15,000 | Raw | Varies | Sailing centre. £5 million improvement scheme. |
| | f ★★ | West | | | | | |
| | ★★★ | East | | | | | |
| | ★★★ | **Ryde** | 2 | 17,000 | Maceration | 3km below LWM | Sandy. Safe swimming. |
| | | Seaview | 4 | 4,000 | Raw | 200 below | Sandy and rocks. Bathing safe. |
| | ★★ | **Bembridge** | 1 | 7,000 | Maceration/tidal tank | 800 below | Sailing centre. |
| | ★★★ | **Whitecliff Bay** | | | | | Sandy. Safe bathing. |
| | ★★★ | Yaverland | 1 | 50,000 | Primary | 250 below | Sandy. Safe bathing. |
| 52 | ★★★ | **Sandown** | | | | | Sandy. Safe bathing in calm weather. |
| | ★★ | **Shanklin** | | | | | Sandy. Safe bathing. |
| | ★★ | **Ventnor** | 2 | 5,300 | Maceration | At LWM | Sandy. Safe bathing. |
| | ★★★ | **Compton Bay** | | | | | Pebbles. |
| | ★★ | **St Helens** | 1 | 1,500 | Raw | | Sandy. |
| | f ★★ | **Seagrove Bay** | 1 | 500 | Raw | | Sandy. |

## 1 Woolacombe Sand, Woolacombe, Devon   OS Ref: SS4500

Two rugged headlands, Morte Point and Baggy Point, bound this magnificent long, straight, west-facing beach. 2 miles (3.3km) of flat sands extend south from the rocky shore at Woolacombe to the sandstone cliffs of Baggy Point at Putsborough. This end of the beach has again achieved a four-star Good Beach Guide grading for its water quality. The 380 yard (350m) wide sands are backed by extensive dunes behind which the shrub-covered slopes of Woolacombe Down rise. The beach is popular with surfers because of the crashing waves that wash the shore and with families wanting to relax on the beach. After building sand castles and exploring the rock pools you can escape from the crowds by taking a stroll on the headlands at either end of the bay. On the northern side of Woolacombe there is a pocket-sized beach, in complete contrast to the long sweeping sands to the south. The small sandy Barricane beach nestles among the rocky shore stretching to Morte Point and is overlooked by the hotels and guest houses of Woolacombe.

*Water quality* Beach monitored by the NRA and found to meet the EC standard for clean bathing water in 1990. One outfall serving 5,000 people discharges fully treated sewage 22 yards (20m) below low water, north of the beach.

*Bathing safety* It is dangerous to swim near the rocks or at low tide due to undertow currents. Lifeguards patrol the beach from Whitsun to the second week in September.

*Access* A turning off the approach road to Woolacombe from the B3231 leads to car parks behind the beach. There are paths through the dunes to the sands.

*Parking* There are several car parks behind the dunes which provide over 1,000 spaces. National Trust car park close to Baggy Point.

*Toilets* There are toilets in the car park behind the dunes and at the Putsborough end of the beach.

*Food* Cafés and shops at the Woolacombe end of the beach; shop at Putsborough car park.

*Seaside activities* Swimming, surfing, windsurfing, diving, sailing and fishing. Surfboards are available for hire. Hang gliding from Woolacombe Down.

*Wildlife and walks* The North Devon Coast Path leads in both directions from Morte Bay. To the south, the gorse-clad Baggy Point affords excellent views across the bay, as does the jagged slate headland of Morte Point. On a clear day you can see Lundy Island lying 15 miles (24km) away in the Bristol Channel. This island is a Marine Nature Reserve, renowned for the rich marine wildlife around its rocky shores. The steep cliffs that soar 130 yards (120m) above the sea are the haunt of numerous seabirds. Trips to the island to explore its superb shore in greater detail are available from Ilfracombe harbour.

## 2 Croyde Bay, Croyde, Devon   OS Ref: SS4439

A good flat scenic beach of soft sand. The mile (1.6km) of sand is separated from the picturesque village of Croyde by sand dunes. The pale sandstone cliffs of Baggy Point stretch away at right angles from the northern end of the beach. The southern side of the beach is flanked by a grassy headland which is the seaward end of Saunton Down. The rocky shore below the low cliffs at either side of the bay contains rock pools perfect for exploring. The beach is noted for the variety of shells that are washed up. It is popular with surfers, and a surfing centre in the village caters for their needs.

**Water quality** Beach monitored by the NRA and found to meet the EC standard for clean bathing water in 1990. One outfall serving 6,431 people discharges macerated raw sewage at low water mark on the southern side of Baggy Point.

**Litter** Some marine litter is washed up on the beach.

**Bathing safety** Strong undertows make bathing unsafe, particularly at low tide; the beach is patrolled by lifeguards from Whitsun to the second week in September.

**Access** Croyde Bay is signposted from Croyde village. Road leads to the car park from which the beach is signposted. A path leads through dunes to the beach.

**Parking** The holiday park behind the dunes has a car park with 100 spaces open to the public.

**Toilets** At beach entrance.

**Food** Shop, beach club and café on path through dunes.

**Seaside activities** Swimming, surfing, windsurfing, diving, sailing and fishing. There is a surf centre in the village from which boards may be hired.

**Wet weather alternatives** The Croyde Rock and Gem Museum.

**Wildlife and walks** Baggy Point provides excellent walks from this beach; there are numerous flowers to be seen and the steep cliffs are home to many types of seabird. The point provides excellent views south across the extensive sands of Bideford Bay. The path skirts the headland leading north to Morte Bay and Woolacombe.

## 3 Shipload Bay, Hartland, Devon   OS Ref: SS2428

Far removed from the seaside resort or the quaint tourist attraction, this is a small unspoilt cove on the northern side of Hartland Point. 110 yard (100m) cliffs rise sharply above the half moon of shingle and low tide sand. There are rocky reefs at either side of the beach below the grass-covered cliffs. The steps down to this sheltered beach are steep and quite difficult.

**Water quality** No sewage is discharged in the vicinity of this beach.

**Bathing safety** Safe bathing from the centre of the beach but beware of currents that may cause problems.

**Access** From Hartland take the road signposted to Hartland Point lighthouse. The bay lies just off the road a mile before the Point; there are steps down the steep cliffs.

**Parking** There is a National Trust car park on the cliff top.

**Toilets** None.

**Food** None.

**Seaside activities** Swimming.

**Wildlife and walks** The North Devon Coast Path leads along the cliff path to Hartland Point; the strenuous walk is rewarded with excellent views along the rocky shore to the south and to Lundy Island on the far horizon. From the point, you look down on to a lighthouse standing on a lower promontory (the lighthouse is not open to the public).

## 4 Widemouth Sand, Widemouth Bay, Cornwall   OS Ref: SS2002

In contrast to a lot of the beaches in North Cornwall the mile of flat sands at Widemouth Bay is backed by low cliffs and undulating grassy fields which stretch down to the beach from the whitewashed houses of Widemouth village. Flat rocks, which can be too hot to lie on, stretch away in either direction from this popular surfing beach. The relatively easy access, which can be so important if you do not wish to negotiate steep cliff paths, unfortunately often means that in summer the beach also becomes very congested. The cliffs that rise on either side of the beach provide walks away from the busy sands.

**Water quality** Beach monitored by the NRA and found to meet the EC standard for clean bathing water in 1990. No sewage is discharged in the vicinity of the beach.

**Litter** There are reports of bottles and containers being washed up on the beach. The beach is cleaned by the local authority.

**Bathing safety** Surf bathing is dangerous at low tide, and beware of currents near the rocks at each side of the beach. Lifeguards patrol the beach during the summer.

**Access** Widemouth Bay is signposted from the A39 south of Bude. Sandy slopes and steps lead from the car parks on to the beach.

**Parking** There are two car parks behind the beach, at either end of the bay, with spaces for approximately 200 cars in each.

**Toilets** At the car parks.

**Food** A café at the southern car park and a beach shop at the northern car park.

**Seaside activities** Swimming, surfing, windsurfing and fishing. Surf-boards are available for hire.

**Wildlife and walks** The coast path leads off the road south of the beach, climbing Penhalt cliff towards Dizzards Point. There are superb views looking back along the straight coast stretching north of Bude.

## 5 Crackington Haven, Cornwall    OS Ref: SX1496

A steep-sided valley opens to the coast at Crackington Haven. At its mouth is a small 'V' shaped sandy beach, flanked on either side by sheer, dark cliffs. Those of Pencarrow Point on the north-eastern side of the beach rise 400 feet (120m) above the sands, which are edged with rocky outcrops. Surfers ride the waves that wash this beach, although anyone swimming or surfing should steer well clear of the rocks on either side of the bay. A perfect little beach for the family who want to spend a day on a beach with a lovely setting; there are superb walks along the coast path for those that tire of the sand and surf. Unfortunately the village can be rather congested in summer. Dogs are banned from the beach between Easter Sunday and 1st October.

**Water quality** Beach monitored by the NRA and found to meet the EC standard for clean bathing water in 1990. No sewage is discharged in the vicinity of this beach.

**Bathing safety** Bathing is safe in the centre of the bay, but the rocks on the southern shore are very dangerous. Lifeguards patrol the beach in summer.

**Access** Signposted from the A39, steep lanes lead down to the village where there is a small car park; it is a short walk to the sands. Grass slopes and rocky outcrops edge the beach and a road runs parallel.

**Parking** There is a car park in the village which fills very quickly in summer. A Parish Council car park, with picnic facilities, is situated close to the beach.

**Toilets** There are public toilets in the village.

**Food** There is a shop, café and two pubs in the village.

**Seaside activities** Swimming, surfing and fishing.

**Wildlife and walks** The stretch of coast that lies both north and south of this bay must be one of the wildest and most magnificent in the country. The coast path follows the grass slope which rises south of the bay: the path leads over National Trust land to High Cliff – a stretch of extremely rugged shale cliffs that rise 731 feet (222m) above the waves. As its name suggests, this is one of the highest cliffs in England. Below is a sandy beach known as The Strangles because of the numerous boats that have found their final resting place on this shore. The rock-studded sands can be reached down an extremely steep and rough path, which is not to be recommended. Bathing from the beach is very dangerous. There are superb views all along the coast path from Crackington to Boscastle; the path can be reached from the National Trust car park south of Trevigue. There is also an information point at this site.

## 6  Trebarwith Strand, Treknow, Cornwall   OS Ref: SX0587

The lane through a deep wooded valley ends at what can appear to be a tiny rocky cove with cliffs framing an attractive view to Gull Rock. But as the tide recedes an expanse of sand stretching north below steep cliffs is revealed. From the lane end smooth rocks must be crossed to reach the rock-studded sands. A most impressive beach but one on which great care must be taken as the rising tide can cut off the unwary visitor; signs at the entrance to the beach warn of the dangers.

*Water quality*  No sewage is discharged in the vicinity of this beach. There are, however, concerns about the quality of the stream which flows across the sands.

*Bathing safety*  Swimming can be dangerous at low water and close to rocks. Great care must be taken when surfing. The beach is patrolled by lifeguards during the summer months.

*Access*  Trebarwith Strand is signposted from the B3236, Camelford to Tintagel road. The road ends at the shore, with smooth rocks leading down on to the sand.

*Parking*  There are two car parks off the road with about 140 spaces; it is a 2 minute walk down to the beach.

*Toilets*  At the entrance to the beach.

*Food*  There is a café, hotel, restaurant and pub at the beach entrance.

*Seaside activities*  Swimming and surfing. There is a surf school based on the strand.

*Wildlife and walks*  From the coast path which follows the cliffs there are good views of the rocky cliffs, beach and the Gull Rock (in appearance a small version of the Ailsa Craig rock on the Clyde coast). North, the path leads to Tintagel with its cliff-top castle, the legendary seat of King Arthur. In the village the Old Post Office and King Arthur's Hall can also be visited. Tintagel is a honeypot for visitors and becomes very congested in summer. The Heritage Coast Mobile Visitor Centre comes to the area regularly in the summer.

## 7  Harlyn Bay, Harlyn, Cornwall   OS Ref: SW8776

A wide bite into the cliffs on the sheltered eastern side of Trevose Head contains the sandy arc of Harlyn Bay, ⅔ mile (1km) in length. A bank of soft sand overlaid with a scattering of pebbles gives way to gently shelving surf-washed sand, backed by the dunes of Harlyn Warren which are themselves bounded by the dark grey and brown flecked cliffs towards Cataclews Point. There is a small indent in the cliffs, forming Big Guns Cove. Access to the beach is from the south-eastern corner at Harlyn Village, where a stream flows on to the beach and curves to St Cadoc's Point. The remains of an Iron Age cemetery were found below the sands behind the beach.

47

**Water quality** Beach monitored by the NRA and found to meet the EC standard for clean bathing water in 1990. One outfall serving 3,202 people discharges secondary treated sewage at low water mark east of Cataclews Point. In winter sewage only undergoes maceration.

**Litter** Some sea-borne litter is washed on to the shore. The beach is cleaned by the local authority.

**Bathing safety** Safe bathing. Patrolled by lifeguards in summer.

**Access** The road from the B3276 to Harlyn runs along the south-eastern corner of the beach. There is a footpath from the car park to the sand.

**Parking** There is a car park off the road directly behind the beach.

**Toilets** At the car park.

**Food** Refreshments available close to the beach.

**Seaside activities** Swimming, surfing and fishing.

**Wildlife and walks** The walk along the cliffs north-east of the bay skirts Mother Ivey's Bay; a lifeboat house stands on the northern shore of this rocky cove. The footpath continues along the cliffs to the point of Trevose Head where a lighthouse stands sentinel. There are superb sea views towards Pentire Head in the north-east and south towards Newquay, with several small, rocky islands lying just east of the head.

## 8 Constantine Bay, Treyarnon, Cornwall OS Ref: SW8575

One of the new four-star rated beaches in 1990, this wide sweeping arc of gently shelving soft pale sands, backed by large marram covered dunes and bounded on either side by low headlands with rocky outcrops stretching seawards, is a picture to behold. There is very limited parking and there are few facilities available at the beach.

**Water quality** Beach monitored by the NRA and found to meet the EC standard for clean bathing water in 1990. No sewage is discharged in the vicinity of this beach.

**Bathing safety** Bathing is dangerous near the rocks.

**Access** A road off the B3276 at St Merryn is signposted Constantine Bay.

**Parking** A private car park with space for 200 cars is located 2 minutes from the beach.

**Toilets** At the entrance to the beach.

**Food** None.

**Seaside activities** Swimming, surfing.

**Wildlife and walks** The dunes behind the beach are under restoration, with marram grass being planted to stabilise the sands. There are interesting rock pools to explore. The coast path skirts the bay but the low cliffs do not provide the spectacular views that can be found elsewhere on this coastline.

## 9 Bedruthan Steps, Trenance, Cornwall OS Ref: SW8469

The beach that lies below the towering grey cliffs is a visual marvel, best appreciated from the cliff top. The steep slopes of the granite cliffs are reflected in the many islands and rock stacks that have been left isolated by the retreating cliff line. At low tide the rock stacks which punctuate the beach are separated by golden sands. At high tide the beach completely disappears and the rocks are pounded by the waves that have created this wonderful scenery. From Carnewas Island the sands stretch 1¼ miles (2km) north to Park Head. Steep steps lead down the cliff to the beach. Visitors should note that swimming from the beach is dangerous and that there are areas of the beach that are quickly cut off by the rising tide. Legend says that the rocks were used by a giant, Bedruthan, as stepping stones and this gives the beach its name. The National Trust owns this section of coastline and it has provided good facilities for the numerous visitors that come to view the lovely scenery.

*Water quality* No sewage is discharged in the vicinity of this beach.

*Bathing safety* Bathing is dangerous, particularly at low tide.

*Access* Signposted from B3276 north of Trenance, the road ends at the car park. A path leads from the car park to steep steps down the cliff.

*Parking* There is a National Trust car park on the cliff top with space for approximately 100 cars.

*Toilets* Public toilets at car park.

*Food* There is a National Trust shop and café near the car park.

*Seaside activities* Swimming.

*Wet weather alternatives* There is a National Trust Information Centre close to the beach.

*Wildlife and walks* The Cornwall North Coast Path provides good walking north and south of the beach, with fine views along this beautiful rocky coastline.

## 10 Fistral Beach, Newquay, Cornwall OS Ref: SW8262

Originally a fishing port with a busy harbour, Newquay is now one of the foremost holiday resorts in Cornwall with all the facilities of a good holiday centre. Newquay boasts several safe, sandy beaches with booming surf that has made Newquay the surfing capital of Britain, and the World Championships are regularly held here. On the western side of Towan Head lies the ⅔ mile (1km) sweep of Fistral Bay; it is backed by low dunes and a golf course. It is particularly good for surfing as it is exposed to the full force of the Atlantic.

*Water quality* Beach monitored by the NRA and found to meet the EC standard for clean bathing water in 1990. No sewage is discharged in the vicinity of this beach.

*Litter* Beach cleared daily during the summer.

**Bathing safety**  Safe bathing, unless there is a red flag flying. The beach is patrolled by lifeguards from mid-May to the end of September. There are strong currents when the sea is rough.

**Access**  Beach is signposted from Newquay.

**Parking**  There is a car park at the end of the Headland road adjacent to the Headland Hotel.

**Toilets**  In Newquay there are toilets at the North and South piers of the harbour, at Fore Street (with disabled facilities), and at Narrowcliff and Trebarwith Crescent.

**Food**  Snacks are available on the beach and in the town there is a full range of catering outlets to suit every taste and pocket.

**Seaside activities**  Swimming, surfing, sailing, diving and fishing.

**Wet weather alternatives**  Newquay sports centre, aquarium, Trenance Cottages Museum, Tunnels Through Time, Dairyland and Lappa Valley Railway. Trenance Leisure park and Zoo, including Water World – a water centre with fun pool, toddlers' pool and 25m lane pool. Blue Lagoon Leisure Complex, water rides, disco, ten-pin bowling.

**Wildlife and walks**  There are some pleasant walks only a short distance from Newquay. The coast path north of the town climbs on to a headland which overlooks the Whipsiderry, a small cove walled by high cliffs. On the headland there are two Bronze Age burial mounds and the remains of a fortress. Continuing along the coast there are excellent views back across Newquay Bay and of Watergate Bay. There are also walks south on to Towan Head where you are rewarded with excellent views north along the coast. The coast path continues along Fistral Beach to Pentire Head East which overlooks Crantock Beach.

## 11  Crantock, Cornwall   OS Ref: SW7761

An excellent sandy beach nestles between the twin headlands of Pentire Point East and Pentire Point West. The beach is backed by high dunes and Rushy Green, an area of undulating grassland behind the dunes. The tidal channel of the River Gannel bounds the northern side of the beach, below Pentire Point East. There is a deep inlet in the low cliffs on the south side of the bay, Vugga Cove, which can only be reached at low tide. There are also a number of caves; the one closest inshore – Piper's Hole – can be explored at low tide. There are many signs of man's activities around the bay; two slipways are cut into the rocks of Vugga Cove, a poem is carved on a rock in Piper's Hole and there is evidence along the Gannel of its past use as a natural harbour.

**Water quality**  Beach monitored by the NRA and found to meet the EC standard for clean bathing water in 1990. There is no sewage discharged in the vicinity of this beach.

**Bathing safety** Bathing is dangerous at low tide and near the Gannel. Red flags indicate where and when it is safe to swim. The beach is patrolled by lifeguards between mid-May and mid-September.

**Access** Crantock is signposted from the A3075 south of Newquay. A lane from the village leads to a car park behind the dunes. There is a path through the dunes to the beach. The beach can also be reached from West Pentire; a path leads from the village to steps down the cliffs. The Gannel can be crossed from Newquay by either ferry or tidal bridge at Fern Pit or Trethellan.

**Parking** There is a National Trust car park behind the dunes and another in West Pentire.

**Toilets** There are toilets at both car parks.

**Food** There are cafés, shops and pubs in Crantock and West Pentire.

**Seaside activities** Swimming, surfing and fishing.

**Wildlife and walks** There is a network of paths south of the beach providing pleasant circular walks. The footpath which follows the cliffs on the southern side of the beach passes Piper's Hole, a deep crevice in the cliffs where fulmars may be seen nesting. The path continues to the end of the headland where there is a collapsed cave and beautiful views to be enjoyed. Tucked below the headland is a tiny unspoilt cove, Porth Joke. The walker can either continue around the next headland, Kelsey Head, toward Holywell beach or make the return journey across Cubert Common.

## 12 Holywell Bay, Holywell, Cornwall    OS Ref: SW7559

Holywell Bay gets its name from two wells in the area said to contain waters with healing powers. ⅔ mile (1km) of lovely sands sweep south from the low cliffs of Kelsey Head to Penhale Point. The beach is backed by dunes that rise to 200 feet (60m). At the southern end a stream flows through the dunes and across the sands. A narrow cave entrance in the cliffs, at the northern end of the bay, can be explored at low tide. It contains one of the holy wells.

**Water quality** Beach monitored by the NRA and found to meet the EC standard for clean bathing water in 1990. No sewage is discharged in the vicinity of this beach.

**Bathing safety** Bathing is only safe between the orange and red flags. Surfing is dangerous at low tide. Lifeguards patrol the beach during the summer months.

**Access** Holywell is signposted from the A3075 south of Newquay. A path leads from the village along the side of the stream to the beach.

**Parking** There is a car park in Holywell village.

**Toilets** There are toilets in Holywell.

**Food** There are shops and pubs in Holywell.

**Seaside activities** Swimming and surfing.

***Wet weather alternatives*** Holywell Bay Leisure Park on the approach road to the village.

***Wildlife and walks*** A path north along the beach follows the cliffs on to Kelsey Head, where the scant remains of a castle can be seen. From the headland there are excellent views back across the beach, north to the adjacent Pentire Point West and also over 'The Chick', a small rocky island offshore. Seals may often be seen around the island. To the south of the bay the path leads to Penhale Sands, an extensive area of sand hills stretching to Perranporth 3½ miles (5.5km) away. Unfortunately the path is sometimes closed because parts of the dunes are used by the Ministry of Defence as a range. A red flag indicates when access is restricted.

## 13 Hayle, St Ives, Cornwall   OS Ref: SW5639

St Ives Bay has a magnificent necklace of golden beaches, backed on its southern edge by high dunes and some rocky outcrops. The approach to the beach at Hayle is uninspiring; there has been a lot of development on the landward side of the dunes which is rather unattractive and an army of telegraph poles marches across the scene. However, once down on these lovely sands all is forgotten; the 3 miles (5km) of rippled pale golden sands remain untouched by the development behind. From the mouth of the River Hayle the sands, fringed by magnificent dunes and rocky outcrops, stretch north towards Godrevy Point where Godrevy lighthouse stands on an island just offshore. Dogs are banned from Easter to 1st October.

***Water quality*** Beach monitored by the NRA and found to meet the EC standard for clean bathing water in 1990. No sewage is discharged in the vicinity of this beach; an outfall is to be constructed at Gwithian to discharge St Ives and Penzance sewage.

***Litter*** The beach is cleaned regularly.

***Bathing safety*** There are strong currents around the river mouth which make bathing dangerous. Lifeguards patrol the beach during the summer.

***Access*** The beach is signposted from the A30 through Hayle. The road leads up to the car parks behind the dunes and the sands are less than 5 minutes' walk away.

***Parking*** Car parks behind the dunes provide plenty of spaces.

***Toilets*** At the car parks.

***Food*** Beach shop and café at the car parks. A hotel provides snacks and meals.

***Seaside activities*** Swimming and surfing. Surfboards are available for hire.

***Wet weather alternatives*** Hayle Paradise Park and West Cornwall Leisure and Bowling Club.

***Wildlife and walks*** Following the beach north brings you to the rocky shore towards Godrevy Point where the coast path leads along the cliffs to Navax Point. There are lovely views back across St Ives Bay and numerous seabirds can be seen nesting on the cliffs.

## 14 Porthmeor, St Ives, Cornwall   OS Ref: SW5241

The delightful old buildings which are crowded together on the narrow streets around the harbour spill directly on to the beach at Porthmeor. A row of stone houses faces on to the sands but they in no way spoil this most attractive of beaches. Below St Ives Head, also known as the Island, ⅔ mile (1km) of soft sand backed by low cliffs stretches west. Unlike the more sheltered beaches on the other side of the headland, Porthmeor is a surfer's beach with the waves from the Atlantic rolling on to the shore. A promenade at the foot of the cliffs provides all the facilities needed for a day on this lovely beach which was awarded a Blue Flag in 1990. St Ives is famous for its quality of light which has made it popular with artists, a fact reflected in the numerous art galleries and craft workshops to be found in the town. Dogs are banned from the beach from Easter until 1st October.

**Water quality** Beach monitored by the NRA and found to meet the EC standard for clean bathing water in 1990. One outfall serving 50 people discharges fine screened sewage into the sea 155 yards (150m) from the harbour wall.

**Litter** The beach is cleaned daily in the summer.

**Bathing safety** Care must be taken. The beach is patrolled by lifeguards in the summer. An area for use of surfboards is marked with buoys.

**Access** The beach is signposted within the town but it is best to use the large car park above the town and walk down to the beach. There are steps and a lane down on to the sands.

**Parking** The main car park for the town is signposted on the approach roads. There are car parks at either end of the beach; each has space for about 40 cars.

**Toilets** At the car parks.

**Food** Beach shop and café on the promenade.

**Seaside activities** Swimming and surfing. Deck chairs, surfboards and beach huts are available for hire. Boat trips around St Ives Bay are available from the harbour.

**Wet weather alternatives** Art galleries, craft workshops, Barbara Hepworth Museum, St Ives museum, St Ives Leisure and Squash Club.

**Wildlife and walks** From the beach a coastal path leads west along the low rocky cliffs to a series of sandy and rocky coves.

## 15 Priest's Cove, St Just, Cornwall  OS Ref: SW3532

Cape Cornwall was recently presented to the National Trust by Heinz as part of their Guardians of the Countryside programme with the World Wide Fund for Nature. The headland and surroundings remain unspoilt, having escaped the commercialisation of Land's End. A tall chimney stands sentinel on the domed headland, a disused ventilation shaft for the mines far below. The rocky Priest's Cove shelters on the southern side of the Cape, its 200 feet (60m) of shingle ringed by low rugged cliffs. There are numerous quiet and unspoilt coves around the toe of Cornwall – rocky shores with a small fishing boat or two drawn up on to the pebbles. A good starting point to enjoy this rugged, windswept coastline and explore the exposed rocky shore where marine life is plentiful.

**Water quality** No sewage is discharged in the vicinity of this beach.

**Bathing safety** Bathing can be unsafe due to the rocky nature of the shore and the large swell that develops.

**Access** A narrow lane from St Just leads to a car park behind the beach. There is a path and concrete ramp to the shore.

**Parking** Car park with about 70 spaces behind the beach.

**Toilets** At the car park.

**Food** Occasionally an ice-cream van at the car park.

**Seaside activities** Swimming and fishing.

**Wet weather alternatives** North of St Just at Trewellard is Geevor Mine and Mining Museum and at Pendeen there is a mineral and mining museum.

**Wildlife and walks** There is a pleasant walk on to the Cape where you can enjoy good views along the coast towards Land's End and out to the Brison Rocks where seals can be seen. The coast path provides good walking both north and south along the rugged granite cliffs which are dotted with the remains of mines.

## 16 Whitesand Bay, Sennen Cove, Cornwall  OS Ref: SW3626

On the rugged Land's End Peninsula the splendid sweep of Whitesand Bay is in sharp contrast to the many rocky coves that indent the cliffs. From the picturesque little harbour of Sennen Cove the beach stretches north 1 mile (1.6km) to Aire Point, with steep cliffs ringing the northern section. The southern end of this moderately shelving beach is good for swimming and surfing, being sheltered by offshore reefs. The northern end is open to the full force of the Atlantic and conditions can be wild and dangerous. The beach gained Blue Flag status in 1989 and 1990. Dogs are banned from the beach between Easter and 1st October.

**Water quality** Beach monitored by the NRA and found to meet the EC standard for clean bathing water in 1990. One outfall serving 1,489 people discharges macerated sewage at low water mark by the harbour. There have been some complaints of sewage slicks in the bay.

**Bathing safety** Bathing and surfing are safe at the southern end of the bay. Lifeguards patrol the beach during the summer months.

**Access** A road from the A30 to Land's End leads steeply down to Sennen Cove. There is easy access to the beach.

**Parking** There is a car park in Sennen Cove and another on the approach road.

**Toilets** There are toilets in the village.

**Food** There are shops, cafés and a pub in the village.

**Seaside activities** Swimming, surfing and angling. Fishing trips are available from the harbour. Surfboards can be hired.

**Wildlife and walks** The granite cliffs south from Sennen Cove to Land's End are owned by the National Trust. The coast path follows the cliff top which can be wild and windswept. It is probably the best way to approach Land's End avoiding the severe summer congestion of the most westerly tip of Britain, which has been rather spoilt by uncontrolled development.

## 17 Praa Sands, Ashton, Helston, Cornwall    OS Ref: GR5827

This most attractive sweep of sand between rocky headlands is a popular beach for the family. Sheltered by Hoe Point cliffs to the west, the 1 mile (1.6km) sandy strip edged by high dunes stretches east to Lesceave cliff and the granite Rinsey Headland. At low water 110 yards (100m) of gently sloping sand is exposed, with rockpools at either end containing an interesting variety of marine life. There is a car park on the headland and a path leads down to the quiet sandy cove of Porthcew. Caravan parks close by make the beach busy.

**Water quality** Beach monitored by the NRA and found to meet the EC standard for clean bathing water in 1990. No sewage is discharged in the vicinity of this beach.

**Litter** Although the beach is cleaned regularly by the National Trust, sea-borne litter is frequently washed ashore.

**Bathing safety** A rip current makes bathing at low tide very unsafe; the beach is patrolled by lifeguards during the summer season.

**Access** Praa Sands are signposted from the A394 between Helston and Penzance. From the car park there is a short walk down a sloping path to the beach. From the car park further up the hill there are steps and a steeper path to the beach.

**Parking** On the road down to the beach there is a car park with 100 spaces. At the bottom of the hill, adjacent to the beach entrance, there is another small car park.

*Toilets* At the entrance to the beach.

*Food* Cafés/takeaways and a pub/restaurant at the beach entrance.

*Seaside activities* Swimming, diving, surfing, windsurfing, sailing, raft racing and fishing.

*Wildlife and walks* The coast path from the eastern end of the beach leads away from the often crowded sands up Lesceave cliff and on to Rinsey Head. Wheal Prosper, the engine house of an old copper mine, stands on the headland; the property and surrounding land is owned by the National Trust. The mine shaft has been capped and the building restored. A mile (1.6km) further east the ruin of another mine stands on Trewavas Head. To the west of Praa Sands the coast path rises over the cliffs at Hoe Point, passing Kenneggy Sands and Prussia Cove before reaching Cudden Point.

## 18 Poldhu Cove, Mullion, Cornwall   OS Ref: GR6620

A stream crosses this sheltered, sandy cove backed by dunes and bordered by steep, turf-covered slopes. At high tide there is a fair-sized beach, and the falling tide reveals wide, gently sloping sands washed by clear green seas. This cove is easily accessible, making it popular and often busy. It can be a good starting point for reaching coves north and south which are quieter. The Cornwall South Coast Path leads south to the Marconi Memorial ¾ mile (1.2km) away, and north to Church and Dollar coves. Both are fine, sandy coves framed by low, rocky cliffs, but they are unsafe for swimming at low tide. On the rocks of Church Cove stands the 15th-century church of St Winwaloe.

*Water quality* Beach monitored by the NRA and found to meet the EC standard for clean bathing water in 1990. There is no sewage discharged into Poldhu Cove.

*Bathing safety* Signs warn that it is unsafe to swim for one hour either side of low tide. The beach is patrolled by lifeguards during the summer season.

*Access* A lane north-west of Mullion, signposted to Poldhu, leads down to the car park behind the beach. There is a path to the sands.

*Parking* There is a car park with 100 spaces close to the beach. There is another car park behind Church Cove.

*Toilets* There are toilets on the beach.

*Food* There is a beach shop/café.

*Seaside activities* Swimming, surfing, windsurfing and fishing from the beach, but no hiring facilities for boards etc.

*Wildlife and walks* There are pools among the rocks that fringe the beach, with plenty of marine life to be examined.

## 19 Kynance Cove, The Lizard, Cornwall   OS Ref: GR6912

A classic Cornish cove which is extremely well known for its magnificent cliff scenery and is therefore popular with visitors. 200 foot (60m) cliffs shadow the golden sands which are revealed at low tide. Softer layers of rock between the richly-coloured serpentine have been eroded to form some spectacular cliff formations, impressive isolated stacks, arches and caves. This includes 'The Devil's Bellows' stacks which tower as high as the cliffs; they are surrounded by the sands of the cove at low tide. The beach completely disappears at high tide, so great care is required not to get cut off by the rising tide.

**Water quality** No sewage is discharged in the vicinity of this beach.

**Bathing safety** Safe bathing away from the rocks.

**Access** A toll road from the A3083 north of The Lizard leads to a car park on the cliff top. It is a 5-minute walk to the cove down a valley path to the north of the car park.

**Parking** There is a National Trust car park on the cliff top.

**Toilets** In the car park.

**Food** Beach café. Seasonal refreshments in the car park.

**Seaside activities** Swimming.

**Wildlife and walks** There is good walking on the coast path along the cliffs from which the seabirds nesting on the cliffs and stacks can be best appreciated. There are caves that can be explored at low tide.

## 20 Polpeor, The Lizard, Cornwall   OS Ref: SW7012

The Lizard Peninsula is beautiful and remote, with much of interest for the naturalist. Unfortunately, in the summer it is overwhelmed by visitors and the narrow roads become congested with traffic. If you want to appreciate the lovely coves around the headland, make your visit early or late in the season to avoid some of the crowds. Polpeor is a small rock and shingle cove at the southernmost tip of the Lizard, framed by the cliffs of the Lizard Head and the Lizard Point, a rocky promontory that shelters the beach. The 110 yard (100m) beach disappears at high water. A former lifeboat house and slipway adjoins the beach on to which a few boats are still drawn. The turning of the local marble-like serpentine rock has become a small local industry with many of the items sold locally.

**Water quality** No sewage is discharged from this beach.

**Bathing safety** Safe bathing.

**Access** There is a path from the car park 500 yards (450m) from the beach.

**Parking** There are two car parks with 100+ spaces.

**Toilets** On the beach.

**Food** Cafés close to the beach.

**Seaside activities** Swimming and fishing.

**Wet weather alternatives** Museum of Cornish history in the village, lighthouse and lifeboat house open to the public.

**Wildlife and walks** Several rare plant species flourish in the mild climate of the Lizard Peninsula, particularly those of the maritime heathland which is a feature of the headland.

## 21 Kennack Sands, Kuggar, Cornwall   OS Ref: SW7316

Probably the best swimming beach on the Lizard, Kennack Sands gained a four-star water quality rating in 1990. Two separate 550 yard (500m) beaches merge at low tide to form one wide, gently sloping sandy beach. The pale sands, on the sheltered eastern side of the Lizard Peninsula, are fringed by dunes. At either end of the bay the sand gives way to shingle, which is bounded landwards by cliffs. This is a popular family beach.

**Water quality** Beach monitored by the NRA and found to meet the EC standard for clean bathing water in 1990. No sewage is discharged in the vicinity of this beach.

**Bathing safety** Safe bathing.

**Access** A road from Kuggar village signposted for Kennack ends behind the beach; there is a short walk through dunes to the sands.

**Parking** There is a car park at the beach entrance with 250 spaces.

**Toilets** There is a toilet in the car park.

**Food** Cafés at the entrance to the beach.

**Seaside activities** Swimming, surfing, diving, windsurfing and fishing. Surfboards are available for hire adjacent to the beach.

**Wildlife and walks** The Cornwall South Coast Path proceeds east from the beach along the cliff tops towards Black Head with good sea views.

## 22 Towan Beach, Portscatho, Cornwall   OS Ref: SW8733

A safe and sandy beach south of the fishing village of Portscatho. 550 yards (500m) of sand and pebbles are encircled by low shale cliffs on which wild flowers abound. St Anthony Head, south-east of the beach, guards the entrance to Carrick Roads.

**Water quality** No sewage is discharged in the vicinity of this beach.

**Litter** Fishing materials and a lot of plastics are frequently washed up on the beach; however, it is cleaned by the owners, the National Trust.

**Bathing safety** Safe bathing.

**Access** From Portscatho take the road to St Anthony Head. The car park is off this road. There is a 330 yard (300m) level walk from the car park behind the beach to the sands.

**Parking** There is a National Trust car park behind the beach at Porth Farm with 200 spaces.

**Toilets** Toilets, including disabled facilities, 275 yards (250m) from beach.

**Food** None.

**Seaside activities** Swimming, windsurfing, diving and fishing.

**Wildlife and walks** The beach lies on the Cornwall South Coast Path, which can be followed in either direction. There is a 6 mile (9.6km) circular route starting at the beach; follow the path inland along Froe Creek, turning east along the Percuil to Carricknath Point and beach. From there continue to the lighthouse on St Anthony Head, where there is a superb panorama of Falmouth Bay and the Black Rock. The path returns to Towan beach along the cliff top.

## 23 Pendower Beach, Veryan, Cornwall   OS Ref: SW9038

A lovely, unspoilt beach with an attractive setting facing Gerrans Bay; there are good views from the beach towards the gorse-covered cliffs of Nare Head. There is a ⅔ mile (1km) strip of coarse sand fringed by dunes which have suffered from erosion. In order to repair the damage, access is restricted with areas fenced off. Further west the sand gives way to the rocky outcrops and sand of Carne Beach. There are rocky platforms below the steeply sloping cliffs towards Nare Head. A good family beach with easy access.

**Water quality** Beach monitored by the NRA and found to meet the EC standard for clean bathing water in 1990. No sewage is discharged in the vicinity of the beach.

**Bathing safety** Safe bathing.

**Access** A turning off the A3078 leads to the car park behind the beach. Do not take cars right to the end of road as there is only parking for hotel patrons. There are board walks across the dunes suitable for wheelchairs.

**Parking** A National Trust car park behind the dunes has about 200 spaces.

**Toilets** There are toilets in the car park.

**Food** The Pendower House Hotel and café overlooks the beach.

**Seaside activities** Swimming, windsurfing, diving, sailing, canoeing, waterskiing and fishing.

**Wet weather alternatives** Veryan Sports Club.

**Wildlife and walks** There is abundant marine life to be found in the rockpools along the shore. The coast path follows the cliffs that rise to the south-east of the beach. There are excellent views from Nare Head and from Carne Beacon. The panorama along the coast stretches from Zone Point in the west to Dodman Point in the east.

## 24  Bow or Vault Beach, Gorran Haven, Cornwall   OS Ref: SX0141

Sheltered on the eastern side of Dodman Point is the superb Vault Beach, a sweep of sand and shingle below steep, bracken- and heather-clad cliffs. From Maenease Point the beach curves for ⅔ mile (1km) to the rock outcrop of Penover Point. The cliffs rise beyond to the impressive 370 foot (110m) bulk of Dodman Point.

**Water quality**  Beach monitored by the NRA and found to meet the EC standard for clean bathing water in 1990. One outfall serving 2,487 people discharges untreated sewage at low water mark on the north side of Maenease Point.

**Litter**  There is only a very small amount of litter on this beach.

**Bathing safety**  Bathing is safe with care.

**Access**  The coast path must be followed south from Gorran Haven to reach a steep path down the cliffs. Alternatively, there is a path down from Lamledra Farm.

**Parking**  There is a National Trust car park at Lamledra Farm, above the beach.

**Toilets**  None.

**Food**  None.

**Seaside activities**  Swimming.

**Wildlife and walks**  The coast path along the cliff top leads on to Dodman Point; there is evidence of an Iron Age fort with a ditch and bank. At the point, a granite cross stands as a memorial to all the ships that have been wrecked around the point. There are superb views along much of the Cornish coast.

## 25  Lantic Bay, Polruan, Cornwall   OS Ref: SX1451

A superb cove framed by high turf- and shrub-covered cliffs which can only be reached by a 10-minute walk from the nearest road. The shingle and sand beach shelves steeply. The undulating land approaches and the smooth-profiled cliffs give the area an impression of gentleness in comparison to the jagged outlines of the cliffs to the east. This is a fine bathing beach owned by the National Trust, but much care is needed when swimming due to a strong undertow.

**Water quality**  No sewage is discharged in the vicinity of this beach.

**Litter**  A lot of plastic bottles, caps and rope are regularly washed up on to the beach which is cleaned by the National Trust.

**Bathing safety**  Strong undertow.

**Access**  From the car park off the Polruan to Polperro road there is a 10-minute walk along the coast path towards Pencarrow Head to reach a very steep path down to the cove. This path can be dangerous when wet.

**Parking** There is a National Trust car park on the cliff-top road east of Polruan.

**Toilets** None.

**Food** None.

**Seaside activities** Swimming.

**Wildlife and walks** The 400 foot (120m) Pencarrow Head rises east of the beach and from its summit you can see from Devon to The Lizard on a clear day. The coast path that skirts the headland leads to the adjoining Lantivet Bay. West of Lantic Bay the coast path follows the cliffs to St Saviour's Point and Polruan at the mouth of the Fowey. Grey seals can often be seen in the bay.

## 26 Lansallos Bay, Cornwall   OS Ref: SX1651

This lovely small shingle and sand cove owned by the National Trust is completely unspoilt. This cove, shadowed by high cliffs, is reached by a 15-minute walk from Lansallos and this ensures that it remains relatively secluded even during high summer. The grass-topped cliffs slope gently to the rock-studded beach below. There are many rockpools full of interesting marine life, and seals are a common sight offshore.

**Water quality** No sewage is discharged in the vicinity of this beach.

**Bathing safety** Safe bathing.

**Access** From the A387 north of Polperro there is a side road to Lansallos. It is approximately 15 minutes' walk from the village down the valley path to the cove.

**Parking** There is a National Trust car park in Lansallos village.

**Toilets** None.

**Food** Cream teas available in Lansallos Barton.

**Seaside activities** Swimming and fishing.

**Wildlife and walks** The coastal path west of the beach leads to Pencarrow Head, a 400 foot (120m) high headland which provides magnificent views of the Cornish coast. East of the beach the path leads along the cliffs to Polperro some 4 miles (6.4km) away.

## 27 Whitsand Bay, Freathy, Cornwall   OS Ref: SX4052

A 3 mile (5km) sweep of sand backed by 250 foot (75m) cliffs stretches from Portwrinkle south-east to Rame Head. The rugged slate cliffs slope gently down to the beach where rocky outcrops dot the pale grey sands. Portwrinkle, with its tiny harbour, overlooks the rocky shore at the western end of the bay. Once a pilchard fishing village, it is now given over to the

THE GOOD BEACH GUIDE

holiday industry with holiday development ranging over the cliff top. Further east the beach remains unspoilt by development. Access points to this long stretch of beach are few; there are paths down the cliffs at Tregantle and Freathy, the former providing the easiest route down, but this part of the beach lies below the Tregantle Fort which is used as a firing range. There have also been reports that this section of beach suffers considerably from marine litter washed on to the shore. At Freathy the path is steeper but the reward is a superb clean and quiet beach. There are excellent views along the bay to Rame Head, its seaward-pointing finger ending in a knoll topped by a small chapel. On a calm day the water may look very inviting but beware of strong rip currents.

**Water quality** Portwrinkle monitored by the NRA and found to meet the EC standard for clean bathing water in 1990. One outfall serving 768 people discharges macerated sewage at low water mark. A £0.9 million scheme for a long sea outfall should be completed in 1995.

**Litter** There is a problem in some parts of the bay, with marine litter being washed on to the beach. There is a considerable amount of plastic including bottles, old buckets and packaging.

**Bathing safety** Bathing is unsafe; the beach is valleyed which causes a tidal race and undertow. Two life-saving clubs patrol the beach at weekends.

**Access** Whitsand is signposted from the B3247. There are paths down the cliffs at Portwrinkle, Tregonhawke, Tregantle and Freathy. The area around Tregantle Barracks is used by the army as a firing range and a red flag indicates when access is prohibited.

**Parking** There are clifftop car parks at the access points; there are 150 spaces at Freathy.

**Toilets** There are public toilets on the beach at Freathy.

**Food** At Freathy there is a café on the cliff top.

**Seaside activities** Swimming, surfing and fishing.

**Wildlife and walks** Tregantle Cliffs and Rame Head are owned by the National Trust and provide good walks over the scrub headland with fine sea views.

## 28 Cawsand Bay, Cawsand, Cornwall   OS Ref: SX4451

Cawsand Bay is at the approaches to Plymouth Sound, the largest of the series of rias (drowned river valleys) along the south coast. The bay overlooks the Plymouth breakwater, built in the 19th century to provide a safe and sheltered anchorage, and there is a continually changing scene of traffic, naval and civilian, plying in and out of the Sound. The bay curves 3 miles (5km) from Picklecombe Point to Penlee Point. The two villages of Cawsand and Kingsand fringe the southern end of the bay, their colourful houses overlooking the sand and shingle beach which is sheltered by the Rame Head Peninsula to the south. The beach is a series of moderately shelving sandy pockets between rocky outcrops. At either end of the beach the sand gives way to rocky foreshore backed by wooded slate cliffs.

**Water quality** Two outfalls serving 489 people discharge untreated sewage, one at low water mark and the other 55 yards (50m) below. Three other outfalls exist in the bay, but they appear to be redundant or negligible in their discharges.

**Bathing safety** Bathing is safe except when there are south-east winds.

**Access** A launching ramp leads from the village to the beach.

**Parking** There is a pay and display car park in the village with 100 spaces.

**Toilets** There are public toilets adjacent to the beach.

**Food** There is a beach shop and there are hotels and cafés in the village.

**Seaside activities** Swimming, windsurfing, sailing, diving and fishing. There are boats available for hire.

**Wet weather alternatives** Cremyll and Rame Churches, Mount Edgcumbe House and Country Park.

**Wildlife and walks** 2 miles (3km) north along the coast path lies the Mount Edgcumbe Country Park, 800 acres (323 hectares) of wooded parkland with superb views of Drake Island and Plymouth Sound. The park contains the original Tudor house and a deer park. South of the beach the coastal path follows the wooded slopes to Penlee Point and continues westwards along the cliffs to Rame Head.

## 29 Wembury, Devon    OS Ref: SX5248

Wembury is a Marine Protected Area set up to maintain its diverse marine wildlife. It is a particularly attractive and unspoilt bay. A valley opens to the back of the beach where the only development is a car park and a small shop and café. Flanked on either side by low cliffs, a narrow strip of sand curves round the bay. Low tide reveals a series of sandy pockets between rocky reefs which contain numerous pools. This area is of significant marine biological interest and, while beach users should take the opportunity to investigate the shore life, a great deal of consideration is required so that the area remains unspoilt. The disturbance or collection of marine life should be avoided, as should littering, or any other type of damage to the beach and its surroundings. The view from the beach is dominated by the Great Mew Stone just off shore. There is excellent snorkelling in the area.

**Water quality** Beach monitored by the NRA and found to meet the EC standard for clean bathing water in 1990. One outfall serving 4,383 people discharges primary treated sewage 3m (10 feet) below low water mark west of the bay. A £100,000 scheme for a sewage treatment works is due for completion in 1992.

**Litter** A small amount of marine litter.

**Bathing safety** Safe bathing but beware of rocks off-shore.

**Access** Wembury is signposted from the A379. A lane from the village leads down to the car park behind the beach, and a path approaches the beach about 33 yards (30m) away.

**Parking** National Trust car park behind the beach.

**Toilets** There are toilets at the car park.

**Food** National Trust café and shop adjacent to beach.

**Seaside activities** Swimming, windsurfing, diving, sailing and fishing.

**Wildlife and walks** The South-West Peninsula Coast Path skirts the bay, but the path to Wembury Point is frequently closed when the firing range around the point is in use.

## 30 Bigbury-on-Sea, Devon    OS Ref: SX6544

A new entry with four-star water quality in 1990, Bigbury-on-Sea is a pretty village with a sandy beach at the mouth of the South Devon Avon. Burgh Island, just off the beach, is connected by a causeway which is passable at low tide; at high tide there is a unique sea tractor which transports passengers to and from the island. The hotel on Burgh Island is reputed to have been the inspiration for Agatha Christie's *'Ten Little Indians'*. Dogs are not banned from the beach but must be kept under control.

**Water quality** Beach monitored by the NRA and found to meet the EC standard for clean bathing water in 1990. One outfall, serving 1,286 people, discharges primary treated sewage at low water mark.

**Bathing safety** Safe bathing except near river mouth. Lifeguards patrol between May and September.

**Access** From the village and car park.

**Parking** Car parking for 900 cars.

**Toilets** In the village and on the island.

**Food** Kiosk and café in the village, pub and hotel on the island.

**Seaside activities** Swimming, surfing, windsurfing, fishing, jetskiing.

**Wildlife and walks** Bigbury is on the South Devon Coast Path and leaflets are available describing the area. Between the rivers Avon and Erme, the path follows the undulating cliff-line passing Burgh Island and the beaches of Bigbury and Challaborough. It leads on through one of the most strenuous sections of the coast path: after rounding Beacon Point walking becomes easier as the path drops down to Wonwell Beach and the Erme estuary. The many wild flowers attract numerous butterflies in summer.

## 31 Slapton Sands, Devon    OS Ref: SX8445

A 2½ mile (4.5km) stretch of shingle beach extending from Pilchard Cove in the north to Torcross in the south. The main road from Dartmouth to

Kingsbridge runs along the edge of the beach, with a large, reed-rimmed freshwater lake (Slapton Ley) on the other side. The village of Slapton itself is about a mile (1.6km) inland. The beach was used in 1943-44 as a practice area for the D-day landings and all the local villages were evacuated while the US army took over the area. A Sherman tank has been salvaged from the sea and is on display in Torcross as a memorial, and opposite the lane to Slapton there is a stone obelisk put up by the US army as a 'thank you' to the local people. As can be expected on such a long, open beach, it is often very windy but the views all round Start Bay are spectacular. At low tide it is possible to walk round the headland from Torcross to Beesands, the next cove along, but if you get cut off there is an arduous walk back on the cliff path.

**Water quality** Beach monitored by the NRA and found to meet the EC standard for clean bathing water in 1990. Two outfalls serving 1,582 people discharge untreated sewage, one at low tide and the other 33 yards (30m) below low water mark.

**Bathing safety** Safe bathing but beach shelves steeply – beware of the undertow.

**Access** The A379 runs along the edge of the beach; access is easy.

**Parking** There are car parks at Strete Gate, Torcross and approximately half-way down the length of the beach.

**Toilets** In Torcross and at the car parks.

**Food** Shops, cafés and pubs in Torcross.

**Seaside activities** Swimming, fishing, and a children's play area at Strete Gate.

**Wet weather alternatives** Field Study Centre at Slapton Ley.

**Wildlife and walks** The area is rich in differing habitats and the Slapton Ley Field Centre organises guided walks throughout the summer. On the edges of the beach itself the unusual Yellow Horned Poppy can be found, which should be admired, not picked. Slapton Ley itself is the largest body of fresh water in the south-west of England and as a result is a mecca for many species of wildfowl and other animals. At Torcross there is a hide (with disabled access) to allow panoramic observation across the Ley and also a corner where children can feed the ducks and swans.

## 32 Blackpool Sands, Stoke Fleming, Devon   OS Ref: SY8747

Blackpool Sands is a complete contrast to its Lancashire cousin. The only development of this beach, an unspoilt cove at the northern end of Start Bay, comprises a car park, a building serving takeaway food and drink and a toilet block. A crescent of coarse pink sand ⅔ mile (1km) long is flanked by steep, wooded cliffs. On the southern side of the cove below Matthews Point a valley opens to the shore, from which a stream, Blackpool Lake, flows across the moderately shelving sands into a pool, very popular among families with small children. This lovely beach with a most attractive setting was awarded a

Blue Flag in 1988 and 1989; it had to be withdrawn from the scheme in 1990 due to extensive storm damage early in the year. It is hoped however that the Blue Flag will be flying again in 1991. Easy access and safe bathing make it very popular. Dogs are banned from the beach between May and September.

**Water quality** Beach monitored by the NRA and found to meet the EC standard for clean bathing water in 1990. No sewage is discharged in the vicinity of the beach.

**Bathing safety** Safe bathing, but care is required because the beach shelves steeply.

**Access** The A379 south of Stoke Fleming leads to Blackpool Sands. A side road leads to the car parks where there is a promenade to the sands.

**Parking** There are three car parks adjacent to the beach.

**Toilets** There are toilets at the car park.

**Food** Takeaway with off-licence and beach barbecue.

**Seaside activities** Swimming, windsurfing, sailing, fishing and diving. Windsurf boards and canoes are available for hire. Windsurfing school with RYA instructors. Beach shop offers deckchairs, parasols etc. for hire.

**Wildlife and walks** North of the beach the South Devon Coast Path can be followed, passing through Stoke Fleming to the entrance to the Dart Estuary. South, the footpath leads to Strete Gate and along the 5 mile (8km) sweep of Start Bay, fringed by shingle beaches, and on towards Start Point.

## 33 Torbay, Devon    OS Ref: SY9057–SX9366

Torquay, Paignton and the old fishing port of Brixham combine to make Torbay, one of Britain's most popular areas for seaside holidays and known as the English Riviera on account of the mild climate and abundant palm trees. The large bay has numerous beaches, all of which passed the EC standard for clean bathing water, and boasts five Blue Flags in 1990 (Paignton Sands, Torre Abbey Sands, Meadfoot Beach, Anstey's Cove and Oddicombe Beach). There is a beach to suit every taste around Torbay, from the wide expanses of sand at Paignton and Goodrington to small sheltered coves on the north side of Torquay. As should be expected in a large holiday area, there are lots of things to do locally, and for trips inland Dartmoor is not many miles away. Dogs are banned from most of the beaches between May and September.

**Water quality** All the beaches were monitored by the NRA and found to meet the EC standard for clean bathing water in 1990. See the Golden List for details of sewage outlets in the area.

**Litter** Most beaches are cleaned daily during the summer season.

**Bathing safety** Safe bathing generally. All beaches fly red flags when bathing is unsafe, and beach inspectors patrol with loud hailers.

**Parking, toilets, food** These facilities are not too far from any of the beaches in the area.

**Seaside activities** Swimming, fishing, sailing, pedalo and boat hire, boat trips.

**Wet weather alternatives** English Riviera Centre in Torquay. Kent's Cavern show caves, Paignton Zoo, Torbay Aircraft Museum, Compton Castle, Berry Pomeroy Castle, the Dart Valley Railway and the beautiful village of Cockington are all within easy reach. Leaflets are available from Beach Offices and Tourist Information Centres in Torquay, Paignton and Brixham, with details of activities and places to go.

**Wildlife and walks** The South Devon Coast Path extends round the bay and offers glorious views. More information may be obtained from Tourist Information Centres.

## 34 Teignmouth, Devon   OS Ref: SX9473

A 200 foot (60m) wide beach of red sand stretches for just over a mile (1.6km) from the Point at the mouth of the river Teign eastwards to the Parson and Clerk headland. The river mouth gives access to the busy harbour on the estuary side of the Point and provides an ever-changing boating scene. On the seaward side of the Point the steeply shelving beach is backed by a promenade and the Den Green Gardens. East of the Victorian pier, the promenade gives way to a sea wall with the British Rail Inter-City line, backed by steep cliffs, running parallel to it. Across the river mouth, reached by ferry from the Point, is Shaldon. Its strip of beach is unsafe for bathing but the Ness headland provides excellent views of Teignmouth and the estuary. Teignmouth was awarded the Blue Flag for the first time in 1990.

**Water quality** Beach monitored by the NRA and found to meet the EC standard for clean bathing water in 1990. Two outfalls serving 17,400 people discharge screened sewage through a tidal tank at low water mark.

**Litter** A very small amount of litter is reported on this beach.

**Bathing safety** Currents from the mouth of the river Teign affect bathing from the west end of the beach. Signs indicate the danger areas. The beach is patrolled by lifeguards from the end of May to September.

**Access** Links to the national rail and bus network. Local bus services from the Triangle on the promenade. Easy access to the beach with steps and ramps from the promenade.

**Parking** Car parks at the Point and at Eastcliff accommodate 350 and 200 cars respectively, and there are additional car parks within the town.

**Toilets** There are toilets at Eastfield promenade, near the pier, next to the children's paddling pool and at all the car parks.

**Food** There is a good selection of pubs, cafés, snack bars and ice-cream kiosks on or near the promenade.

**Seaside activities** Swimming and windsurfing from certain areas of the beach. Floats are available for hire during the summer. Facilities for playing tennis, bowls and crazy golf are provided at the Den. There is a botanical garden and children's zoo at Shaldon. There is an open bowls tournament in June and a regatta in August. Carnival week is in July and there is a fair during August.

**Wet weather alternatives** Pier amusements, local museum.

**Wildlife and walks** Set in beautiful countryside, cliff walks to the east and north provide excellent views seawards and over the town to the Ness. The wooded headland of the Ness also provides good views from the summit.

## 35 Dawlish Warren, Devon  OS Ref: SX9778

From the Langstone rock a 220 yard (200m) wide sandy beach extends just over a mile (1.6km) north-east and forms the seaward-facing edge of a double sandspit at the mouth of the River Exe. The south-west end of the beach is backed by a promenade with shops, cafés, amusements and a grassy picnic area, contrasting sharply with the main body of the beach. This forms part of the Dawlish Warren nature reserve which includes the dunes that lie behind the beach and the mudflats on the estuary side of the spit. There are good views across the mouth of the Exe to Exmouth and the red sandstone cliffs beyond. This beach provides something of interest for everyone, from swimming, surfing and family fun to beachcombing and birdwatching. Great care must be taken to ensure that the dunes and sandspit are not damaged. Dogs are banned between 1st May and 30th September.

**Water quality** Beach monitored by the NRA and found to meet the EC standard for clean bathing water in 1990. No sewage is discharged in the vicinity of the beach.

**Litter** Waste paper and plastic left by tourists are a constant problem on this beach, which is cleaned regularly by the local authority.

**Bathing safety** Currents from the mouth of the Exe affect parts of the beach; signs indicate where it is safe to swim. The beach is patrolled by lifeguards from May to September.

**Access** Dawlish Warren is signposted from the A379 north of Dawlish and the beach is signposted from the village. There is a short walk from the car parks to the beach; steps and a ramp lead from the promenade.

**Parking** Four car parks close to the beach provide 1,700 spaces.

**Toilets** There are toilets behind the promenade and at the car park entrance.

**Food** A selection of cafés, snack-bars and ice-cream stalls behind the promenade.

**Seaside activities** Swimming and surfing. Windsurfers and surf canoes available for hire.

***Wet weather alternatives*** Amusement arcade. Dawlish has all the usual facilities of a seaside town.

***Wildlife and walks*** Dawlish Warren Nature Reserve is a Site of Special Scientific Interest owned by Teignbridge District Council and Devon Trust for Nature Conservation. It covers 505 acres (204 hectares) on the spit at the mouth of the Exe and includes a wide variety of habitats: sandy shore, mud-flats, saltmarsh and dunes. Together these provide a diverse flora and fauna. Over 180 types of birds can be seen annually at the reserve, with thousands of waders, geese and ducks over-wintering on the mud-flats. There are 778 species of plants and fungi, including some rare ones. The reserve is also a bird sanctuary and a hide overlooks the mud-flats. Guided walks of the reserve begin at the visitors' centre, signposted from the north-east end of the promenade.

## 36 Exmouth, Devon   OS Ref: SX9980

At the mouth of the river Exe lies the elegant town of Exmouth, a holiday resort popular since the 18th century, and a Blue Flag winner in 1989 and 1990. The 2½ mile (4.5km) long sandy beach becomes rocky at the eastern end, where National Trust land extends to Sandy Bay and the Devon Cliffs holiday camp. A good beach for children, with rockpools at the eastern end containing seaweeds, crabs and sea anemones. There is a passenger ferry to and from Starcross on the west bank of the Exe. Dogs are banned from the beach between May and September from Maer Rocks in the east to a point opposite the Octagon Café in the west.

***Water quality*** Beach monitored by the NRA and found to meet the EC standard for clean bathing water in 1990. One outfall serving 43,009 people discharges primary treated sewage 181 yards (166m) below low water mark, and an improvement scheme is planned. Complaints have been received from sailors about the water quality in the estuary.

***Litter*** The beach is cleaned regularly and there are beach supervisors and dog wardens.

***Bathing safety*** Safe bathing except near the estuary, and a 300 yard (250m) area clearly marked by flags. The Exmouth Beach Rescue Club patrols the beach at weekends and bank holidays.

***Access*** Access to the beach is easy from the promenade.

***Parking*** There are several large car parks adjacent to the beach and also on-street parking.

***Toilets*** There are five toilet blocks along the front.

***Food*** Cafés, restaurants and kiosks.

***Seaside activities*** Swimming, fishing, windsurfing, sailing. Windsurf boards available for hire.

***Wet weather alternatives*** Indoor swimming pool/sports centre, various other sporting activities, cinema.

*Wildlife and walks* Exmouth is on the South-West Way but care should be taken because the sandstone cliffs are crumbly.

## 37 Budleigh Salterton, Devon   OS Ref: SY0782

The beach and sea wall have changed little since Millais painted *The Boyhood of Raleigh* here. The town remains a quiet resort. From the mouth of the River Otter, the wide red shingle beach extends 3 miles (5km) westwards past the promenade to the sandstone cliffs of West Down Beacon, known as the Floors. Small boats are winched up on to the flat pebbles, of which several hundred yards remain exposed at high tide. The Blue Flag was awarded for the first time in 1990. Dogs are banned from the beach between May and September.

*Water quality* Beach monitored by the NRA and found to meet the EC standard for clean bathing water in 1990. One outfall serving 5,066 people discharges untreated sewage 55 yards (50m) below high water mark.

*Bathing safety* Bathing safe. Beach patrolled at weekends by the Beach Rescue Club.

*Access* From the promenade.

*Parking* There is a large car park at the mouth of the river Otter (Lime Kiln) and a smaller one in the town centre 3 minutes' walk from the beach.

*Toilets* Blocks at each end of the promenade.

*Food* One refreshment kiosk with some chairs outside, by the Otter Mouth car park, and another at the Steamer steps at the west end of the beach. One small café on Marine Parade.

*Seaside activities* Swimming, diving, windsurfing and fishing from the beach. Indoor and outdoor bowling, East Devon golf course.

*Wet weather alternatives* Otterton mill – a water-powered mill still used to grind flour. Bicton Park 2 miles (3.3km) from Budleigh Salterton towards Otterton includes narrow gauge railway, countryside museum and other facilities.

*Wildlife and walks* Budleigh Salterton lies on the South Devon Coast Path. This can be followed west along the sandstone cliffs known as the Floors towards Exmouth. This route, offering excellent views, passes Littleham and Otter Coves before reaching Sandy Bay, which as the name suggests is a good sandy beach. East from Budleigh Salterton the coastal path leads to Ladram Bay. Here, the sandstone cliffs have been eroded into some spectacular shapes with huge blocks isolated by the waves. There are also several good walks in the Otter Valley, part of which is a conservation area with good bird life. A guide to 12 walks in the Otter Valley is available from the local tourist office.

## 38 Sidmouth, Devon   OS Ref: SY1287

An elegant Regency seaside resort overlooking Lyme Bay which has escaped over-commercialisation. Sidmouth has two beaches: the town beach and Jacob's Ladder beach to the west. The commitment of the local authority towards the maintenance of their beaches is illustrated in the fact that both these sites were awarded Blue Flags in 1990. The town sits in an open hollow between impressive sandstone cliffs facing a ⅔ mile (1km) long pebble beach. To the west are the Chit Rocks and the Connaught Gardens, which give access to the 1¼ mile (2km) shingle and sand beach of Jacob's Ladder backed by the 500 foot (160m) west cliff. Sidmouth has all the amenities one may require of a quiet resort and is an ideal place for relaxing on the beach or walking in the surrounding countryside, but not a spot for those seeking bright lights and amusements. However, the town comes alive during the first week of August when it hosts an International Folk Festival. Dogs are banned on the town beach between 1st May and 30th September.

**Water quality** Beach monitored by the NRA and found to meet the EC standard for clean bathing water in 1990. One outfall serving 15,880 people discharges screened and macerated sewage through a tidal tank 440 yards (400m) offshore.

**Litter** Generally a clean and litter-free beach, cleaned by local authority.

**Bathing safety** Safe bathing. The beach is patrolled at weekends by the Sidmouth Inshore Rescue Club.

**Access** Steps and slope from the promenade lead on to the town beach; a sloping ramp gives access to Jacob's Ladder beach.

**Parking** Ham, Manor, and Bedford car parks close by in the town.

**Toilets** In the Connaught Gardens and Port Royal.

**Food** Cafés and kiosks at the town beach and a kiosk at Jacob's Ladder beach.

**Seaside activities** Swimming, windsurfing, sailing and fishing. There are paddle floats, windsurf boards and deck-chairs available for hire. Putting and golf courses.

**Wet weather alternatives** Sports centre, museum and theatre.

**Wildlife and walks** There are some excellent walks on the surrounding hills and cliffs; the views of Sidmouth and the Heritage Coast from Peak Hill, Fire Beacon and Salcombe Hill are excellent.

## 39 Branscombe, Devon   OS Ref: SY2188

A quiet, undeveloped 3 miles (5km) of pebble beach stretches from Beer Head to Weston Mouth. A wide valley opens to the coast at Branscombe Mouth with grassland stretching down to the edge of the beach. The cliffs and crags to the east are chalk, whereas to the west there are steep red sandstone cliffs. At Weston Mouth, a stream flows down a steep grassy valley to the beach which is more secluded due to the restricted access (pedestrian only).

**Water quality** No sewage is discharged in the vicinity of this beach.

**Litter** A clean beach normally free of litter.

**Bathing safety** Safe bathing.

**Access** Branscombe is signposted off the A3052 between Sidmouth and Seaton. At Branscombe Mouth there is a short level walk from the car park to the beach.

**Parking** There is a car park adjacent to Branscombe beach with 400 spaces; limited parking in Weston village (20 spaces).

**Toilets** Public conveniences.

**Food** Café on beach.

**Seaside activities** Swimming, windsurfing, sailing, diving and fishing. Boats available for hire. Snorkelling and fishing competitions.

**Wet weather alternatives** Roman camp, pottery, forge and bakery all open to the public.

**Wildlife and walks** East of Branscombe, walks along the Hooken Cliffs take you to Beer Head. In the other direction the South West Way follows the cliffs to Weston, Sidmouth and beyond. The area is geologically very interesting with landslips, deep cut valleys and fossils. There is a varied and interesting flora and rock pools on the shore abound with marine life.

## 40 Seatown, Bridport, Dorset   OS Ref: SY4292

This is an undeveloped and completely unspoilt beach in a most attractive setting. The green and lush Winniford valley opens to the coast at Seatown, where a lovely shingle beach shelves steeply to some sand at low tide. Steep sandstone cliffs rise on either side of the valley, the mellow coloured sandstone making a pleasing contrast to the green grassland above. The cliffs show the distinctive signs of the sea's continual attack – sheer exposed rock at their summit with rock slumped at their base. To the west lies Golden Cap, the highest point on the southern coast, where the cliffs rise 626 feet (190m) above the shore. The beach is very popular with fishermen.

**Water quality** Beach monitored by the NRA and found to meet the EC standard for clean bathing water in 1990. No sewage is discharged in the vicinity of the beach.

**Bathing safety** The beach shelves steeply and great care is required when bathing.

**Access** A narrow lane from Chideock on the A35 leads to the shore.

**Parking** Car park behind the beach.

*Toilets* In the car park.

*Food* The pub overlooking the beach serves food.

*Seaside activities* Swimming and fishing.

*Wildlife and walks* On either side of the beach the rugged sandstone and shale cliffs rise and fall steeply where river valleys cut through to the sea. To the west of the beach the Dorset coast path climbs on to the Golden Cap and from its flat table summit there are terrific views along the coastline and inland over the undulating patchwork of fields. To the east is Thorncombe Beacon, where a fire used to be lit to warn of potential invasion.

## 41 Burton Bradstock, Dorset   OS Ref: SY4890

One of Dorset's four-star rated beaches, Chesil Beach officially begins here and runs the whole length of the coast as far as Portland. The shingle beach is backed by dramatic sandstone cliffs which are owned by the National Trust. At low tide a band of sand is revealed. The highly picturesque village of Burton Bradstock is worth exploring too, with its thatched, stone-built cottages set around a 15th-century church. Dogs (except guide dogs) are banned from the beach from June to September inclusive.

*Water quality* No sewage discharged in the vicinity of this beach, which was monitored by the NRA and found to meet the EC standard for clean bathing water in 1990.

*Bathing safety* The beach shelves steeply and there is a strong undertow which can make bathing dangerous.

*Access* The beach is signposted off the B3157 in Burton Bradstock, 3 miles (5km) east of Bridport.

*Parking* There is a 500-space car park close to the beach.

*Toilets* Public toilets with facilities for the disabled.

*Food* Beach café.

*Seaside activities* Swimming.

*Wildlife and walks* The coast path follows the cliff with fine views over Lyme Bay. As with most stretches of the Dorset coast, there are good geological exposures to be admired.

## 42 Weymouth, Dorset   OS Ref: SY6779

The wide sweep of soft sand overlooked by the elegant Georgian houses of the Esplanade makes this a very popular beach. To the north of the town, the beach is backed by the Lodmoor Country Park which extends round the bay to Overcombe and Bowleaze Cove. The Lodmoor end of the beach gained a four-star water quality rating in 1990. To the south lies Weymouth harbour which combines the old and the new; the modern berths used by cross-channel ferries, hydrofoils and luxury yachts contrast with the picturesque 17th-century fishing harbour. This is set in the old town which provides a pleasantly different atmosphere to the busy sea front. Through the lift-bridge in the old town lies a marina for 1,000 craft, beyond which lies Radipole Lake. There are views from the beach of the Isle of Portland and Portland Harbour. A Blue Flag winner in 1989 and 1990, with a reputation for sand highly suitable for building sand castles. Dogs are banned from the main beach areas but are permitted on a lead in a designated area near the Weymouth Pavilion Complex. Poop scoops are available free.

**Water quality** Beach monitored by the NRA and found to meet the EC standard for clean bathing water in 1990. No sewage is discharged in the vicinity of this beach.

**Bathing safety** Very safe swimming from all of the beach, which is patrolled by lifeguards throughout the holiday season, April to October. There is a lost children's hut on the beach near the King's Statue. From March to October there is a full-time beach supervisor and staff equipped with two-way radios.

**Access** There are steps and ramps from the promenade to the sand. There is an hourly open-top bus service along the esplanade to Overcombe and Bowleaze Cove, and also to Portland.

**Parking** There are car parks at Swannery (800 spaces), Lodmoor (1000 spaces) and Pavilion (300 spaces).

**Toilets** Public conveniences with facilities for the disabled at three points along the beach.

**Food** Cafés all along the Esplanade.

**First aid** St John's Ambulance post on the beach near the King's statue.

**Seaside activities** Swimming and boating from the beach, with rowing and motor boats available for hire. There are organised sailing and windsurfing regattas throughout the season. Sand sculpture, Punch and Judy, merry-go-rounds, swings, bumper boats and a free children's beach club provide traditional entertainment. The Weymouth Country Park at Lodmoor offers a number of seaside attractions including mini golf, model world, miniature railway and leisure ranch.

**Wet weather alternatives** Pavilion Theatre and complex. Swimming pool, Diving and Shipwreck Centre, Nothe Fort museums, Sea Life Centre, butterfly farm, Portland Bill lighthouse and open days at the Portland navy base. Time walk at Hope Square.

**Wildlife and walks** Radipole Lake and swannery is a nature reserve with a wide variety of habitats from freshwater lagoon to grassland and scrub. There are many walks through the reserve where numerous types of birds can be seen, including the bearded tit and Cetti's warbler. There are conducted tours from the RSPB visitors' centre. The Lodmoor Country Park also contains a nature reserve with walks providing views across Weymouth Bay. There are cliff top walks on Portland which provide excellent views across the bay. Other paths allow access on to The Ridgeway and to the White Horse.

## 43 Ringstead Bay, Dorset   OS Ref: SY760814F

Chalk cliffs and undercliffs produced by chalk landslips surround Ringstead Bay and at their foot a pebble beach with scattered rockpools curves 1¼ miles (2km) round the bay. 'Burning Cliff', to the east of the beach, is so named because oil shale smouldered for several years in the 19th century. There are magnificent views from White Nothe at the eastern side of the bay.

**Water quality** Beach monitored by the NRA and found to meet the EC standard for clean bathing water in 1990. No sewage is discharged in the vicinity of this beach.

**Bathing safety** Care is required when swimming as the beach shelves steeply.

**Access** Ringstead is signposted off the A353, 3 miles (5km) east of Weymouth. The road leads to a National Trust car park on the crest of the down or, alternatively, a toll road can be taken to the car park in Ringstead.

**Parking** There are two car parks with approximately 400 spaces.

**Toilets** Public conveniences in the village.

**Food** Small café and shop.

**Seaside activities** Swimming, windsurfing, sailing, diving and fishing.

**Wildlife and walks** The area is of interest for its geology, fossils and the vegetation and wildlife of the undercliffs, particularly invertebrates. The White Nothe Undercliff Nature Reserve is run by the National Trust. The Dorset Coast Path skirts the cliff top. To the east, Durdle Door and Lulworth Cove are reached and westwards the path leads past the medieval village site towards Bowleaze and Weymouth, 5 miles (8km) away.

## 44 Durdle Door, Dorset   OS Ref: SY8280

This beach is famous for Durdle Door Arch, created by the great erosive power of the sea and probably the most photographed view along the Dorset coast. The eastern end of the beach (Durdle Door Cove) is protected by the arch while the rest of the beach is partially protected by a submerged offshore reef that dries in places along its length. The beach is a steep, narrow strand of mixed shingle, gravel and sand which makes a strenuous ⅔ mile (1km) walk to the western end where Bats Head, a chalk headland, forms an attractive boundary to the beach itself. All the cliffs backing the beach are steep and prone to occasional rockfalls – thus climbing or sheltering underneath them is not advised.

**Water quality** Beach monitored by the NRA and found to meet the EC standard for clean bathing water in 1990. No sewage is discharged in the vicinity of this beach, which gained a four-star grade water quality status by meeting both imperative and guideline standards for coliform levels.

**Litter** A small amount of marine litter, including plastic, rope and wood is washed up in Durdle Door Cove.

**Bathing safety** Care required as with most shingle and gravel beaches since there can be sudden steep slopes underwater. The western end of the beach may be cut off under certain tide and wave conditions.

**Access** Beach approached by steep ½ mile (800m) footpath from cliff top car park. Access on to the eastern end of the beach down a steep flight of steps cut into the bay cliff can be slippery in wet weather.

**Parking** Large cliff top car park at Durdle Door Caravan Camping Park (with excellent views across Weymouth Bay to the Isle of Portland).

**Toilets** At the caravan park.

**Food** Café and store in the caravan park.

**Seaside activities** Swimming, diving, snorkelling and fishing. The steep access to the beach means that heavy equipment, including picnic tables, should not be carried down.

**Wildlife and walks** The undulating cliffs form a challenging section of the Dorset Coast Path. To the east lies Lulworth Cove and the Isle of Purbeck, to the west White Nothe headland. However, the reward for tackling this stretch of Heritage Coast is a fine view across Weymouth Bay and to the glorious beaches below. The chalk habitat creates picturesque downland with its accompanying flora and fauna.

## 45 Lulworth Cove, West Lulworth, Dorset    OS Ref: SY8380

The spectacular scenery along the Dorset coast attracts large numbers of visitors and this is particularly true of Lulworth Cove. The dramatic cliffs and rock formations are famous among geologists. There is a series of layers of different rock types parallel to the shore; the band on the seaward edge is hard Purbeck Limestone which is very resistant to erosion. At Lulworth this hard rock has been breached and the invading sea has eroded the softer clay behind to form the impressive cove. A narrow shingle beach forms a margin to the round bay which is ringed by rugged cliffs. The eastern edge of the cove marks the edge of the Lulworth Army Firing Range. Access to the range is restricted to weekends and August. Local notices indicate when it is safe.

**Water quality** Beach monitored by the NRA and found to meet the EC standard for clean water in 1990. One outfall serving 2,000 people discharges screened and macerated sewage several yards below low water mark just outside the cove. There have been reports that the waste is sometimes visible and is washed back into the cove. A £11.9 million improvement scheme should rectify the problem.

**Bathing safety** Bathing is only safe close inshore because of strong currents and rocks within the cove.

**Access** The road from West Lulworth leads down to the shore.

**Parking** There is a privately owned car park (Weld Estate) on the cliff top with about 1,300 spaces.

**Toilets** Public toilets including facilities for the disabled.

**Food** Beach café; several cafés, restaurants and hotels in West Lulworth.

**Seaside activities** Swimming, windsurfing, diving, sailing, canoeing, rowing and fishing. There are rowing boats available for hire and boat trips along the coast to Durdle Door.

**Wildlife and walks** Rockpools abound below the cliff and contain a wealth of marine life – between 20 and 30 different types of animals and plants can be seen. The surrounding area is also rich in wildlife, for a wide variety of flowers, butterflies and birds complement the unique geological features. There is a series of circular walks starting at the main car park. Clearly marked paths lead west over Hambury Tout to Durdle Door, a magnificent rock arch. There is a short walk from the car park to Stair Hole, a second cove in the early stages of development. Waves break through a series of arches in the hard limestone and are eroding the softer rock lying behind. There are some excellent rock folds and faults exposed in the hole. When the Lulworth Army Range is open, marked paths can be followed east to Mupe Bay. It is worth stopping at Pepler Point to view the superb prospect across the cove from its narrow entrance. After entering the range a short detour leads to the remains of a fossil forest. Steps lead down the cliff where fossilised remains of trees can be seen in the cliff. In the range it is dangerous to leave the marked paths. Leaflets which describe the walks in detail are available at the information centre close to the beach.

## 46 Kimmeridge, Nr Wareham, Dorset   OS Ref: SY9078

The beach has no sand and is formed of cobbles, stones and smooth flat rocks sheltered below crumbling shale cliffs. It is a good spot for combining a coastal walk with exploration of the excellent rockpools. Better for older children than the young. The bay is part of the Purbeck Marine Wildlife Reserve, and a wealth of marine life abounds on the shore and in the shallow waters. On the eastern headland of this square bay stands the Clavell Tower, which was built as a folly and was for a time used as a coastguard look-out post. The tower now stands empty. The opposite side of the bay marks the edge of the army firing range, which covers the land between the bay and Lulworth Cove to the west. The shale cliffs around the bay are very unstable and beach users should not climb on the cliffs or sunbathe below them because of the danger of falling rocks. The bay provides some of the best conditions for windsurfing in the south of England.

**Water quality** Beach monitored by the NRA and found to meet the EC standard for clean bathing water in 1990. No sewage is discharged in the vicinity of this beach.

**Litter** A lot of plastic rubbish is frequently washed up on to the beach; it is cleaned occasionally.

**Bathing safety** Bathers must beware of submerged rocks that can make swimming dangerous. There are, however, no strong currents or dangerous tides. A coastguard's hut is manned by auxiliary coastguards at weekends and sometimes in rough weather during the summer.

**Access** A toll road from Kimmeridge village leads to the bay, and a track leads from the car park to the beach.

**Parking** There are two car parks on the cliff top with about 700 spaces.

**Toilets** There are two toilet blocks near the beach and a toilet for the disabled in Kimmeridge village, 1 mile (1.6km) from the beach.

**Food** Ice-cream kiosk. There is a shop/restaurant in Kimmeridge village.

**Seaside activities** Swimming, diving, windsurfing and fishing. There are two slipways for launching small boats from the beach.

**Wildlife and walks** There is an information centre at the eastern end of the bay run by the Dorset Trust for Nature Conservation which sponsors the Purbeck Marine Wildlife Reserve. The centre can provide information on the numerous animals and plants to be found around the bay. In addition, it produces a leaflet describing a nature trail which is laid out in the area. There are well-marked walks across the firing range to the west which are open at weekends, for a few days at Christmas, the two public holidays in May and for the whole of August. Information about opening days can be obtained by ringing the Range Office on Bindon Abbey 462721.

## 47 Swanage, Dorset   OS Ref: SZ0379

Swanage beach has frequently received Blue Flags for its high standard of cleanliness and facilities. The safe sheltered bay is flanked by magnificent chalk headlands on either side: Ballard Point in the north and Peveril Point to the south of the bay. The gently sloping sands form a good 1¼ mile (2km) family beach with a promenade providing all the facilities of a small seaside resort. The development has not spoilt the sea front. Swanage is an ideal spot for a holiday combining days on the beach with explorations of the superb Dorset coastline. Dogs are banned from the beach between 1st May and 30th September.

**Water quality** Beach monitored by the NRA and found to meet the EC standard for clean bathing water in 1990. One outfall serving 20,000 people discharges screened and macerated sewage 110 yards (100m) below low water mark off Peveril Point.

**Litter** A clean beach with only a small amount of litter left by visitors; the beach is cleaned daily. There are reports that marine litter can be a problem after an east wind.

**Bathing safety** Safe bathing. No lifeguard, but a beach inspector patrols the beach during the summer. There is a first aid post on the promenade adjacent to the tourist information centre.

**Access** Steps and ramps from the promenade lead to the sand.

**Parking** There are car parks at Broad Road, De Moulham Road, Victoria Avenue and one in the town centre.

**Toilets** Public toilets with facilities for the disabled at several points along the promenade.

**Food** Numerous cafés, restaurants, and take-aways within easy reach of the beach.

**Seaside activities** Swimming, windsurfing, diving, sailing and fishing. There are pedalos and motor boats for hire. Fishing and boat trips are available from the quay, where there is also a diving school.

**Wet weather alternatives** Tithe Barn Museum and Arts Centre, Railway Station Steam Museum, indoor bowling complex. The lifeboat house is open to visitors.

**Wildlife and walks** The Dorset Coast Path extends in both directions from Swanage Bay, passing through beautiful countryside along this section of coast. To the north of the beach Ballard Cliff rises on to Ballard Down, and the path follows the cliffs round to Handfast Point, which provides excellent views of Old Harry Rocks lying just off shore, and across Poole Bay. South of Peveril Point above Durlston Bay and Head is the Durlston Country Park. There is parking within the park and an information centre provides details of a series of walks in the area. The long-distance coast path follows the cliffs beyond Anvil Point Lighthouse, passing the Dancing Ledge, Seascombe cliff and continuing to St Aldhelm's Head and beyond. There is a series of shorter circular routes starting from the country park that explore both the coast and the beautiful scenery inland. A leaflet produced by the Dorset Heritage Coast Project describes the various walks.

## 48 Studland, Dorset   OS Ref: SZ0483

A lovely clean beach that is an Area of Outstanding Natural Beauty. 3 miles (5km) of excellent sandy beach is backed by unspoilt dunes. The beach sweeps south from the entrance to Poole harbour to the splendid chalk cliffs of Handfast Point, once connected to the Needles of the Isle of Wight, which are visible on the horizon most days. The beach can be divided into three areas – south beach, middle beach and the north or Knoll beach. Behind the Knoll beach there is a brackish lake and marsh area which forms the Studland Heath National Nature Reserve. Visitors should note that a section of the beach is used by naturists. Bye-laws require that dogs are kept on leads and all faeces must be removed by the owners from the beach. Jetskiing is banned.

**Water quality** Beach monitored by the NRA and found to meet the EC standard for clean bathing water in 1990. No sewage is discharged in the vicinity of this beach.

79

**Litter** This is a very clean beach due to the excellent efforts of the National Trust. In summer 4-5 tons of litter are removed daily from the litter bins and sands.

**Bathing safety** Safe bathing off the main beach; strong currents at the entrance to Poole harbour make bathing at the northern end of the beach unsafe. The beach is patrolled by National Trust wardens from Easter to September.

**Access** Each section of the beach is signposted from Studland village. It is a short walk from the car parks to the sands. There is a wheelchair ramp at the Knoll beach.

**Parking** Four car parks provide space for 3,500 cars.

**Toilets** Five blocks. New toilets at Middle and Knoll beach have facilities for the disabled with provision for nursing mothers at Knoll beach.

**Food** Cafés and kiosks.

**Seaside activities** Swimming, windsurfing, sailing and fishing. Windsurf boards are available for hire.

**Wildlife and walks** The Studland Heath National Nature Reserve containing a brackish lagoon, Little Sea, lies on the landward side of the beach. The reserve cannot be reached from the beach but must be entered from the road which bounds its western edge. There is a wide variety of wildlife including the rare smooth snake and adders. Walkers are advised to wear stout shoes and stick to the marked paths. A leaflet describing seven local walks is available from the National Trust Information Centre at Knoll beach. A leaflet which describes the local wildlife and guided walks in the area is produced by the Dorset Heritage Coast and Dorset Trust for Nature Conservation and is available locally. The Dorset Coast Path starts, or alternatively finishes, at the entrance to Poole Harbour. It follows the bay south and on to the Foreland. There are splendid views of the cliffs and the chalk pillars, Old Harry and Old Harry's wife, isolated from the adjacent headland by the ever-eroding waves. The path continues south towards Ballard Point where there are fine views of Swanage Bay.

## 49 Sandbanks, Poole, Dorset   OS Ref: SZ0487

A Blue Flag winner for two years which only just failed to achieve a Good Beach Guide four-star rating again in 1990. From North Haven Point at the end of the Sandbank spit, the fringe of golden sand stretches 3 miles (5km) north-east to merge with the beaches of Bournemouth. The pedestrian promenade is backed by the steep pine- and shrub-covered Canford Cliffs. Flaghead Chine, Cranford Chine and Branksome Chine cut through the cliffs to the beach. South-west, the cliffs give way to the low-lying Sandbanks peninsula at the mouth of Poole Harbour. Here the beach is edged by dunes and overlooked by holiday development and the Sandbanks Pavilion and recreation area. The whole of Poole Harbour is a centre for sailing and water sports, and there is an ever-changing boating scene at the harbour entrance.

There are excellent views across the harbour and of Brownsea Island from Evenning Hill off the western shore road. A removal of canine faeces bye-law and dog ban between Sandbanks and Branksome Chine is in force from May to September, and dogs must be kept on a lead on the promenade.

**Water quality** Beach monitored by the NRA and found to meet the EC standard for clean bathing water in 1990. No sewage is discharged in the vicinity of this beach.

**Litter** The beach is cleaned daily.

**Bathing safety** Safe bathing except at the extreme western end of the beach near the harbour entrance. Warning signs indicate where not to swim. Segregation of bathers and powered vessels is actively encouraged with a buoyed area in which boats must observe a strict speed limit. The beach is patrolled by lifeguards at weekends and on bank holidays from May to September and there is a first aid post manned by St John Ambulance at weekends.

**Access** There is easy access along the length of the beach; paths lead down the cliffs to the promenade. Disabled access is available to the promenade at Sandbanks, Branksome Chine and Branksome Dene Chine.

**Parking** There are seven car parks along the length of the beach with 1,400 spaces. There is also parking available on adjacent streets.

**Toilets** There are toilets (with facilities for the disabled) along the beach.

**Food** There are cafés, and kiosks close to the beach.

**Seaside activities** Swimming, windsurfing, sailing, and fishing. There are windsurf boards and boats for hire. Poole harbour has several windsurfing and sailing schools. There is also a putting green, crazy golf and a variety of children's amusements.

**Wet weather alternatives** Tower Park leisure complex incorporating Splashdown, Ice-Trax, Mega-Bowl, multi-screen cinema and sports centre; swimming pool, aquarium, Guildhall Museum, Archaeological Museum, Royal National Lifeboat Museum, Maritime Museum, Waterfront Museum, Arts Centre and Poole Pottery, Poole Park.

**Wildlife and walks** There is a car and pedestrian ferry from North Haven Point to Shell Bay, where the extensive Studland Heath National Nature Reserve backs an excellent beach. There is also a pedestrian ferry to Brownsea Island. 200 acres (80 hectares) of this 500 acre (202 hectare) National Trust-owned island is a nature reserve run by the Dorset Trust for Nature Conservation. There are many different types of habitat to be found on the island including heathland, woodland, freshwater lakes, salt marsh and the sea shore. There is a nature trail and guided walks are available during the summer. Further information is available from the National Trust shop on the island's landing quay.

## 50 Bournemouth, Dorset   OS Ref: SZ4109

Bournemouth is often referred to as 'the garden city by the sea' because of its many parks, including the upper and lower Bourne Gardens. These wind their way through the town centre following the Bourne Valley and emerge at the sea front. Bournemouth has an excellent family beach, which was awarded a Blue Flag again in 1990. Throughout the summer the wide promenade, which backs the golden sands, is traffic-free. The steeply sloping shrub-covered cliffs that rise above the promenade are bisected by a series of deep wooded glades, known as chines. These valleys all have their own individual characters and divide the long sea front into distinctive sections. This is not merely a seaside town, but truly a holiday centre. You may just want to enjoy the sun, sea and sand, but you can also take advantage of the resort's numerous facilities. There are two piers, amusements, and a beach club to entertain children. In addition there is a full programme of events staged throughout the summer including carnivals, regattas and competitions.

**Water quality** Beach monitored by the NRA and found to meet the EC standard for clean bathing water in 1990. No sewage is discharged in the vicinity of this beach.

**Litter** Beach cleaned daily.

**Bathing safety** Hoisted red flags indicate when conditions are unsafe for swimming. Lifeguards, using inflatable safety boats, patrol the beach. All the deckchair attendants are qualified in life-saving. The Beach Leisure Department surveys the beach by closed circuit television during the season and all staff are first aid trained. There are two St John Ambulance first aid posts, and voluntary lifeguard stations at Southbourne and Burley Chine.

**Access** The promenade is reached by zig-zag pathways down the cliff. There is a cliff-lift to the east and west of the pier and at Fisherman's Walk.

**Parking** There are several car parks close to the beach and in the town, plus spaces along the roads.

**Toilets** There are 15 public conveniences along the promenade.

**Food** There are numerous catering outlets along the promenade.

**Seaside activities** Swimming, surfing, windsurfing, sailing and fishing. There are rowing boats and pedalo floats available for hire. There are boat trips from the pier. A land train operates along the promenade between Bournemouth and Boscombe Piers.

**Wet weather alternatives** Bournemouth International Conference Centre. Leisure centre 110 yards (100m) from the beach with indoor swimming pool, Russel-Cotes Art Museum, Transport Museum and the Shelley Museum. The Pier leisure centre and sea front amusements. The Littledown Centre with swimming pools, water slides, sports hall and gym.

**Wildlife and walks** Stretching east from Bournemouth is the 1¼ mile (2km) long Hengistbury headland which separates Poole Bay and Christchurch Bay, and encloses Christchurch Harbour on its landward side. Most of the headland remains undeveloped and has been designated as a Site of Special Scientific Interest because of the wide variety of plant and animal life it supports. The headland is a nature reserve owned by Bournemouth Borough Council. It contains a wide variety of habitats including grassland, heath, woods, salt marsh, freshwater marsh, dunes, rocky and shingle shore. There is a nature trail on the eastern slopes of the headland. The summit of Warren Hill on the landward end of the headland provides good views of Christchurch Bay, Poole Bay, the Solent and the Isle of Wight beyond. There is a south-facing 1 mile (1.6km) pebble beach below the imposing sandstone cliffs. In sharp contrast to this undeveloped beach is the sandspit stretching north from the headland to the entrance of Christchurch harbour, where the groyne-ribbed sands are backed by beach huts. A small land train takes passengers from the Hengistbury Head car park to the tip of the headland.

## 51  Highcliffe Castle, Highcliffe, Dorset   OS Ref: SZ2093

From Highcliffe Castle (which resembles the ruins of an impressive cathedral rather than a castle), steps lead down the gently sloping shrub- and tree-covered cliffs directly on to the sand. A lovely, long beach of sand and pebble extends from Highcliffe Castle to Highcliffe Crow's Nest. This is a clean, unspoilt stretch of beach which is ideal for a day relaxing in the sunshine. Between 1st May and 30th September dogs are permitted on Highcliffe Castle beach but not on Highcliffe Crow's Nest. On the promenade, cliff paths and adjacent car park, dogs must be kept on a lead. Owners are asked to clean up after their dogs and receptacles are provided.

**Water quality** Beach monitored by the NRA and found to meet the EC standard for clean bathing water in 1990. No sewage is discharged in the vicinity of this beach.

**Litter** During the summer the local authority employs a team of litter pickers to clean the beaches and surrounding area.

**Bathing safety** Safe bathing but care is required because the beach shelves quite quickly. The beach is patrolled by lifeguards and a patrol boat daily from mid-July to early September. This stretch of coast has separate designated areas for swimming and windsurfing, which are signposted on the beach. There is a slight problem with weever fish.

**Access** From the A337 through Highcliffe a side road leads to Highcliffe Castle. There are steps and a path down the cliff. The steps are quite gentle but access may be difficult for the elderly and the disabled, particularly the walk back up.

**Parking** Car park at Highcliffe Castle with 100 spaces, 110 yards (100m) walk to beach. Car park at Steamer Point with 172 spaces, 330 yards (300m) walk to beach and car park at Highcliffe top with 600 spaces, 440 yards (400m) walk to the beach.

**Toilets** In Highcliffe Castle grounds and Highcliffe Crow's Nest.

**Food** Shop/café in the grounds of Highcliffe Castle. During the summer there is often someone selling ices along the beach from a cool box. Café on the cliff top at Highcliffe Crow's Nest.

**Seaside activities** Swimming and windsurfing; the latter is restricted to Highcliffe Crow's Nest; swimming is confined to Highcliffe Castle. Fishing.

**Wildlife and walks** There are woodland and nature walks on the cliffs at Steamer Point, where an information centre can provide details of the flora and fauna to be seen in the area.

## 52 Sandown Bay, Isle of Wight   OS Ref: SZ5984

The twin resorts of Sandown and Shanklin face Sandown Bay, the largest bay on the Isle of Wight. From Shanklin Chine, a deep wooded cleft cutting through the cliffs, a safe and sandy beach curves gently northwards to Sandown and the white cliffs of Culver Down beyond. Almost 2 miles (3km) of unbroken sands separate these busy holiday resorts made popular by the Victorians. Houses and hotels perch on the cliffs and downs which ring the bay, sloping down to the esplanades which edge the beach. There are pleasant walks at each end of the bay, and the old village of Shanklin can be explored.

**Water quality** Beach monitored by the NRA and found to meet the EC standard for clean bathing water in 1990. One outfall serving 50,000 people discharges secondary treated effluent at Yaverland.

**Litter** The beach is cleaned by the local authority and licensed beach operators.

**Bathing safety** Safe bathing.

**Access** Steps and ramps from the esplanade in both Sandown and Shanklin. There is a lift down the cliff to the esplanade in Shanklin.

**Parking** In Shanklin two car parks off the esplanade. In Sandown several car parks off the High Street.

**Toilets** At either end of the esplanade in both resorts.

**Food** Shops, cafés, pubs and restaurants along the esplanades.

**Seaside activities** Swimming, windsurfing and fishing. Beach huts, boats and deck chairs for hire. Jetski hire at Shanklin.

**Wet weather alternatives** Pier and amusements, Sandown Leisure Complex, zoo and museum. Putting and crazy golf, tennis courts. In Brading, just outside Sandown, a wax museum, dolls' museum, animal world and Roman villa.

**Wildlife and walks** The Shanklin Chine provides a pleasantly contrasting walk away from the sea-front. A footpath south of Shanklin leads along the cliffs to Luccombe. Here another chine gives access to Luccombe Bay – a small and undeveloped beach. North of Sandown the cliffs can be followed on to Culver Down. There are excellent views back across the bay.

# South-East England

The south-east of England is rich in sharp coastal contrasts. There are long shingle banks, sand dunes, saltmarshes and the wide open skies of Norfolk. Low clay cliffs predominate in Suffolk, powerless to resist the forces of the invading sea. The creeks and mud flats of Essex and the Thames estuary provide yet another type of coastline while the striking white cliffs of the south coast form an impressive backdrop to many busy holiday resorts and ferry terminals that are the gateway to Europe. Long empty sands and crowded promenades are both to be found.

The south-east has some of the most heavily developed coastal regions and with people and popularity come problems. The heavy traffic in the Channel creates a continual problem with marine litter and oil being washed up on to the beaches. Extensive stretches of the coastline suffer from pollution by sewage. Sludge dumping off the Thames Estuary, nuclear and industrial discharges are all causes for concern. The disturbance around Shakespeare Cliff from the construction of the Channel Tunnel will have a severe long-term impact on marine and coastal life. On a coastline under pressure from every type of human activity, tourism, industry, and residential development, continual effort is needed to ensure that those areas left unspoilt will remain so for future generations.

### Beaches receiving European Blue Flags in 1990:

Hill Head, Stokes Bay, Eastbourne, Bexhill, West Beach Clacton, Southwold, South Beach Lowestoft.

# South-East England

**16** Wells-next-the-Sea — Blakeney Point — Sheringham — Cromer — **15** Happisburgh — **14** Sea Palling

Hunstanton — Heacham — Brancaster — Holkham Bay — Mundesley

Kings Lynn

Great Yarmouth – North/Pier
Great Yarmouth – South **f**

Norwich

**13** Lowestoft

**f** = failed to meet EC standard for clean bathing water in 1990.
Numbered beaches appear in the following chapter.

**12** Southwold
**11** Dunwich

## Coastal walks
Saxon Shore Way
Gravesend to Rye 143 miles (230km).

**10** Aldeburgh

Norfolk Coast Path
Hunstanton to Cromer (part of Peddar's Way and Norfolk
Coast Path).

Ipswich

Felixstowe
Dovercourt

Colchester

Walton-on-the-Naze
Frinton-on-Sea
Holland-on-Sea
**9** Clacton-on-Sea
Jaywick
Brightlingsea

Southend – Thorpe Bay
Southend – Westcliff
Leigh-on-Sea
Shoeburyness

London

St Mildreds
Leysdown
**7** Margate
Joss Bay
Broadstairs
Ramsgate **f**
Sandwich Bay **f**
Deal Castle **f**
**6** St Margaret's Bay

Chatham

Minnis

Minster Leas
**8** Whitstable (west beach)
Heme Bay
Dover

Hythe **f**
Dymchurch **f**
Folkestone **f**
Sandgate
St Mary's Bay
Littlestone

Hove **f**
Brighton **f**
Saltdean
Newhaven **f**
Camber Sands

Pagham
Bognor Regis
Middleton-on-Sea

Brighton

**5** Bexhill-on-Sea
Norman's Bay **f**
Pett Level/Winchelsea
Hastings
Pevensey Bay **f**

**1** Lee-on-the-Solent
**2** Stokes Bay
Southsea

Southwick
Lancing
Worthing **f**

Eastbourne

Selsey **f**
Littlehampton
Bracklesham Bay
West Wittering

West Hayling

**4** Eastbourne
**3** Cuckmere Haven
Seaford **f**

# The Golden List  *See page 25 for further details*

| Beach No on Map | Rating. The more stars the better. f=failed | Resort | Sewage outlets | Population discharging from outlet | Type of treatment | Discharge point relative to low water mark, unless otherwise stated. Distance given in metres | Remarks |
|---|---|---|---|---|---|---|---|
| **HAMPSHIRE** | | | | | | | |
| | ★★ | **Barton-on-Sea** | 1 | 17,400 | Flow transfer | At LWM | Pebbles and shingle. Scheme under construction. |
| | ★★ | **Milford-on-Sea** | | | | | Pebbles. As above. |
| | ★★★★ | **Lepe** | | | | | Sand and shingle. |
| | ★★ | **Calshot** | 1 | 448 | Maceration/ tidal tank | | Mud. Improvement scheme. |
| | ★★★ | **Hill Head** | | | | | |
| *1* ★★★ | | **Lee-on-the-Solent** | 1 | 200,000 | Primary | 1100 below | Sand and shingle. Improvement scheme under construction. |
| *2* ★★★ | | **Stokes Bay** | | | | | As above. |
| | ★★★ | **Southsea** | | | | | Shingle. |
| | ★★★ | **Eastney** | 1 | 200,000 | Maceration screens/ tidal tank | At LWM | Shingle. Sewage discharged into channel between Eastney and Hayling. New outfall under construction. |
| | ★★★ | **Eaststoke** | | | | | Sandy. |
| | ★★★ | **West Hayling** | | | | | Sandy. |
| **WEST SUSSEX** | | | | | | | |
| | ★★★ | **West Wittering** | | | | | Sandy. Safe bathing. |
| | ★★★ | **East Wittering** | | | | | |
| | ★★★ | **Bracklesham Bay** | | | | | Sandy. |
| f ★★ | | **Selsey Bill** | | | | | Shingle. Bathing unsafe. |
| | ★★ | **Pagham** | | | | | Shingle. |
| | ★★★ | **Bognor Regis** | 1 | 71,500 | Maceration/ screens | 3km below LWM | Sandy. Safe bathing. |

| Beach No on Map | Rating. The more stars the better. f=failed | Resort | Sewage outlets | Population discharging from outlet | Type of treatment | Discharge point relative to low water mark, unless otherwise stated. Distance given in metres | Remarks |
|---|---|---|---|---|---|---|---|
| | *** | **Middleton-on-Sea** | | | | | Sand and shingle. |
| | *** | **Littlehampton** | 1 | 53,000 | Maceration/screens | 2.5km below LWM | Sandy. Safe bathing. |
| | | Goring-by-Sea | 1 | 39,000 | Primary | At LWM | Sand and shingle. Safe bathing. |
| | *** ** | **Worthing** | 1 | 75,000 | Primary | 335 below LWM | Shingle and sand. Improvement scheme planned. |
| | f ** | **Lancing** | | | | | Shingle and sand. £29 million improvement scheme. |
| | *** ** | Shoreham-by-Sea | 1 | 52,000 | Tidal tank | 600 below | Commercial port. Improvement scheme. |

**EAST SUSSEX**

| Beach No on Map | Rating | Resort | Sewage outlets | Population discharging from outlet | Type of treatment | Discharge point | Remarks |
|---|---|---|---|---|---|---|---|
| | f ** | Southwick | | | | | Shingle. |
| | f ** | **Hove** | | | | | Pebbles and sand. £42 million improvement scheme. |
| | f ** | **Brighton** | 5 | | | | All storm water overflows. |
| | ** | **Saltdean** | | | | | Rocky with some sand. |
| | | Portobello | 1 | 300,000 | Screens | 1900 below | New long sea outfall. |
| | f ** | **Newhaven** | | | | | Sandy beach within breakwater. New long sea outfall. |
| | f ** | **Seaford** | 1 | | | At LWM | Shingle beach is steep. New long sea outfall. |
| 3 | | Cuckmere Haven | | | | | Pebbles. |
| 4 *** | | **Eastbourne** | 1 | 87,000 | Maceration/screens | 650 below | Shingle with sand. £16.7 million improvement scheme. |
| | f ** | **Pevensey Bay** | 1 | 9,590 | Maceration/tidal tank | 360 below | Shingle with sand. Improvement scheme as above. |

| Beach No on Map / Rating. The more stars the better. f=failed | Resort | Sewage outlets | Population discharging from outlet | Type of treatment | Discharge point relative to low water mark, unless otherwise stated. Distance given in metres | Remarks |
|---|---|---|---|---|---|---|
| f ★★ | **Normans Bay** | | | | | Shingle with sand at low water. |
| | Cooden Beach | 2 | | | 150 above | Shingle with sand at low tide. Storm water overflows. |
| 5 ★★★ | **Bexhill** | 3 | 32,500 | Maceration/tidal tank | 400 below | Sand and shingle. Beware sand holes. New long sea outfall. |
| ★★★ | St Leonards | 2 | 23,000 | Maceration/screens | 2000 below | Shingle sand and rocks. New long sea outfall as above. |
| ★★ | **Hastings** | 4 | 68,000 | Screens/maceration tank | 140 below | Shingle and sand. New long sea outfall as above. |
| ★★★ | **Winchelsea** | | | | | Shingle. Bathing only safe in calm weather. |
| ★★★ | **Camber Sands** | | | | | Sand dunes. Ridges in sand can be a danger. |
| | Broomhill Sands | 1 | 9,500 | Secondary | 300 above | Sandy and coarse shingle. |
| **KENT** | | | | | | |
| ★★ | **Littlestone-on-Sea** | | | | | Sandy. |
| ★★ | **St Mary's Bay** | | | | | Sandy. |
| ★★ | **Dymchurch** | 1 | 20,800 | Secondary | Between HWM & LWM | Shingle and sand. |
| | Dymchurch Redoubt | 1 | 3,000 | Primary | At LWM | Pebbles and sand. |
| f ★★ | **Hythe** | | | | | Shingle and sand. New long sea outfall. |
| ★★★ | **Sandgate** | | | | | Shingle. £14.5 million improvement scheme. |
| f ★★ | **Folkestone** | 1 | | Screens | At HWM | Shingle. Improvement scheme. |
| | The Warren | 1 | 20,000 | Raw | 584 below | Danger from falling rocks. Improvement scheme. |

| Beach No on Map | Rating. The more stars the better. f=failed | Resort | Sewage outlets | Population discharging from outlet | Type of treatment | Discharge point relative to low water mark, unless otherwise stated. Distance given in metres | Remarks |
|---|---|---|---|---|---|---|---|
| | | Shakespeare Cliff | 1 | 30,000 | Maceration | 635 below | Sand and shingle. Improvement scheme. Start of the tunnel. |
| 6 ★★★ | | St Margaret's Bay | | | | | Shingle and rocks. |
| f ★★ | | Deal Castle | 3 | 10,000 | Screens/ maceration tank | 731 below | Steep shingle. Improvement scheme. |
| f ★ | | Sandwich Bay | | | | | Sandy. Improvement scheme. |
| f ★★ | | Ramsgate | 3 | 20,000 | Screens/ maceration | 150 below | Sandy. Improvement scheme. |
| f★★ | | Broadstairs | | | | | Sandy. Improvement scheme. |
| ★★★ | | Joss Bay | 1 | 12,000 | Screens/ maceration | 100 below | Sandy. |
| | | Botany Bay | 1 | 40,000 | Screens/ maceration tank | 100 below | Sandy. |
| 7 ★★★ ★★ | | Margate | 3 | | Screens | At LWM | Sandy. New long sea outfall. |
| ★★ | | St Mildreds Bay | | | | | Sandy. |
| ★★★ | | Minnis Bay | | | | | Sand and rocks. |
| f ★★ | | Herne Bay | 1 | 10,000 | Screens | 460 below | Pebbles and sand. Improvement scheme. |
| 8 ★★ | | Whitstable | 1 | 10,000 | Screens/ maceration | 1500 below | Shingle. |
| ★★ | | Leysdown-on-Sea | | | | | Sand, shingle and mud. |

**ESSEX**

| | | | | | | | |
|---|---|---|---|---|---|---|---|
| ★★★ | | Canvey Island | 1 | 45,500 | Secondary | At LWM | Muddy sand. |
| ★★★ | | Leigh-on-Sea | | | | | Small sandy beach. |
| ★★★ | | Westcliff-on-Sea | | | | | Sandy. |

| Beach No on Map | Rating. The more stars the better. †=failed | Resort | Sewage outlets | Population discharging from outlet | Type of treatment | Discharge point relative to low water mark, unless otherwise stated. Distance given in metres | Remarks |
|---|---|---|---|---|---|---|---|
| | ** | **Southend-on-Sea** | 1 | 210,000 | Primary | 500 below LWM | Sand, shingle and mud. |
| | ** | **Thorpe Bay** | | | | | |
| | *** | **Shoeburyness** | | | | | Sand and shingle. |
| | ** | **Brightlingsea** | 1 | 10,000 | Secondary | To the colne | Muddy sand. Bathing dangerous. |
| | ** | **Jaywick** | 1 | 38,000 | Maceration | 650 below LWM | Sandy. |
| 9 | *** | **Clacton-on-Sea** | 2 | | | 300 below LWM 50 below LWM | Sandy. Stormwater outfalls only. |
| | *** | **Holland-on-Sea** | 1 | 70,000 | Maceration | 750 below LWM | Sandy. Safe bathing. |
| | *** | **Frinton-on-Sea** | 2 | | | 50 below | Sandy. Safe bathing. Storm overflows only. |
| | *** | **Walton-on-the-Naze** | 1 | 29,000 | Secondary | 50 below LWM | Sandy. Safe bathing. |
| | ** | **Dovercourt** | 1 | 11,000 | Primary | At LWM | Sandy. Safe bathing. |

### SUFFOLK

| Beach No on Map | Rating | Resort | Sewage outlets | Population | Type of treatment | Discharge point | Remarks |
|---|---|---|---|---|---|---|---|
| | | **Felixstowe:** | | | | | |
| | *** | **South Beach** | 1 | 4,262 | Maceration | 630 below LWM | Red shingle and sand. Another outlet to docks serving 30,000. |
| | *** | **North Beach** | | | | | Improvement scheme for both beaches. |
| 10 | | Aldeburgh | 1 | 4,000 | Maceration | 1300 below LWM | Shingle. |
| 11 | | Dunwich | | | | | Pebbles. |
| 12 | | Southwold | | | | | Sandy. |
| 13 | | **Lowestoft:** | | | | | |
| | *** | **South beach** | 1 | 80,000 | Maceration | 1,000 below LWM | Sandy. |
| | ** | **North Beach** | | | | | |

**NORFOLK**

| Beach No on Map | Rating. The more stars the better. f=failed | Resort | Sewage outlets | Population discharging from outlet | Type of treatment | Discharge point relative to low water mark, unless otherwise stated. Distance given in metres | Remarks |
|---|---|---|---|---|---|---|---|
| | | **Great Yarmouth:** | | | | | |
| f ★★ | | **South Beach** | 1 | 180,000 including discharge to river | Fine screening | 1050 below LWM | Sandy. Macerated sewage is discharged into the River Yare. |
| ★★ | | **Pier** | | | | | |
| ★★★ | | **North Beach** | | | | | |
| 14 | | Sea Palling | | | | | Sandy. |
| 15 | | Happisburgh | | | | | Sandy. |
| ★★★ | | **Mundesley** | 1 | 14,000 | Secondary/other | 1420 below LWM | Sandy. |
| ★★★ | | **Cromer** | 1 | 13,500 | Tidal tank | 100 below LWM | Sandy. Improvement scheme planned. |
| | | East Runton | 1 | 1,400 | Maceration | At LWM | Sandy. Improvement scheme planned. |
| | | West Runton | 1 | 1,400 | Maceration | At LWM | Sand and pebbles. Improvement scheme planned. |
| ★★★ | | **Sheringham** | 1 | 10,000 | Maceration | 260 below LWM | Sand and shingle. Improvement scheme planned. |
| 16 ★★ | | **Wells-next-the-Sea** | 1 | 3,700 | Secondary | To inland drain | Sandy. Improvement scheme planned. |
| ★★★ | | **Hunstanton** | 1 | | | | Sand, stones and shingle. Storm overflow only. Sewage to Heacham STW. |
| ★★ | | **Heacham** | 1 | 24,000 | Secondary/tertiary | To river | Gravel. Private beach. New STW completed 1990. |

## 1 Lee-on-the-Solent, Hampshire   OS Ref: SU5700

A long, gently curving ribbon of groyne-ribbed shingle with sand at low tide faces the Solent, with views of Southampton Water and across to the Isle of Wight. The residential development along Marine Parade overlooks this uncommercialised beach. Marine Parade West is separated from the beach by the Solent Gardens, which slope down to a promenade on two levels edging the shingle. Another promenade and flat lawns separate Marine Parade East from the beach. The steep shingle may not be the most comfortable for sunbathing on but it is popular with the more active beach user. There is a designated area for water skiing, and recommended launching areas for windsurfers. There is always something to watch off shore, whether it is the water sports or the continual shipping traffic plying the Solent. Dogs are banned from the central section of the beach. Dogs on the promenade must be kept on a lead and must not foul the footpaths or the adjoining grass verges.

**Water quality** Beach monitored by the NRA and found to meet the EC standard for clean bathing water in 1990. One outfall serving 200,000 people discharges primary treated sewage ⅔ mile (1km) below low water mark off Peel Common, north of the beach. There is a £0.6 million sewerage improvement scheme under construction.

**Litter** The beach is cleaned regularly by the local authority. Heavy usage of the Solent leads to problems on the beaches, with marine debris and oil being washed ashore.

**Bathing safety:** Safe bathing. Water skiers must use the area buoyed near the Daedalus slipway and windsurf boards should be launched from the Hill Head end of the beach.

**Access** Lee-on-the-Solent is signposted from the A32; the B3385 leads to Marine Parade running parallel with the shore. There is level access and ramps to the promenade from which there are steps and ramps to the shingle.

**Parking** Two car parks with approximately 250 spaces are signposted off Marine Parade; two other car parks with approximately 150 spaces are located at the Hill Head end of the beach.

**Toilets** At the Solent Gardens and the Daedalus slipway (Marine Parade East and Marine Parade West).

**Food** There are shops and cafés on Marine Parade opposite the Solent Gardens. There is a café and sheltered terrace garden off the promenade and a pub at Hill Head.

**Seaside activities** Swimming, waterskiing and windsurfing.

**Wet weather alternatives** In Gosport there is a local museum, Fort Brockhurst and the submarine museum.

**Wildlife and walks** The Solent Way coastal footpath can be followed in either direction from the beach. To the north it skirts the Titchfield Haven Nature Reserve and continues along the shore to the River Hamble, an extremely popular yachting centre. To the south it can be followed to Stokes Bay. A section of the grassland adjacent to the Daedalus slipway has been set aside as a conservation area.

## 2 Stokes Bay, Gosport, Hampshire   OS Ref: SZ5998

The arc of Stokes Bay, with its almost manicured shingle, curves from the No 2 Battery Fort south to Fort Gilkicker, fortifications built in 1860 to protect the western approaches to Portsmouth docks. The narrow band of shingle, which shelves quite steeply to some sand at low tide, widens landward towards the south-east of the bay; the long shore drift currents continually move the shingle in this direction and this has led to the build-up of a wide area of flat shingle stretching towards Fort Gilkicker. The beach, overlooking Ryde on the Isle of Wight, has a wide-open feel about it. The promenade is level with the shingle and is backed by flat grassed recreational areas which are in turn bordered by the trees and shrubs of the adjacent park and school. Popular for water sports; windsurfers can be seen throughout the year. Dogs are banned from the beach. Dogs on the promenade must be kept on a lead and should not be allowed to foul. Stokes Bay received a Blue Flag in 1990.

**Water quality** Beach monitored by the NRA and found to meet the EC standard for clean bathing water in 1990. One outfall serving 200,000 people discharges primary treated sewage ⅔ mile (1km) below low water mark off Peel Common, to the north of Lee-on-the-Solent.

**Litter** The beach is cleaned regularly by the local authority. Heavy use of the Solent by shipping leads to problems on the beaches; marine debris is frequently washed ashore.

**Bathing safety** Safe bathing. Swimming and windsurfing is restricted to specific areas of the beach which are signposted. First aid post near sailing club. Inshore rescue boat station at southern end of the bay.

**Access** Stokes Bay is signposted from the B3333 between Lee-on-the-Solent and Gosport. There is easy parking off the road behind the beach and level access on to the shingle.

**Parking** Car parks are signposted at each end of the beach and at its centre, with over 300 spaces. There is also some parking along the promenade.

**Toilets** At the car park adjacent to the No 2 Battery Fort, on the promenade near the sailing club and at Gilkicker.

**Food** Café on the promenade.

**Seaside activities** Swimming, windsurfing, sailing, canoeing and diving. Two public slipways. Children's paddling pool, miniature golf and tennis courts behind the beach.

**Wet weather alternatives** In Gosport there is a local museum, the submarine museum and Fort Brockhurst.

***Wildlife and walks*** The Solent Way footpath can be followed south-east past Fort Gilkicker towards Portsmouth Harbour or north-west to Lee-on-the-Solent and beyond.

## 3 Cuckmere Haven, Westdean, East Sussex  OS Ref: TV5298

A path from the Seven Sisters Country Park Centre leads through the lovely Cuckmere valley to this quiet pebble beach. The river, which meanders through the valley, disappears below the pebbles. The impressive white chalk cliffs of the Seven Sisters stretch away east to Beachy Head. Below them there are numerous rockpools which abound with marine life. This is an ideal spot for those who want to combine sun bathing with exploring the shore and surrounds. The nature trail starting from the superbly restored flint barn which houses the Country Park Interpretative Centre is well worth following.

***Water quality*** No sewage is discharged in the vicinity of this beach.

***Litter*** A lot of plastic and metal cans and bottles both washed up and left by visitors.

***Bathing safety*** The swiftness of the incoming tide and associated currents can cause problems.

***Access*** Pedestrian access only; a 1 mile (1.6km) walk on a marked path through the Cuckmere Valley from the Country Park Centre at Exceat on A259 leads to the beach.

***Parking*** Car park at Country Park Centre.

***Toilets*** At Country Park Centre.

***Food*** Pub at Exceat Bridge provides food.

***Seaside activities*** Swimming and diving.

***Wet weather alternatives*** The Country Park Centre and The Living World exhibition of animals from the countryside and seashore.

***Wildlife and walks*** A 1½ mile (2.5km) or 3 mile (5km) circular trail through the country park covers a selection of wildlife habitats, saltmarsh, river meadows and the chalk grassland above the cliffs. Leaflets which describe the route are available at the Country Park Centre. The South Downs Way follows the cliffs and cuts through the valley. Survey work by the Marine Conservation Society showed that the shallow seas of this stretch of coast are particularly rich in marine life and the area has been designated as a Voluntary Marine Nature Reserve.

## 4 Eastbourne, East Sussex  OS Ref: TV6199

The 1989 and 1990 Blue Flag beach is at the centre of 3 miles (5km) of accessible beach and 2 miles (3km) of promenades with splendid gardens backed by a parade of elegant hotels and houses. Access to the beach is by steps and ramps. Wooden groynes hold the pebbles at the high tide level and give way to sand at low tide. The promenades provide easy walking from the foot of the white chalk cliffs of Beachy Head at the western boundary via the Martello Tower, Bandstand, Pier, Redoubt Fortress, Treasure Island and the Butterfly Centre to the fishing and boating beaches at the eastern end. Ample seating on all promenade levels. Dogs are banned from the central beach area between 1st May and 30th September, with lead restrictions and poop scoop regulations elsewhere.

**Water quality** Beach monitored by the NRA and found to meet the EC standard for clean bathing water in 1990. One outfall serving 87,000 people discharges macerated and screened sewage 710 yards (650m) below low water off Langney Point. Macerated sewage has been observed off the beach and there have been complaints about smell. A new £17 million long sea outfall may rectify the problem.

**Bathing safety** Restricted bathing west of the Wish Tower because of rocks. Mixed bathing and boating east of the Redoubt requires extra care. The central area, Wish Tower to Redoubt, provides safe bathing unless the red warning flags are flying. Seasonal lifeguard cover is based at the Wish Tower from June to September.

**Access** Steps and ramps lead down from the esplanade to the beach. There are beach wheelchairs available from the bathing station on the lower esplanade.

**Parking** Pay and display car parks at the fishing station, Princes Park and Wish Tower. Free parking on the promenade, in some areas restricted between May 20th and September 20th to four hours. Multi-storey car park in Trinity Place off the sea-front and Ashford Road in the town centre.

**Toilets** Adjacent to the bandstand, Pier, Wish Tower, Holywell, Redoubt and the fishing station.

**Food** Ice cream and refreshment kiosks on promenades and cafés at Holywell, Wish Tower and the Redoubt. Also cafés on the Pier and in town.

**Seaside activities** Swimming, sailing, windsurfing and angling. Sailing and canoeing lessons at the sailing clubs. Two pleasure boats cruise from the beach west of the Pier to Beachy Head and the Lighthouse with fine views of the Seven Sisters. The Pier provides amusements, dances, boat trips and angling. Beach cabins and canoes for hire at the Wish Tower. Military bands and entertainments at the bandstand. Children's entertainment at Treasure Island, the Fort Fun playgrounds and at the Wish Tower and bandstand. Putting and mini-golf at Holywell, Princes Park and Treasure Island. Boating lake at Princes Park. Dotto rail-less train runs from the Wish Tower to Holywell.

**Wet weather alternatives** Sovereign Centre all-weather 'beach' recreation centre, Redoubt Fortress Military Museum and Aquarium, Butterfly Centre, pier amusements and dances, Winter Garden dances. The town provides theatres, cinemas, local history museums and art gallery.

**Wildlife and walks** To the west of the town rises Beachy Head and the South Downs. The view is of rolling chalk hills and cliffs and there is a Visitors Centre at Beachy Head. The Downs also offer fine views across the town to the east where lie the Crumbles, Pevensey Marshes and the Sussex Weald.

## 5 Bexhill-on-Sea, East Sussex  OS Ref: TQ7407

Bexhill has 2 miles (4.2km) of beach, meticulously maintained and a deserving winner of the Blue Flag in 1989 and 1990. The beach consists of shingle between recently replaced sea-defence groynes with safe exposed sands at low tide. There are excellent facilities for recreation and very tight control over graffiti, vandalism and litter. Behind the beach lie wide, clean promenades with cafés, shelters and amusements. The De La Warr Pavilion on the sea front caters for all tastes, with plays, concerts and exhibitions. Old Bexhill is slightly inland from the sea and nearby are the Manor Gardens. Dogs are banned from the beach during the summer.

**Water quality** Beach monitored by the NRA and found to meet the EC standard for clean bathing water in 1990. A new long sea outfall deals with the sewage from Bexhill, St Leonard's and Hastings.

**Litter** The beach is cleaned regularly.

**Bathing safety** Safe bathing. Lifeguards at weekends in the summer.

**Access** Easy access to the beach from the promenade.

**Parking** Extensive parking on the sea-front.

**Toilets** Two blocks on the promenade and at the De La Warr Pavilion.

**Food** Cafés, restaurants and kiosks.

**Seaside activities** Swimming, fishing, sailing, windsurfing.

**Wet weather alternatives** De La Warr Pavilion, museum, amusement arcades, nearby shops.

**Wildlife and walks** The local authority have erected interpretation boards on local wildlife and fossils to be found in the area. Galley Hill, at the eastern end of the town, offers splendid views. From the small car park it is a short walk down the hill to a secluded shingle beach at Glyne Gap.

## 6 St Margaret's Bay, St Margaret's at Cliffe, Kent  OS Ref: TR3644

A picturesque little cove, once home for both Noël Coward and Ian Fleming, sheltered by towering chalk cliffs which form part of the white cliffs of Dover. A narrow lane leads past terraces of holiday homes to the promenade which backs the shingle, kept in place by iron groynes. The cove has been the starting point for many of the cross-Channel swims. The Pines, gardens on the slopes above the beach, are near-tropical because of the mild climate of the area. A 'dog-free zone' is being established on the beach and the local council regularly cleans the beach and empties the litter bins.

**Water quality** Beach monitored by the NRA and found to meet the EC standard for clean bathing water in 1990. No sewage is discharged in the vicinity of the beach.

**Bathing safety** Safe bathing except at high tide. Safety equipment on site.

**Access** St Margaret's at Cliffe is signposted from the A258. From the village a narrow road twists to the sea but it is easier to park on the cliff top and walk down the hill.

**Parking** Large car park behind sea wall and also at Dover Patrol memorial on cliff top.

**Toilets** Ladies and gents.

**Food** Public house, ice-cream kiosk.

**Seaside activities** Swimming, diving and fishing. Dover District Council operates a boat plot with slipway. Beach huts for hire.

**Wildlife and walks** The cove is on the Saxon Shore Way with cliff top walks to Dover and Kingsdown, but there is restricted access to some areas at times due to a Marines rifle range. There are good views from the cliff top where the rolling heathland is owned by the National Trust.

## 7 Margate, Kent    OS Ref: TR3571

Kent's Leisure Coast – Margate, Broadstairs, Ramsgate – is fringed by a series of sandy bays between low chalk cliffs. The main sands at Margate stretch west from the harbour. The bright lights of amusement arcades and the fun fair along Marine Terrace overlook the promenade which edges the gently sloping crescent of sand. Margate has a long history as a popular seaside resort; it was here that the covered bathing machine was first used in the 18th century and it remains a traditional resort with lots to do on and off the beach. Dog bins are provided on the promenade and bye-laws relating to dogs and dog access should be in force for the 1991 season.

**Water quality** Beach monitored by the NRA and found to meet the EC standard for clean bathing water in 1990. A new long sea outfall has recently been completed.

**Litter** The beach is cleaned daily by the local authority. The sale of glass bottles is banned.

**Bathing safety** Safe bathing. The beach is patrolled by lifeguards throughout the summer. Inshore rescue boat and lifeboat station and coastguard lookout.

**Access** From the promenade there are several sets of steps and ramps to the beach.

**Parking** Several pay-and-display car parks within easy reach of the beach, including those at College Square, Mill Lane and Trinity Square. Short-term parking in Marine Parade, opposite the beach.

**Toilets** On the promenade with facilities for the disabled.

**Food** There is a wide range of cafés, restaurants and takeaways within easy reach of the beach and there are several beach cafés.

**Seaside activities** Swimming, windsurfing, fishing.

**Wet weather alternatives** Aquarium, show caves, shell grotto, lifeboat house, local history museum, Tudor House, sports and leisure centre with swimming pool. Tourist information points carry details of walks and trails. Nearby resorts of Ramsgate and Broadstairs.

## 8 Whitstable, Kent   OS Ref: TR1166

This is a quiet resort that retains much of its traditional seafaring atmosphere around the harbour and in the old town with its narrow streets, alleyways and weather-boarded cottages. Whitstable was famous for its oysters which are still produced and celebrated annually with an oyster week and carnival. Whitstable's main beach lies to the east of the harbour. Undulating grassy slopes lead gently down from Marine Parade to the promenade and sea wall which edge the pebble beach. A long bank of shingle known as the Street extends seawards from the west end of the beach. ⅔ mile (1km) of the bank is exposed at low water and is a good spot for collecting shells, but is dangerous to swim from. From the slopes at Tankerton there are good views east along the curving beach to Swalecliff and Herne Bay, with excellent sunsets. Swalecliff at the eastern end of the Tankerton slopes is used by water skiers as a launching area. The sport is very popular in the bay and the World Water Skiing Championships have been held here.

**Water quality** Beach monitored by the NRA and found to meet the EC standard for clean bathing water in 1990. One outfall serving 10,000 people discharges screened and macerated sewage 1 mile (1.6km) below low water mark.

**Bathing safety** Bathing is safe except near the Street where there are unpredictable currents. Warning notices indicate where it is unsafe. There is a mobile coastguard lookout.

**Access** Steps and ramps from promenade.

**Parking** Free car parking on Marine Parade and Gorrell Tank opposite harbour.

**Toilets** At Priest and Sow Corner (near the sailing club), Beach Walk at the end of Tankerton Slopes, the Harbour and Island Wall.

**Food** A wide variety of cafés, restaurants, ice-cream kiosks and snack bars in the town within easy reach of the beach.

**Seaside activities** Swimming, windsurfing, sailing, water skiing and fishing. Bowling green, tennis courts and golf course.

**Wet weather alternatives** Heritage Museum, sports centre, bowling.

**Wildlife and walks** The Saxon Shore Way follows the banks of the Swale passing through the South Swale Local Nature Reserve on the edge of Graveney Marshes, just west of Whitstable. It continues through the town, along the shore to Herne Bay and the Bishopstone mud cliffs beyond.

## 9 Clacton-on-Sea, Essex    OS Ref: TM1814

Clacton is a bright and popular resort, justly proud of its lovely gardens. Several miles of sandy beach extend from Holland-on-Sea to Jaywick and all the facilities of a major resort are to be found; a pier, golf course, watersports facilities and the newly undeveloped Mantello Bay area. A carnival is held at the beginning of August. Dogs are banned on the beach from the 1st May to the 30th September. A Blue Flag winner in both 1989 and 1990.

**Water quality** Beach monitored by the NRA and found to meet the EC standard for clean bathing water in 1990. Two outfalls discharge 328 yards (300m) and 55 yards (50m) below low water mark: they are storm water overflows only.

**Bathing safety** Safe bathing except in one or two areas which are clearly marked. The beach is patrolled by lifeguards during the summer months; there is a safety patrol boat and beach inspectors.

**Litter** The beach is regularly cleaned by the local authority.

**Access** Direct from the promenade.

**Parking** Free parking along the sea-front and car parks in the town.

**Toilets** Several near the beach.

**Food** Catering outlets to suit all tastes and pockets.

**Seaside activities** Swimming, fishing, sailing, windsurfing, jetskiing. Windsurfer hire available.

**Wet weather alternatives** Pier, amusements, theatre and leisure centre.

**Wildlife and walks** Two booklets listing varying walks are available free from the Tourist Information Centre just off the sea-front.

## 10 Aldeburgh, Suffolk    OS Ref: TM4757

The long strip of unspoilt shingle beach falls within the Suffolk Coast and Heath Area of Outstanding Natural Beauty and the Suffolk Heritage Coast. A wide sea wall protects the charming town from the continual attack of the North Sea. Colour-washed houses and hotels face this 'working' beach from which a considerable number of boats fish, selling most of their catch of crabs, lobster and a variety of fish from sea-front huts. The local lifeboat can also be seen drawn up on the shingle. The beach has steep shingle ridges with some sand at low tide and stretches 2 miles (3km) north to Thorpeness. This Edwardian holiday village built around a man-made lake, The Meare, is a mixture of traditional weather-boarding combined with Tudor elegance.

The working windmill standing on the heathland behind the beach is also the Heritage Coast visitors' centre and it is well worth a visit to find out more about this curious village and adjacent stretch of unspoilt coast.

**Water quality** One outfall serving 4,000 people discharges macerated sewage ¾ mile (1.3km) below low water mark.

**Litter** The beach is generally very clean, but subject to occasional spotting with tar and oil from passing ships. It is cleaned by the local authority.

**Bathing safety** The beach shelves quite steeply but evenly except at Thorpeness, where some ridges and pits in the sea bed can be dangerous. It is dangerous to swim near the groynes.

**Access** Level access from the road on to the promenade and across the shingle to the north.

**Parking** Pay-and-display car parks at each end of town adjacent to the beach.

**Toilets** Public toilets at the Moot Hall and by the coastguard station at the southern end of the promenade.

**Food** Several cafés, pubs and hotels overlook the beach. Ice-cream vendor on the promenade. Tea shop and inn at Thorpeness.

**Seaside activities** Swimming, diving, windsurfing, sailing and fishing.

**Wet weather alternatives** Moot Hall Museum, Thorpeness Windmill and House-in-the-Clouds water tower, Heritage Coast Visitors' Centre. Snape Maltings concert hall on the banks of the River Alde, a short distance inland, is the home of the Aldeburgh Festival. Gallery, craft centre, shops and restaurants at the Maltings.

**Wildlife and walks** A very good map is available from tourist information which details the network of paths that covers Aldeburgh and its surrounding area. Aldeburgh lies on the Suffolk Coastal Path which runs from Felixstowe to Lowestoft. From the village of Snape the route follows the banks of the River Alde and joins the Sailors' Path. This crosses Snape Warren and the marshes north of the town to reach Aldeburgh beach, where shingle plants such as sea holly and the sea pea abound. The path continues north along the beach to Thorpeness and beyond. North Warren RSPB reserve includes The Meare at Thorpeness, the remnant heath, with dry reedbeds, scrub and birch woodland which supports a wide variety of birdlife.

## 11 Dunwich, Saxmundham, Suffolk   OS Ref: TM4770

A stretch of pebble beach forming part of a long coastal strip that is continually under attack from the waves. Dunwich village, for example, was once a sizeable town but it is progressively falling into the sea. Between Dunwich village and Minsmere, the RSPB reserve to the south, the shingle-ridged beach is backed by low sand cliffs and heathland owned by the National Trust. The heather and heath plants that thrive on the cliffs provide an attractive splash of colour when in full bloom. The steep banks of shingle which give way to sand at low tide curve northwards, protecting the low-lying meadows behind. Care is needed to ensure that these coastal defences remain undamaged. This is a quiet beach in an area frequented for the wildlife interest rather than for any holiday beach atmosphere.

**Water quality** No sewage is discharged to the beach.

**Litter** Some flotsam is washed up on to the beach.

**Bathing safety** War remains between low and high tide can be dangerous for swimmers.

**Access** The beach car park is signposted from the village; there is direct access on to the shingle from the car park.

**Parking** There is a public car park adjacent to the beach, plus National Trust and RSPB car parks at Dunwich Heath and Minsmere Reserve respectively.

**Toilets** In the public car park, Dunwich Heath and Minsmere.

**Food** Beach café at the car park.

**Seaside activities** Swimming, windsurfing and fishing.

**Wet weather alternatives** Museum of local history in Dunwich. Bird hides in the Minsmere Reserve are open to the public free of charge. The Coastguard cottages at Dunwich Heath have an exhibition area along with shop, tearooms and toilets.

**Wildlife and walks** There is a marked footpath around the edge of Dunwich Heath which gives the visitor a tour of all the various habitats that the 214 acre (86.6 hectare) site contains. South of the heathland the 1,500 acre (607 hectare) RSPB reserve includes reedbeds, lagoons, heath and woodland. Over 100 different species have been recorded breeding within the reserve which makes it one of the most important in Great Britain. There is a shop and information centre at the northern end of the reserve.

### 12 Southwold, Suffolk   OS Ref: TM5076

Southwold once had a pier but all that remains is a short skeleton and the buildings on the promenade. Nevertheless, it is still the focal point for this 3 mile (5km) long beach of sand and shingle. This beach was awarded the Blue Flag for the first time in 1990. To the north rainbow-coloured beach huts line the sea wall which edges the groyne-ribbed beach of soft sand. The beach curves northwards below sand cliffs rising to replace the sea wall. South of the pier the groyne-ribbed beach of sand and shingle stretches to the harbour at the mouth of the River Blyth. Wheeled changing huts line the promenade below scrub-covered slopes. The attractive town of Southwold sits aloft, built around seven greens and shadowed by its lighthouse.

**Water quality** Beach monitored by the NRA and found to meet the EC standard for clean bathing water in 1990. No outfalls discharge in the vicinity of the beach.

**Bathing safety** Safe bathing except near the groynes and at the river mouth. Life-saving equipment provided.

**Access** The sea front is signposted within the town; car parks adjacent to the promenade/sea wall. There are steps and a steep ramp on to the beach.

**Parking** Three car parks with a total of 300 spaces adjacent to the pier and harbour.

**Toilets** On the promenade, including facilities for the disabled.

**Food** Café, bar, shop and takeaway at the pier.

**Seaside activities** Swimming, surfing, windsurfing, sailing and fishing. Amusement arcade. Boating lake.

**Wet weather alternatives** St Edmund's Hall and museum.

**Wildlife and walks** There are walks along the river and across the meadows. The climb to the summit of Gun Hill is well worth the effort for the reward of some good views. The Suffolk Coastal Path runs north towards Lowestoft and south to Dunwich Forest and Minsmere, approximately 3 miles (5km) from Southwold.

## 13 South Beach, Lowestoft, Suffolk  OS Ref: TM5491

Lowestoft is a popular resort and a busy port which is split in half by the narrow strip of Lake Lothing. The two sides are linked by a bridge which is occasionally raised to admit large merchant ships into the heart of town. South beach is a 5 mile (3km) long pleasure beach, offering golden sand and all the normal paraphernalia of piers, stalls and amusements. Cleaned every day by the local authority, this beach picked up a Blue Flag in both 1989 and 1990.

**Water quality** Beach monitored by the NRA and found to meet the EC standard for clean bathing water in 1990. One outfall serving 80,000 people discharges screened and macerated sewage 1,500 yards (1,200m) below low water mark.

**Bathing safety** Safe bathing except near the harbour entrance. The beach is patrolled by lifeguards during the summer months.

**Access** Direct from the promenade.

**Parking** There are four car parks near the beach with approximately 800 spaces.

**Toilets** Four sets of toilets including one with facilities for the disabled. Another set has showers and baby changing area.

**Food** There is a full range of catering outlets at a variety of prices.

**Seaside activities** Swimming, surfing, fishing, windsurfing, sailing. Punch and Judy shows, two piers.

**Wet weather alternatives** Multi-sports centre, large central library, Maritime Museum, two cinemas and theatres.

*Wildlife and walks* Guided walking tours of the fishing harbour start from the Tourist Information Centre on the Esplanade. Lowestoft marks the northern end of the Suffolk Coastal Path which runs for 50 miles (90km) south to Felixstowe. Lowestoft Ness is Britain's easternmost point.

## 14 Sea Palling, Norfolk    OS Ref: TG4327

Ten miles (16km) of coastline that is undeveloped and not readily accessible. From Sea Palling the fine stretch of sandy beach to Waxham can be reached. A beautiful unspoilt beach, the gentle sloping sands are fringed by substantial marram-covered dunes. The beach is ideal for a quiet day by the sea; no facilities, no razzmatazz, just sand, sea and sky. 3 miles (5km) south, the Broads come within a couple of miles of the dunes, the only protection that the flat, low-lying land has against the sea. The beach is cleaned daily during the season. Oil on the sand has been observed in winter.

*Water quality* No outfalls in the vicinity of this beach.

*Bathing safety* Bathing can be dangerous on the ebb tide because of undertow currents.

*Access* From the village of Sea Palling, on the B1159, a road leads to a concrete ramp over the dunes.

*Parking* Car park behind dunes provides spaces for 100 cars.

*Toilets* In Sea Palling village.

*Food* A tea shop and two pubs in the village serve food.

*Seaside activities* Swimming, windsurfing and fishing.

*Wildlife and walks* Fossils have sometimes been found in the area of the beach, also jet and amber. The more remote parts of the beach are popular for birdwatching.

## 15 Happisburgh, Norfolk    OS Ref: TG3831

The stretch of coastline from Happisburgh (pronounced Haysboro) east to Winterton is one of the cleanest in Norfolk. There is a continuous gently sloping sandy beach backed by clay cliffs and sand dunes. This attractive stretch of coastline remains undeveloped. Happisburgh, dominated by its red and white lighthouse and the 110 foot (33m) spire of St Mary's Church, is a good family beach, offering safe swimming for children between the groynes that hold the sands in place. The village is set back from the beach on the 50 foot (15m) clay cliffs, an advantage in an area where the ravages of the sea are much in evidence.

*Water quality* No outfalls in the vicinity of this beach.

*Bathing safety* Safe bathing. Inshore lifeboat. Coastguard's lookout.

*Access* From the village on the B1159 a side road leads to parking above the beach. A concrete ramp leads past the inshore lifeboat hut to the beach.

**Parking** Two car parks with 100 spaces.

**Toilets** On cliff top, includes facilities for the disabled.

**Food** Ice-cream van.

**Seaside activities** Swimming, windsurfing, diving, sailing and fishing.

## 16 Wells-next-the-Sea, Norfolk    OS Ref: TF9146

This beach lies approximately 1 mile (1.6km) north of Wells-next-the-Sea, a quaint Norfolk port. Although popular, its extensive sands mean that you can always find a quiet position on the beach. The adjacent pinewoods give it a beautiful backdrop as well as providing cover for walks. The surrounding marsh countryside is famous for its birds. Bye-laws are being drawn up banning dogs from the beach. The small town of Wells has an assortment of shops, cafés and amusements.

**Water quality** Beach monitored by the NRA and found to meet the EC standard for clean bathing water in 1990. No outfalls in the vicinity of this beach.

**Bathing safety** Care is required in certain tidal conditions: a siren is sounded when it is dangerous. The safe and dangerous areas are marked on a large plan at the entrance to the beach. The beach is patrolled by lifeguards at weekends from May to September, with full-time cover in the school holidays.

**Access** Either by road, on foot along the sea wall or by miniature railway.

**Parking** Car park behind the dunes provides space for 300 cars: there is an overflow car park when that is full.

**Toilets** By the car park and in the pinewoods.

**Food** Kiosk on beach, small takeaway adjacent to car park.

**Seaside activities** Swimming, windsurfing, sailing. Miles of walks, good birdwatching, two steam railways.

**Wet weather alternatives** Wells is full of Norfolk charm and worth exploring. Holkham Hall (home of the Earl of Leicester) has magnificently decorated rooms and a bygones section. Also close by is Walsingham with its famous Christian shrine and medieval buildings.

**Wildlife and walks** Wells is on the Norfolk Coastal Path. The beach is incorporated into an SSSI, adjoins a national nature reserve and is part of a designated area of outstanding natural beauty and heritage coast. Inland, Pensthorpe Waterfowl Park is a fascinating place to visit.

# The East Coast

Fabulous, spectacular, dramatic, remote, wild and mysterious have all been used to describe the east coast. The beautiful sweeping bays of golden sand, unspoilt fishing villages and clifftop castle ruins of Northumberland; the rugged cliffs and sandy crescents of Yorkshire; the magnificent chalk cliffs of Flamborough with mile upon mile of sand stretching south, backed by the fast-retreating mud cliffs of Humberside; the everchanging sand banks of Lincolnshire. Unfortunately, less complimentary terms have also been used to describe parts of this coastline. Industry comes to the shore, with steel works, power stations, oil and chemical works. They discharge a cocktail of toxic chemicals, polluting the coastal waters and their wildlife. Millions of tonnes of dredged spoil, sewage sludge and fly ash dumped offshore add to the problem. Waste from coal mines still blackens the beaches of Tyne and Wear, Durham and Cleveland, although the practice is diminishing. Sewage pollution contaminates many of the bathing waters, particularly around the Tyne and Tees. None of the beaches in the region escapes the problem of marine litter.

### Beaches receiving the Blue Flag in 1990:

Sandhaven (South Shields).

Berwick-
upon-Tweed ■
Spittal **f**
**14** Cocklawburn

**13** Bamburgh
Seahouses
**12** Beadnell Bay
**11** Newton Haven
**10** Embleton Bay

**9** Alnmouth
**8** Warkworth
**7** Druridge Bay
Newbiggin North **f**
Newbiggin South **f**
Seaton Sluice
Whitley Bay
Blyth South Beach
Tynemouth Long Sands North
Tynemouth Long Sands South
Cullercoats
Tynemouth King Edward's Bay **f**
Newcastle ■
South Shields **f**
Marsden Bay
Roker
Whitburn **f**

Seaham **f**

Crimdon **f**

Seaton Carew **f**
Redcar
Saltburn
Middlesborough ■
Staithes **f**
**6** Runswick Bay
Sandsend
Whitby
**5** Robin Hood's Bay

Scarborough North Bay
Scarborough South Bay **f**
**4** Cayton Bay
**3** Filey Sands
Reighton
Flamborough North Landing
Bridlington North
Flamborough South Landing **f**
**2** Bridlington South
Fraisthorpe
Earls Dyke
Barnston
Willsthorpe
Skipsea **f**
**1** Hornsea

Hull ■
Tunstall
Withernsea **f**

Cleethorpes **f**

**f** = failed to meet EC standard for clean bathing water in 1990.
Numbered beaches are included in the following chapter.

**Coastal walk**
Cleveland Way. Coastal parts of the Cleveland Way mostly in
the North York Moors National Park.

Mablethorpe
Sutton-on-Sea
Moggs Eye
Anderby Creek
Chapel St Leonards
Ingoldmells
Skegness

Boston ■

# The Golden List   *See page 25 for further details*

| Beach No on Map | Rating. The more stars the better. f=failed | Resort | Sewage outlets | Population discharging from outlet | Type of treatment | Discharge point relative to low water mark, unless otherwise stated. Distance given in metres | Remarks |
|---|---|---|---|---|---|---|---|
| **LINCOLNSHIRE** | | | | | | | |
| | ★★ | **Skegness** | | | | | Sandy. Bathing safe. |
| | ★★ | **Ingoldmells** | 1 | 122,000 | Maceration/ screens | 1420 below | Sandy. Bathing safe. |
| | ★★ | **Chapel St Leonards** | | | | | Sandy. Bathing safe. |
| | ★★★ | **Anderby Creek** | | | | | Sandy. Bathing safe. |
| | ★★★ | **Moggs Eye** | | | | | |
| | ★★ | **Sutton-on-Sea** | | | | | Sandy. Bathing safe. |
| | ★★ | **Mablethorpe** | 1 | 37,000 | Secondary | To inland drain | Sandy. Bathing safe. |
| **HUMBERSIDE** | | | | | | | |
| | f ★ | **Cleethorpes** | 1 | 66,000 | Maceration/ screens | At LWM | Sand. Safe bathing at high tide. Improvements planned. |
| | f ★★ | **Withernsea** | 1 | 12,000 | Primary | At LWM | Sand and shingle. £8m improvement scheme to be completed 1992. |
| | ★★★ | **Tunstall** | | | | | Sand and pebbles. Safe bathing, but not at low tide. Improvement scheme as above. |
| *1* ★★ | | **Hornsea** | 2 | 16,000 | Screens/ maceration | 1000 below LWM | Sandy. |
| | f ★★ | **Skipsea Sands** | | | | | Sandy. |
| | ★★★ | **Barmston** | | | | | Sand and shingle. |
| | ★★★ | **Earls Dyke** | | | | | Sandy. |
| | ★★★ | **Fraisthorpe** | | | | | Sandy. |
| | ★★★ | **Willsthorpe** | | | | | Sandy. |
| *2* ★★★ | | **Bridlington South** | 1 | 56,000 | Screens | 1600 below | Sandy. |

| Beach No on Map | Rating. The more stars the better. f=failed | Resort | Sewage outlets | Population discharging from outlet | Type of treatment | Discharge point relative to low water mark, unless otherwise stated. Distance given in metres | Remarks |
|---|---|---|---|---|---|---|---|
| | ★★★ | **Bridlington North** | 2 | | | At LWM | Sandy. Storm water overflows. |
| | f ★★ | **Flamborough South Landing** | | | | | Sewage works discharges to a stream which reaches the sea. |
| | ★★★ | **Flamborough North Landing** | 1 | 200 | | | Sandy. Bathing dangerous. £4m improvement scheme to be completed 1994. |
| | | Thornwick Bay | 1 | 300 | Primary | At LWM | Rocky. Bathing very dangerous. |

### YORKSHIRE

| Beach No on Map | Rating | Resort | Sewage outlets | Population discharging from outlet | Type of treatment | Discharge point | Remarks |
|---|---|---|---|---|---|---|---|
| | ★★★ | **Reighton Sands** | | | | | Sand and boulders. |
| 3 | ★★★ | **Filey** | 2 | 13,800 | Maceration | 200 below | Red sand. 1 storm water overflow. |
| 4 | ★★★ | **Cayton Bay** | | | | | Sandy. Bathing safe. |
| | f ★★ | **Scarborough: South Beach** | 2 | 1,800 / 29,750 | Raw / Raw | At LWM | Sandy. Safe bathing. £30m improvement scheme to be completed early 1991. |
| | ★★ | **Scarborough: North Beach** | 2 | 55,300 / 8,700 | Raw / Raw | At LWM / At LWM | Sandy. Improvement scheme as above. |
| 5 | ★★ | **Robin Hood's Bay** | 1 | 5,500 | | | Rocky. Swimming dangerous. £5m improvement scheme to be completed 1994. |
| | ★★★ | **Whitby** | 1 | 20,000 | Raw | At LWM | Sandy. Swimming safe. |
| | ★★ | **Sandsend** | 1 | 450 | Raw | At LWM | Sand and shingle. |
| 6 | ★★★ | **Runswick Bay** | 1 | 480 | Raw | At LWM | Sand and shingle. |
| | f ★★ | **Staithes** | 1 | 4,000 | Raw | At LWM | Sand and rocks. |

**109**

THE GOOD BEACH GUIDE

## CLEVELAND

| Beach No on Map | Rating. The more stars the better. f=failed | Resort | Sewage outlets | Population discharging from outlet | Type of treatment | Discharge point relative to low water mark, unless otherwise stated. Distance given in metres | Remarks |
|---|---|---|---|---|---|---|---|
| | | Skinningrove | 1 | 7,700 | Raw | At LWM | Sandy. |
| | ★★ | **Saltburn-by-Sea** | 2 | 13,850<br>6,800 | Raw<br>Raw | At LWM<br>At LWM | Sand and pebbles. |
| | | Marske-by-the-Sea | 1 | 12,800 | Raw | At LWM | Sandy. |
| | ★★★<br>★★ | **Redcar** | 1 | 35,000 | Screened/maceration | 1599 below | Sand and rocks. Improvement scheme |
| | ★★★ | Coatham Sands | 1 | 1,200 | Raw | 25 below | Sandy. |
| | f ★<br>f ★★ | **Seaton Carew** | 2 | 31,300<br><br>28,500 | Maceration<br><br>Maceration | At LWM<br><br>25 below | Sandy. £11.4 million improvement scheme. |
| | | Hartlepool | 5 | 22,800 | 4×Raw<br>1×screened/maceration | 2x25 below<br>3xLWM | Sandy. |

## DURHAM

| | | | | | | | |
|---|---|---|---|---|---|---|---|
| | f ★★ | Crimdon Park | 1 | 4,000 | Tidal tank | At LWM | Sandy. |
| | | Blackhall | 1 | 10,500 | Raw | At LWM | Sand and pebbles. |
| | | Denemouth | 1 | 31,500 | Tidal tank | At LWM | Sand with stones and coal waste. |
| | | Horden | 2 | 6,900<br>8,100 | Raw<br>Raw | Above LWM<br>Above LWM | Sand with coal waste |
| | | Easington | 1 | 8,500 | Raw | At LMW | Sand with coal waste. |
| | | Seaham (South of Harbour) | 4 | 36,600 | Raw | 25 below | Improvement scheme. |
| | f ★★ | **Seaham (North of Harbour)** | | | | | Sand. |

## TYNE AND WEAR

| | | | | | | | |
|---|---|---|---|---|---|---|---|
| | | Ryhope | 2 | | Raw | At LWM | Sandy. Storm sewage overflows only. |

| Beach No on Map | Rating. The more stars the better. **f**=failed | Resort | Sewage outlets | Population discharging from outlet | Type of treatment | Discharge point relative to low water mark, unless otherwise stated. Distance given in metres | Remarks |
|---|---|---|---|---|---|---|---|
| | | Sunderland | 2 | 500 | Tidal tank | At LWM | Rocky outfalls situated south of Wear Estuary. |
| | | | | 175,000 | Screened | 300 below LWM | |
| | ★★ | **Roker** | 1 | | Raw | 25 below | Sand. Storm sewage overflow. |
| | | Seaburn | 1 | | Raw | At LWM | Sand. Storm sewage overflow. |
| | **f** ★★ | **Whitburn** | 1 | | Raw | At LWM | Sand. Storm sewage overflow. |
| | ★★ | **Marsden Bay** | | | | | Sand. |
| | **f** ★★ | **South Shields** | 2 | | Raw | At LWM | Sand. Storm sewage overflows only. |
| | **f** ★★ | King Edward's Bay | | | | | Sand. |
| | ★★ ★★ | **Long Sands** South North | 2 | | Raw | At LWM | Sand. |
| | ★★★ | **Cullercoats** | 1 | | Raw | At LWM | Sand. |
| | ★★ | **Whitley Bay** | 5 | | Raw | At LWM | Sand. |
| | ★★★ | **Seaton Sluice** | 1 | 43,000 | Tidal tank | 60 below | Sandy. |

**NORTHUMBERLAND**

| Beach No on Map | Rating | Resort | Sewage outlets | Population discharging from outlet | Type of treatment | Discharge point | Remarks |
|---|---|---|---|---|---|---|---|
| | ★★★ | **Blyth:** **South Beach** North Beach | 1 | 28,500 | Maceration | 30 below | Sandy. Sandy. |
| | **f** ★★ **f** ★ | **Newbiggin** South North | 2 | 29,000 5,000 | Maceration Raw | At LWM At LWM | Sand. |
| | | Cresswell | 1 | 1,800 summer (200 winter) | Other | At LWM | Sandy. |
| 7 ★★★ | | **Druridge Bay** | 1 | 5,500 | Maceration | At LWM | Sandy. |
| | | Amble | 1 | 8,000 | Screens/ maceration | 250 below | Rocky. |

**111**

| Beach No on Map | Rating. The more stars the better. f=failed | Resort | Sewage outlets | Population discharging from outlet | Type of treatment | Discharge point relative to low water mark, unless otherwise stated. Distance given in metres | Remarks |
|---|---|---|---|---|---|---|---|
| 8 ★★★ | | **Warkworth** | | | | | Sand. |
| 9 ★★★ | | **Alnmouth** | | | | | Sandy. |
| | | Longhoughton Steel | 1 | 3,000 | Raw | At LWM | Sandy cove. |
| | | Craster | 2 | 400 | Maceration | 30 below | |
| 10 | | Embleton Bay | | | | | Sandy. |
| 11 ★★★ | | **Newton Haven** | | | | | Sandy. |
| 12 ★★★ | | **Beadnell Bay** | 1 | 2,000 summer (1,200 winter) | Maceration | At LWM | Sandy. |
| ★★★ | | **Seahouses** | 1 | 6,000 | Screens/ maceration/ tidal tank | 100 below | Sandy. |
| 13 ★★★ | | **Bamburgh** | 2 | 1,000 summer (700 winter) 100 | Maceration/ tidal tank Raw | At LWM At LWM | Sandy. |
| | | Holy Island | 1 | 500 summer (200 winter) | Tidal tank | At LWM | Pebbles. |
| 14 | | Cocklawburn Beach | 1 | 300 | Raw | 20 above | Sand and rocks. |
| f ★★ | | **Spittal** | | | | | Improvement scheme. |
| | | Berwick-upon-Tweed | 1 | | Raw | At LWM | Sandy. |

## 1 Hornsea, North Humberside   OS Ref: TA2047

From Barmston just south of Bridlington to the shingle of Spurn Point is the fastest eroding section of coastline in Britain. Tens of feet of the clay cliffs are lost annually. This makes access to the coastline difficult with the erosion of roads, paths and steps. Hornsea is one of the few places where there is a break in the cliffs and sea defences attempt to stop the advancing sea. A sea wall and promenade face the mile (1.6km) long beach of sand and pebbles which virtually disappears when the tide rises. A park and various seaside amusements line the promenade. The quiet town of Hornsea is set back from the sea.

*Water quality*  Beach monitored by the NRA and found to meet the EC standard for clean bathing water in 1990. One outfall serving 16,000 people discharges screened and macerated sewage ⅔ mile (1km) below low water mark. One storm sewage overflow.

*Bathing safety*  Due to strong currents off shore, bathing is only safe close inshore. The central section of the beach is patrolled by lifeguards at weekends.

*Access*  Steps and ramp from promenade to sands.

*Parking*  Several car parks adjacent to the promenade.

*Toilets*  Several on promenade, all with facilities for the disabled.

*Food*  Six cafés at central section of beach, several more in the town centre.

*Seaside activities*  Swimming, windsurfing, sailing, jetskiing and fishing. Golf course nearby.

*Wet weather alternatives*  Hornsea Pottery is situated to the south of the town and has shops selling bargains in pottery, clothing and shoes. There is also a birds of prey collection, butterfly world and children's adventure playground.

*Wildlife and walks*  Hornsea Mere lies just south of the town. This 2 mile (3km) long lake is part of an RSPB reserve whose 5 acres (2 hectares) are an important wintering ground for wildfowl. There is a large population of reed warblers in the reed swamps. A public footpath along the south shore, through woods and open fields, provides good views of the area. There are boat launching facilities on the Mere.

## 2 Bridlington, North Humberside   OS Ref: TA1866

Bridlington is a bustling holiday resort which has won a whole variety of awards in the past, including the Blue Flag. With its two beaches, it combines the traditional seaside holiday entertainments with new up-to-date facilities, and there is easy access to the natural beauty of the adjacent Flamborough Headland Heritage Coast. The safe, sandy beaches are separated by Bridlington harbour; stone quays enclose a tidal harbour which is a continually changing scene of fishing and pleasure craft. The south beach extends for 5 miles (8km) with the busy promenade giving way to steep cliffs south of the town. North beach is the most popular for watersports, being sheltered by the sheer white cliffs that sweep north to Flamborough Head.

**Water quality** Beach monitored by the NRA and found to meet the EC standard for clean bathing water in 1990. One outfall at Bridlington South serving 56,000 people discharges screened sewage 1 mile (1.6km) below low water mark. Two storm water outfalls discharge storm overflow to the north beach at low water: however, this only occurs at infrequent intervals following heavy rainfall.

**Litter** The beach is cleaned by the local council. Bye-laws banning dogs from the beach were successfully introduced in 1990.

**Bathing safety** Safe bathing.

**Access** Steps and ramps from the promenade.

**Parking** Sea-front and adequate spaces within town.

**Toilets** On promenade.

**Food** Selection of cafés and restaurants along promenade.

**Seaside activities** Swimming, windsurfing, diving, fishing, sailing, water skiing and paragliding. Windsurfing and sailing facilities are available for hire. Fishing tackle is also for hire and there are fishing trips daily from the harbour. Bridlington is the venue for the UK windsurfing championship.

**Wet weather alternatives** Leisure World, Fun Parks, Sewerby Hall and Park, Portminian Model Village, Park Rose Pottery, John Bull World of Rock, Harbour Museum, Historic Old Town and the picturesque Yorkshire Wolds, including Burton Agnes Hall and Sledmere House.

**Wildlife and walks** To the north lies Flamborough Head, 300 feet (90m) of towering chalk cliff. The area is rich in magnificent scenery, with natural arches, stacks and caves to be admired or explored. Several guided walks and special events are on offer and details can be obtained from the Heritage Coast Information Centre, South Landing, Flamborough. The RSPB bird sanctuary is situated to the north at Bempton.

### 3 Filey Sands, Filey, North Yorkshire    OS Ref: TA1180

Five miles (8km) of wide flat golden sands at Filey are sheltered by Filey Brigg, a rocky promontory that extends 1 mile (1.6km) out to sea. From the headland you can enjoy good views north to Scarborough and south to Flamborough Head. Below the gently sloping grass-covered cliffs, the beach curves to the coble landing at the north end of the town. Traditional coble fishing boats are drawn up behind the protective wall and the fishermen are often seen busy mending their nets. South of the landing a promenade and gardens face the beach which all but disappears at high tide. The Georgian residences of this elegant resort overlook the bay. The beach is cleaned daily and dogs are banned from the central part of the beach between May and September.

**Water quality** Beach monitored by the NRA and found to meet the EC standard for clean bathing water in 1990. Two outfalls serving 13,800 people discharge macerated sewage 220 yards (200m) below low water mark.

**Bathing safety** Bathing requires caution as there are strong cross-currents. There is a warning flag system in operation. Inshore rescue boat and coastguard lookout.

**Access** Ramps at the southern end of the promenade and the coble landing lead on to the sand.

**Parking** There are three pay and display car parks at West Avenue (880 spaces), Station Avenue (280) and Country Park (3,000). There is street parking on the promenade and on Church Hill.

**Toilets** 'Superloo' at Cargate, toilets at coble landing and Royal Parade.

**Food** Various kiosks and pub at coble landing, Margate Hill and Royal Parade.

**Seaside activities** Swimming, surfing, windsurfing, sailing, diving and fishing (very good off Filey Brigg; boats available for hire). Boating, putting and amusements. Edwardian Festival in June.

**Wet weather alternatives** Amusement arcades at coble landing, Museum.

**Wildlife and walks** The area is renowned for its bird life and interesting geology. A nature trail along Filey Brigg starts at the foot of the cliff below Filey Country Park. The Brigg should be avoided in rough weather when heavy seas can crash over the rocks, making them dangerous for walkers and anglers.

## 4 Cayton Bay, North Yorkshire    OS Ref: TA0685

Steep wooded cliffs surround the small arc of this bay and many of the boulders fringing it bear the imprints of fossil ammonites and belemites. The National Trust owns the northern half of the bay. At low tide, sandbanks are revealed which may trap the unwary if the incoming tide is not watched. It is also dangerous to cross the rocks at the southern end of the bay. The rockpools abound with marine life and will keep the amateur naturalist engrossed for hours.

**Water quality** Beach monitored by the NRA and found to meet the EC standard for clean bathing water in 1990. No sewage is discharged in the vicinity of the beach.

**Bathing safety** Safest at high water; at other times beware of incoming tide.

**Access** Signposted off the A165, path down from the holiday camp at the top of the cliffs.

**Parking** Car park with 50 spaces approximately 1 mile (1.6km) from beach.

*Toilets* Between Spring Bank Holiday and the end of October.

*Food* None.

*Seaside activities* Swimming, surfing, fishing.

*Wet weather alternatives* The woods at the top of the cliff will at least provide some shelter; for the less hardy the resort of Scarborough is less than 3 miles (5km) away.

*Wildlife and walks* The Cleveland Way runs close by the beach; it can be followed north through Scarborough and into the North York Moors National Park.

## 5 Robin Hood's Bay, North Yorkshire   OS Ref: NZ9505

A wide sweeping bay framed by crumbling red cliffs stretches from Ness Point and the village of Robin Hood's Bay south to the 600 foot (180m) headland of Old Peak with its scattered housing of Ravenscar. Magnificent views of the bay can be obtained from the undulating farmland on the cliff top. There is a remnant cliff line inland. A 40 foot (12m) high sea wall protects the cluster of fishing cottages that make up Robin Hood's Bay village. Vehicle access to the older parts of the village is restricted and to get to the beach you have to park at the top of the hill and walk down through the village. Elsewhere there is limited access to the shore of this huge bay. Boggle Hole, where Mill Beck cuts through the cliffs, is a sheltered shingle and rock cove. Stoupe Beck Sands is an 880 yard (800m) stretch of sand in the middle of the bay. This area of the bay is very isolated with no facilities; the beach is reached down a paved track through a wooded valley. The headland at Ravenscar and the rocky shore below are owned by the National Trust and offer excellent views north along the coast. All have a wild feel to them and mats of washed-up seaweed are commonplace, which some may find unpleasant. The National Trust Coastal Centre at Ravenscar features displays including a marine aquarium with specimens borrowed from the rocky shore.

*Water quality* Beach monitored by the NRA and found to meet the EC standard for clean bathing water in 1990. There is one outfall serving 5,500 people: a £5 million improvement scheme will be completed in 1994.

*Bathing safety* Safe bathing but beware of sharp rocks.

*Access* The main access to the beach is from Robin Hood's Bay village, signposted off the A171 south of Whitby. There is a regular bus service to the village and parking above.

*Parking* Pay and display car park at the top of the hill (267 spaces).

*Toilets* By the beach.

*Food* Various cafés, kiosks and pubs.

*Seaside activities* Swimming, diving and fishing.

*Wildlife and walks* The area is famed for its geology and fossils – there is a geological trail from Ravenscar. The Cleveland Way follows the bay and there is a network of paths on the cliffs. There is much to interest the beachcomber with rockpools full of life.

## 6 Runswick Bay, Runswick, North Yorkshire   OS Ref: NZ8016

From the picturesque hillside village of Runswick, the broad sandy beach, backed by steeply sloping clay cliffs, curves south-east to the rocky headland that bounds the bay. The crescent of sand gives way to rocky shore at either end. The old village of Runswick nestles at the base of the cliffs with the new one perched above. There is easy access to the beach and the area is not over-commercialised. There are beach huts and chalets on the scrub-covered cliffs. Good views across the bay are to be had from the village of Kettleness on the southern headland.

*Water quality* Beach monitored by the NRA and found to meet the EC standard for clean bathing water in 1990. One outfall serving 480 people discharges raw sewage at low water mark.

*Bathing safety* Safe bathing.

*Access* A road off the A174 north of Whitby leads down to Runswick village. There is a ramp to the beach.

*Parking* Pay and display at the bottom of the hill with 104 spaces.

*Toilets* By car park.

*Food* Cafés and shops in village.

*Seaside activities* Swimming, sailing and fishing.

*Wildlife and walks* The area is excellent for walking with the Cleveland Way skirting the bay. Following the route north for 2 miles (3km) you reach the tiny harbour of Mulgrave, now falling into disrepair below the cliffs. Further north at the mouth of a tiny rocky inlet is Staithes Harbour. The village with its closely packed houses and network of alleyways nestles in the steep valley.

## 7 Druridge Bay, Cresswell, Northumberland   OS Ref: NZ2993

A 5 mile (8km) curving sweep of golden sand is fringed by dunes with rocky outcrops at either end, at Cresswell and Hadston Carrs. Cresswell is the easiest point of access and may be busy on a sunny afternoon, but a short walk along the shore will bring you to miles of quiet sand. There are views north along the bay to Coquet Island and its lighthouse.

*Water quality* Beach monitored by the NRA and found to meet the EC standard for clean bathing water in 1990. One outfall serving 5,500 people discharges untreated sewage at low water mark.

*Bathing safety* Swim with extreme caution as the tides and currents are strong and unpredictable.

**117**

**Access** The A1068 leads to Cresswell and the Druridge Bay Country Park. It is a short walk from the car parks across the dunes.

**Parking** Near Cresswell there is a car park with 100 spaces; at Cresswell Ponds there is space for 10 cars, and on Druridge Links a National Trust car park has 150 spaces. Druridge Bay Country Park has parking for 200+ cars and also coaches.

**Toilets** In Cresswell village and at Druridge Bay Country Park at the northern end of the bay.

**Food** Café and tea room in village, mobile ice-cream vans.

**Seaside activities** Swimming, sailing and fishing.

**Wildlife and walks** At the northern end of the beach is the Druridge Bay Country Park. There are also nature reserves at Druridge and Hauxley. Cresswell Ponds have been designated as a Site of Special Scientific Interest. It is a superb area for birdwatching; the Northumberland Wildlife Trust has recently opened its Druridge Pools Reserve to the public and hide facilities are available. The Trust also runs the Blakemoor Visitor Centre where details of bird numbers and species can be found. South of the bay, beyond the smaller Broadsands beach and the rocky outcrops of Snab Point, there is the sharply contrasting Lynemouth beach, blackened by coal dust washed from waste tips that line the beach.

## 8 Warkworth, Northumberland   OS Ref: NU2606

Between Warkworth Harbour at the mouth of the Coquet Estuary and the Aln Estuary there lie 3 miles (5km) of fabulous sandy beach. The beach, edged by sand dunes, extends northwards for 2 miles (3km) to merge with Alnmouth Links. The town of Amble lies on the southern banks of the estuary and here fishing cobles may be seen in the harbour and yachts moored in the river or at the Braid Marina – winner for the past four years of a European Blue Flag for ports, awarded for environmental quality and good facilities. Coquet Island lies 1 mile (1.6km) off shore, sheltering the harbour entrance. The island is an RSPB reserve and boat trips are available from the harbour. The views back across the estuary with the backdrop of Warkworth Castle are most impressive. The near-perfect mediaeval village of Warkworth, an idyllic spot with dramatic castle, hermitage and unique fortified bridge is set a mile (1.6km) inland, almost enclosed by a meander of the river Coquet. Warkworth beach is signposted from here. The picnic site by the beach has panoramic views of the Coquet Estuary. There is access to Alnmouth Links south of Bilton on the A1068 but there is very limited parking behind the dunes.

**Water quality** Beach monitored by the NRA and found to meet the EC standard for clean bathing water in 1990. One outfall serving 8,000 people discharges screened and macerated sewage at Amble.

**Litter** Some marine litter and fishing debris is washed on to the beach.

**Bathing safety** Bathing is dangerous at high tide. There is an inshore and offshore rescue boat and coastguard station at Amble.

*Access* North of Warkworth a turning off the A1068 is signposted to the beach.

*Parking* Car park at picnic site with space for 50 cars.

*Toilets* In car park.

*Food* None. Tea rooms in village a mile (1.6km) away.

*Seaside activities* Swimming, golf course (Warkworth), river and sea fishing from Amble.

*Wildlife and walks* The picnic site and surrounding area at Warkworth beach is managed by the Northumberland National Park and the National Trust owns the land to the north. A coastal path stretches the 3½ miles (6km) from Warkworth to Alnmouth and is described in a leaflet available locally. A walk to the south takes you through dunes to the long breakwater serving Warkworth harbour and some interesting salt marshes which were designated as a Site of Special Scientific Interest in 1988. Coquet Island with its prominent lighthouse is frequented by colonies of breeding seabirds – puffins, terns, eider. These may be viewed from boat trips around the island organised by the RSPB and bookable at the Amble Tourist Information Office.

## 9 Alnmouth, Northumberland   OS Ref: NU2410

A 1 mile (1.6km) expanse of sand stretches from the picturesque village of Alnmouth north to the Marsden Rocks. At low tide over 440 yards (400m) of excellent sand is exposed. The beach is bordered by a large car park and golf course, behind which lies the village. Alnmouth was a port of some importance during the 18th century, but due to a change in the course of the river little can be seen of the old harbour; however the old granaries have been carefully converted into pubs, shops, eating places and accommodation, retaining its unspoilt character.

*Water quality* Beach monitored by the NRA and found to meet the EC standard for clean bathing water in 1990. No sewage is discharged in the vicinity of the beach.

*Bathing safety* There are dangerous currents at some states of the tide.

*Access* Alnmouth is signposted off the A1068 south of Alnwick. A road through the golf course north of the village leads to the beach car park.

*Parking* Parking for 150 cars adjacent to beach.

*Toilets* In the village.

*Food* Numerous cafés and restaurants in the village.

*Seaside activities* Swimming, surfing, windsurfing, fishing and sailing in estuary. Two links golf courses north of village.

*Wildlife and walks* There is an excellent coastal walk north from Alnmouth along the rocky shore with its series of small sandy bays to explore.

Fulmars glide effortlessly along these cliffs where a wide range of seabirds can be seen. At Howick Haven you can either continue north along the low cliffs to the fishing village of Craster or turn inland following the wooded valley for 1 mile (1.6km) to the grounds of Howick Hall, where the gardens are open in summer.

## 10 Embleton Bay, Northumberland   OS Ref: NU2329

This scenically outstanding bay is bounded to the south by the craggy headland on which stand the dramatic ruins of Dunstanburgh Castle. The steep basalt cliffs are known as Gull Crag because of the numerous nesting seabirds, especially kittiwakes and fulmars. The excellent sandy Embleton beach, bordered by sand dunes and a golf course, stretches north from the boulder-strewn shore below the Crag to merge with the Newton Haven beach at the northern end of the bay.

**Water quality** No sewage is discharged on to the beach.

**Litter** A clean beach but with some marine debris washed up, especially in winter.

**Bathing safety** Safe bathing on the incoming tide; there are undercurrents on the ebbing tide.

**Access** From Embleton village on the B1339 follow the road leading to the golf course or Dunstan Steads Farm. A path leads directly on to the beach and connects with the coastal footpath.

**Parking** Roadside parking for approximately 100 cars.

**Toilets** In the village.

**Food** In the village.

**Seaside activities** Swimming.

**Wildlife and walks** This stretch of coastline is owned by the National Trust. There are excellent views across the bay from the Heritage Coast path to the south; the path continues along the rocky foreshore to Craster, a classic fishing village with miniature harbour, rows of neat cottages and the stone sheds where the world famous Craster kippers are smoked.

## 11 Newton Haven, Northumberland   OS Ref: NU2525

Newton Haven's ⅔ mile (1km) crescent of sand lies at the northern end of Embleton Bay. Low tide exposes a wide beach which is fringed by dunes. Sheltered by a grass headland to the north and an offshore reef, the beach is popular for watersports. It is overlooked by the village of Low Newton, an attractive square of fishermen's cottages and pub now owned by the National Trust. Behind the dunes lies Newton Pool, a freshwater lagoon which is a nature reserve.

**Water quality** Beach monitored by the NRA and found to meet the EC standard for clean bathing water in 1990. There is no sewage discharged in the vicinity of this beach.

*Litter* Some oil drums and fishing debris are washed up, particularly in winter.

*Bathing safety* Bathing is safe on the incoming tide; there are undercurrents on the ebbing tide.

*Access* From the car park on the approach road to Low Newton, signposted off the B1339 from High Newton. It is a short walk down to the village with direct access to the beach. A path leads along Low Newton beach to Embleton Bay.

*Parking* There is a car park 330 yards (300m) from Low Newton and on the road sides with space for about 100 cars. Parking in the village is for residents and disabled badge holders only.

*Toilets* Adjacent to beach.

*Food* Pub with snacks and tea room in High Newton ⅔ mile (1km) away.

*Seaside activities* Swimming, windsurfing, sailing, diving, canoeing and fishing. Newton Sailing School provides tuition hourly or weekly and has dinghies, canoes and windsurfboards for hire.

*Wildlife and walks* There are bird hides at Newton Pool (one with disabled access) and a wide variety of species can seen, particularly in winter. The Heritage Coast Path stretches south round Embleton Bay to Dunstanburgh Castle and north around Newton Point to the wide sweep of Newton Links and Beadnell Bay.

## 12 Beadnell Bay, Beadnell, Northumberland   OS Ref: NU2229

The golden sands of this superb beach sweep south on a 2 mile (3km) long curve to the rocky outcrop of Snook Point. A stream meanders across the sands in the centre of the bay and to the south is a good area for collecting shells. At the northern end of the beach is the tiny harbour of Beadnell, still used by the traditional east coast fishing cobles. It has the distinction of being the only east coast harbour to actually face west! Standing on the quay are some huge 18th-century limestone kilns. These impressive structures have been restored and are owned by the National Trust.

*Water quality* Beach monitored by the NRA and found to meet the EC standard for clean bathing water in 1990. One outfall serving approximately 2,000 people discharges macerated and screened sewage at low water mark.

*Litter* A very clean beach: two wardens are employed to oversee the maintenance of the beach.

*Bathing safety* Bathing is safe on the incoming tide; there are dangerous undercurrents on the ebb.

*Access* A road from the B1340 in Beadnell village leads to the harbour. Short walk from car park to sand.

**Parking** Large car park at north end of bay near harbour with 200 spaces. Small car park at Newton Links at south end of bay with space for 30 cars.

**Toilets** In Beadnell car park.

**Food** Ice-cream van at car park.

**Seaside activities** Swimming, windsurfing, sailing, diving, water skiing and canoeing. Outdoor sports hire centre at car park.

**Wildlife and walks** This stretch of coastline provides some splendid walking. South, a path around the edge of the bay leads to Newton Haven, the lovely Embleton Bay and the romantic ruins of Dunstanburgh Castle. To the north, the rocky shore gives way to sand that stretches to Seahouses.

## 13 Bamburgh and Seahouses, Northumberland    OS Ref: NU1834

A 150 foot (45m) rock outcrop towers above beautiful long sandy beaches and provides the magnificent setting for Bamburgh Castle. From the castle rock there are spectacular views of the sandy beaches stretching north to Holy Island and south to Seahouses. Seaward lies the panorama of the Farne Islands, their rocky cliffs falling steeply to the water below. It was from the Longstone lighthouse on Outer Farne that Grace Darling set off to rescue the crew of the *Forfarshire*. The row that made her a national heroine is remembered in the Grace Darling Museum in Bamburgh. Today the trip to the Islands is made from the little harbour at Seahouses. Inland, Bamburgh village nestles below the castle among undulating fields. Between Bamburgh and Seahouses there are 4 miles (6.5km) of superb beach with sand which squeaks when walked over. Backed by the St Aidan's and Shoreston Dunes, the sands give way to rocky shore at Seahouses where the rockpools are full of marine life.

**Water quality** Both Bamburgh and Seahouses were monitored by the NRA and found to meet the EC standard for clean bathing water in 1990. There are two outfalls at Bamburgh; one, serving approximately 1,000 people, discharges macerated sewage through a tidal tank at low water mark; the other serves 100 people and discharges untreated sewage at low water mark. One outfall at Seahouses serving 6,000 people discharges screened and macerated sewage through a tidal tank 110 yards (100m) below low water mark.

**Litter** A little wood, plastic and fishing debris is washed on to the beach. Litter left by visitors is cleared by the National Trust.

**Bathing safety** Bathing is safe only on the incoming tide due to under-currents as the tide ebbs; beware of offshore winds. Life belts are available at Seahouses. Inshore rescue boat and lifeboat.

**Access** There is access from both Bamburgh and Seahouses which lie on the B1340, with easy access to the beach across dunes.

**Parking** Bamburgh: Large car park in Bamburgh has over 200 spaces.

Three dune car parks with approximately 25 spaces in each, plus space for about 50 cars along the road above dunes.

Seahouses: Car park in village has 500+ spaces. Space for 30 cars parking on verge of B1340 north of Seahouses.

### Bamburgh

**Toilets** In village.

**Food** Café and hotel in village, and ice-cream vans on or near beach.

**Seaside activities** Swimming, surfing, windsurfing, diving, sailing and fishing.

**Wet weather alternatives** Castle, Grace Darling Museum and her grave in village.

### Seahouses

**Toilets** In village.

**Food** In village.

**Seaside activities** Swimming, golf course, amusements.

**Wet weather alternatives** Marine Life Centre.

**Wildlife and walks** This fantastic section of coastline falls within the Northumberland Heritage Coast and is also designated as an Area of Outstanding Natural Beauty. Below the lofty position of Bamburgh Castle, a walk north along the shore leads to Budle Bay. The salt marsh, mud and sand flats are part of the Lindisfarne Nature Reserve which covers the whole of the Fenham Flats, Holy Island Sands and most of the Island itself. The area provides feeding for thousands of waders and wildfowl. It is dangerous to cross the sands; access to the island is by the causeway which is covered for at least 11 hours each day. With its Castle and Priory, the Island is steeped in history and its distinctive conical shape leaves a lasting impression on the memory. The beaches around the island are wide and sandy but unsafe for swimming because of strong currents. The Farne Islands to the south of Holy Island are of international importance for their large colonies of seabirds and grey seals. The 30 islands that make up the Farnes are a National Trust Nature Reserve and landing is permitted on Inner Farne and Staple Island. Boats make the hour-long trip from the harbour at Seahouses in good weather. Further information about the service is available from the National Trust shop in Seahouses. Access is restricted during the bird breeding season from mid-May until mid-July.

## 14 Cocklawburn, Scremerston, Northumberland   OS Ref: NU0349

The retreating tide exposes rockpools in the rocks which bound this ⅔ mile (1km) long section of sandy beach. This is the accessible end of an extensive sandy beach which stretches south as Cheswick Sands towards Holy Island. The further south-east you venture along the beach the quieter the beach becomes. Wide flat sands revealed at low tide join the island with the mainland. They should not be crossed by foot – use the causeway road from Beal. The influence of man is much in evidence at the Cocklawburn beach with the remains of lime kilns and waste heaps on the edge of the beach. The modern activity of man imposes on the beach at times too, with the sound of trains on the railway line to Edinburgh which runs parallel with the shore.

***Water quality*** One outfall serving 300 people discharges untreated sewage 22 yards (20m) above low water mark.

***Bathing safety*** Safe bathing on the incoming tide; undercurrents on the ebb tide make swimming dangerous; beware also of offshore winds.

***Access*** Turning east from the village of Scremerston, a lane leads down to and then runs parallel with the shore. The beach is reached by a short walk through the dunes.

***Parking*** Cars can be parked at several places along the lane on grassland behind the dunes. There is space for approximately 200 cars.

***Toilets*** None.

***Food*** None.

***Seaside activities*** Swimming, surfing, windsurfing and fishing.

***Wildlife and walks*** The dunes that edge the beach support a very good flora and an area at the southern end of the beach is a Northumberland Wildlife Trust Nature Reserve. The limestone outcrops are favoured by cowslips, cranesbills and vetches which add to the variety of plants to be found. A path north along the rocky shore leads to the mouth of the river Tweed where fishermen netting salmon can often be seen.

# North-West England

For the region which pioneered the concept of the seaside resort, it's rather sad that the role the north-west can play in a guide such as this is so small. The north-west does have some lovely stretches of coastline; birdwatching on Morecambe Bay with the Lake District as a backdrop, or the Victorian elegance of Southport are but two regional attractions.

However, the whole region suffers from major pollution problems which affect nearly all its shores. The Irish Sea is heavily polluted; it is the most radioactive sea in the world and it is more chemically contaminated than the North Sea. The Mersey Estuary and Liverpool Bay have suffered particularly. For example, 8.8 lb (4kg) of mercury and cadmium, and 990 lb (450kg) of lead are released into the bay each day, mostly from industrial and contaminated sewage discharges to the Mersey and its tributaries. In addition at least 1.5 million tons of sewage sludge and 3.5 million tons of dredged spoil (sediments dredged from the estuary usually contaminated with heavy metals and other persistent toxic chemicals) are dumped into Liverpool Bay each year. Blackpool, the most famous (and still one of the most popular) seaside resort of them all, looks out on to this toxic mess. As a result, its beaches remain some of the most grossly polluted in the whole of the UK.

Thus, visitors to the beaches in this region must, unhappily, expect to see strands of foam resulting from excessive algal growth triggered by the very high nutrient inputs from sewage. They will also come across the refuse dumped from the boats and ships which continually use the waterway. Despite a considerable improvement in the water quality results (in 1988 only five of the designated beaches in the region complied with the EC standard for bathing water quality; in 1989 this rose to 10, but in 1990 the figure went down to nine), most people would think twice about swimming. Although work is being undertaken to improve the situation (nearly £60 million for Blackpool alone), without more action it will be many years before there are major improvements.

# North-West England

Silloth **f**
■ Carlisle

Allonby
Allonby South **f**

■ Whitehaven

St Bees
Seascale **f**

Silecroft
Askam-in-Furness **f**
Aldingham **f**
Haverigg **f**
Roan Head **f**
Bardsea
Barrow-in-Furness ■
Newbiggin **f**
Morecambe **f**
Walney Westshore **f**
Walney Sandy Gap
Walney Biggar Bank
Heysham **f**

Fleetwood **f**
Cleveleys **f**

■ Blackpool **f**

Lytham St Annes **f**
Lytham St Annes South **f**
■ Southport **f**
Ainsdale

**1** Formby

New Brighton **f**
Moreton
■ Liverpool
Moels **f**
Birkenhead

**f** = failed to meet EC standard for clean bathing water in 1990.

# The Golden List   *See page 25 for further details*

| Beach No on Map | Rating. The more stars the better. f=failed | Resort | Sewage outlets | Population discharging from outlet | Type of treatment | Discharge point relative to low water mark, unless otherwise stated. Distance given in metres | Remarks |
|---|---|---|---|---|---|---|---|
| | f ** | **Silloth** | 1 | 2,600 | Screened | 60 below | Sand and shingle. Sewage treatment works planned. |
| | f **<br>*** | **Allonby**<br>South<br>West Winds | 1 | 600 | Screened | 50 below | Sand and rock slighty muddy. Popular beach. Safe bathing. Improvements planned. |
| | | Maryport | 1 | 11,500 | Raw | At LWM | Sand, shingle. Fishing port. Improvements planned. |
| | | Flimby | 3 | 500<br>1,500<br><br>100 | Raw<br>Raw<br><br>Raw | 150 above<br>150 above<br><br>150 above | Shingle/sand. Popular beach. Improvements planned. |
| | | Siddick (Low Seaton) | 2 | 4,300<br><br>50 | Raw<br><br>Raw | 200 below<br><br>200 below | Shingle/slag. Mainly used by fishermen. Improvements planned. |
| | | Workington | 4 | 6,000<br>8,000<br>9,000<br>7,500 | Raw<br>Raw<br>Raw<br>Raw | At LWM<br>10 above<br>20 above<br>Below HWM | Sand, shingle and slag. Well used beach.<br>Shingle/mud bank. Derwent Estuary.<br>Shingle/slag. Low amenity.<br>Shingle/slag. Low amenity. Improvements planned. |
| | | Harrington | 1 | 1,500 industry | Raw | At LWM | Shingle/slag. Popular beach. Improvements planned. |
| | | Parton | 1 | 200+ | Screened/maceration | 800 below | Shingle/sand. Low amenity. Industrial. Improvements planned. |
| | | Whitehaven | 3 | 500<br>2,350<br>23,500 | Raw<br>Raw<br>Raw | Above HWM<br>At LWM<br>At LWM | Shingle/black sand and high cliffs. Little used. Improvements planned. |
| | *** | **St Bees** | 1 | 1,750 | Primary | 100 above | Sand/shingle. Strong tank currents. Proposed improvement scheme. |
| | | Nethertown | 1 | 400 | Raw | 50 below | Sand/shingle. |
| | | Braystones | 1 | 7,000 | Raw | 50 below | Sand/shingle. |

| Beach No on Map | Rating. The more stars the better. f=failed | Resort | Sewage outlets | Population discharging from outlet | Type of treatment | Discharge point relative to low water mark, unless otherwise stated. Distance given in metres | Remarks |
|---|---|---|---|---|---|---|---|
| | f ** | **Seascale** | 1 | 2,200 | Raw | Below LWM | Sand/shingle & rocks. £1.6 million improvement scheme. |
| | | Ravenglass | 1 | 250 +heavy tourist trade | Primary | To Esk Estuary at LWM | Shingle and mud. |
| | *** | **Silecroft** | | | | | Sand and shingle. |
| | f ** | **Haverigg** | | | | | Sand dunes. High amenity. Improvement scheme. |
| | | Millom | 1 | 7,500 | Primary | At LWM | Sand and shingle. |
| | f ** | **Askam-in-Furness** | 1 | 2,350 | Secondary | To Duddon Channel | Sand. Bathing safe inshore. Pollution in Duddon Estuary. Improvement scheme planned. |
| | | Barrow-in-Furness | 32 | 73,000 | Raw/other | All discharge to Walney Channel | Beaches to the west of the island have sand dunes and |
| | f ** | **Roanhead** | | | | | normal bathing facilities. Walney Channel and east |
| | | Rampside | | | | | of the island is polluted and |
| | f ** | **Walney Island: West Shore** | | | | | is used for boating only. Imrprovements planned. |
| | ** | **Walney Island: Biggar Bank** | | | | | |
| | *** | **Walney Island: Sandy Gap** | | | | | |
| | f * | Newbiggin | | | | | Sandy. |
| | f ** | Aldingham | | | | | Sandy. |
| | ** | **Bardsea** | | | | | Sandy. Country park. Improvement scheme. |
| | | Grange-Over-Sands & Kents Bank | 3 | 11,500 | Secondary | Discharges to Wyke Beck | Mud, shingle and sand. New sewage treatment works. |
| | | Arnside | 1 | 2,000 | Tidal tank | | Mud, shingle and sand. New pumping station has reduced the number of occasions when overflow operates. |

| Beach No on Map | Rating. The more stars the better. f=failed | Resort | Sewage outlets | Population discharging from outlet | Type of treatment | Discharge point relative to low water mark, unless otherwise stated. Distance given in metres | Remarks |
|---|---|---|---|---|---|---|---|
| | | Hest Bank | 2 | 2,850 | Secondary | One above HWM and one below | Mud flats, sea retreats 4 miles (6.4km). No bathing. |
| f ★<br>f ★★ | | **Morecambe**<br>North<br>South | 1 | 31,000 | Raw | At LWM | North beach mud and shingle. South beach sandy with safe bathing. £20 million improvement scheme. |
| f ★★ | | **Heysham** | 1 | 3,500 | Primary | At LWM | Sand. Popular beach. |
| | | Pilling Sands | 1 | 1,000 | Tidal tank | To Broad-fleet | Mud flats/salt marsh. Outfall has been moved. |
| | | Knott End-on-Sea | 1 | 1,100 | Raw | To Wyre Estuary | Sand/mud flats. |
| f ★ | | **Fleetwood** | 1 | 31,000 | Tidal tank | At LWM | Sand. Stormwater overflow at high water mark which often overflows on to the beach. Linked to Blackpool scheme. |
| f ★★ | | **Cleveleys** | | | | | Linked into Blackpool scheme. Sewage at present to Blackpool. |
| f ★ | | Bispham | | | | | |
| f ★ | | **Blackpool North** | 2 | 75,000 | Screened | 950 below | Sand. Discharges of storm water directly on to the beach occur once or twice a year. Improvement scheme planned, due for completion in 1994, secondary treatment envisaged. |
| f ★ | | **Blackpool Lost Childrens Post Blackpool South** | | 216,000 | Screened | 500 below | |
| f ★/<br>f ★ | | **Lytham St Anne's** | 1 | 37,000 | Screened | At LWM | Sand. Outfall discharges into channel of the Ribble Estuary. Linked to new Blackpool scheme. |

| Beach No on Map | Rating. The more stars the better. f=failed | Resort | Sewage outlets | Population discharging from outlet | Type of treatment | Discharge point relative to low water mark, unless otherwise stated. Distance given in metres | Remarks |
|---|---|---|---|---|---|---|---|
| | f ** | Marshside **Southport** | 5 | 91,500 | Secondary | All above LWM | Sandy beaches. 3 storm sewage overflows used in emergency only, 2 stormwater overflows. Sewage is treated at Southport and Ainsdale sewage treatment works which is being extended in a £21 million scheme. |
| | *** | **Ainsdale** | | | | | |
| 1 | *** | **Formby** | | | | | |
| | | Hightown | 2 | 2,100 | Secondary | | Sand and some muddy areas around Alt estuary. Emergency overflow into Alt Estuary. Sewage is treated at Formby sewage treatment works. |
| | | Blundell Sands | 5 | 48,100 | | | New interceptor sewers carrying the sewage to a treatment works; part of a major scheme to clean up the Mersey. |
| | | Brighton-Le-Sands | | | | | |
| | | Crosby | | | | | |
| | | Waterloo | | | | | |
| | | New Brighton Egremont | 4 | 16,000 | | | All flows now diverted to Wallasey screening plant. |
| | ** | New Brighton Harrison Drive | 5 | 30,000 | | | |
| | *** | **Moreton** | 1 | 65,000 | Maceration | 3000 below | A long sea outfall discharges macerated sewage through diffusers. The coast is normally free from sewage but see remarks above re the Mersey Estuary. |
| | | Hoylake | | | | | |
| | f ** | **Meols** | | | | | |
| | | West Kirby | | | | | |

## 1 Freshfield, Formby, Merseyside   OS Ref: SD2907

Freshfield is the oasis in the desert of polluted, neglected, or industrialised beaches of the north-west. A massive expanse of sand is revealed as the tide retreats across the flat beach. Not an ideal beach for swimming from but good for walking, soaking up the sun or escaping from the surrounding urban sprawl and enjoying the 450 acres (182 hectares) of unspoilt dunes and woodland. These are owned by the National Trust and stretch a mile (1.6km) inland from the beach. The 2½ mile (4km) long stretch of beach extends north to the Ainsdale National Nature Reserve, with views to Southport and Blackpool Tower beyond. To the south is the Raven Meols Nature Reserve, and there are views across the Mersey to the hills of North Wales.

**Water quality** Monitored by the NRA and found to meet the EC standard for clean bathing water in 1990. Formby sewage treatment works serving 34,000 people discharges secondary treated sewage to the channel at Formby Bank off the Signal Station.

**Litter** Litter causes quite a problem on the beach with a lot of plastics and other debris from boats being washed up. Some sewage solids have been observed.

**Bathing safety** Bathing is only safe close inshore; the incoming tide is very swift and can be dangerous.

**Access** A short walk through dunes from car park. Freshfields station 1¼ miles (2km) from beach along Victoria Road.

**Parking** National Trust car park for 770 cars at end of Victoria Road within reserve. Sefton MBC car park at Lifeboat Road.

**Toilets** None.

**Food** Two ice-cream vans during summer.

**Seaside activities** Swimming, fishing and windsurfing. Horse-riding on marked way through dunes, woods and along the beach, by permit only. Golf course at northern end of beach beyond Pinetree Caravan Site.

**Wildlife and walks** The dunes and woodland behind the beach are owned by the National Trust. Throughout the area there are footpaths and board walks which you should use to protect this fragile environment. If followed inland from the beach the footpaths will reveal the whole sequence of habitats associated with the developing dune system. These range from the sand and mud flats exposed at low tide, which provide for large numbers and varieties of migrating and breeding birds, to mature Scots pine woods planted to stabilise the sand. Between, there are mobile dune ridges and slacks (wet troughs) where Britain's largest breeding population of Natterjack toads can be seen and heard in the freshwater pools. Inland, the dunes become fixed by a continuous cover of heath-type vegetation, which is replaced landwards by scrub, characterised by creeping willow, and then deciduous woodland. At the Wicks Lane end of the reserve there is a lake that provides a further range of wetland habitats. Adjacent to Victoria Road there is a red squirrel reserve. They can be seen throughout the year in the pinewoods. This whole area is covered by the Sefton Coastal Management Scheme and there is a programme of work to protect and improve the area and its wealth of wildlife. There is a full programme of guided walks organised by the Rangers – details from the Rangers' Office at Formby Council Offices.

# Scotland

If you are looking for a clean beach in the UK you are most likely to find one in Scotland. That is not to say that Scotland does not have problems around the coast. There are Scottish beaches that have failed to meet the EC bathing water quality standard. Sea-borne rubbish is washed up on to shore. Sewage sludge and dredged spoil are dumped off the Clyde, Forth and Tay estuaries. Industrial waste is discharged into the coastal water, particularly the Clyde and Forth. Nuclear installations at Chapelcross, Hunterston, Torness and Dounreay contribute to pollution of the sea. There is development of the coastline detrimental to scenic value. The west coast lochs are studded with the floating cages of the rapidly expanding fish farming industry. The offshore structures of the North Sea oil and gas industry that dot the horizon have resulted in the growth of onshore terminals. The view along the Cromarty Firth is dominated by a string of massive platforms. By contrast there is probably some of the most spectacular coastal scenery in the country, including the long sand dunes of the east coast, and the rocky shore of Fife with its series of picturesque fishing villages. There are also the cliffs and stacks of Caithness, and of course the west coast, Highlands and Islands, sea lochs, towering mountains and fantastic sunsets. There are hundreds (if not thousands) of beaches, tiny sandy bays, mostly remote, deserted and beautiful. Many can only be reached by the keen walker but without a doubt the effort is well worth while. The beaches that follow are those which are relatively easily accessible for a day at the sea or as a starting point to explore the delights of this coastline further. The sands of the Western Isles have not been included in the section; if you take the boat to the outer islands, beaches abound and every one is a good beach. If you are looking for peace and solitude combined with traditional hospitality then try Scotland.

*Scotland*

14 Sandside Bay
Dunnet Bay
16 Balnakeil Bay
Thurso
13 Duncansby Head
Farr Bay
17 Sandwood
15 Coldbackie
Sinclair's Bay
Wick

18 Scourie

20 Clachtoll    19 Clashnessie Bay
21 Achmelvich
22 Achnahaird
23 Achiltibuie
Ullapool

27 The Coral Beaches
24 Gruinard Bay
12 Dornoch
Lossiemouth Silversands
Inverboyndie Bay
25 Gairloch
Lossiemouth East
Banff f    Fraserburgh
Invergordon
8 Strathbeg
26 Applecross
11 Burghead    9 Sandend    Peterhead
Nairn
10 Cullen    Cruden Bay
Inverness

Balmedie
Aberdeen Ballroo
Aberdeen    Aberdeen Footdee
28 Morar
7 Muchalls
29 Camusdarrach
6 Stonehaven

30 Sanna Bay
St Cyrus f
5 Montrose

31 Calgary Bay
Arbroath f
Camoustie f
32 Erraid
4 Tentsmuir Point
Oban
St Andrews West    St Andrews East f

2 Thorntonloch
Dunglass
1 Pease Sand
Edinburgh    White Sands    Coldingham
Eyemouth

Glasgow

Saltcoats f
34 Brodick
Bay
Irvine f
33 Machrihanish    36 Troon
35 Blackwaterfoot    Prestwick f
Ayr f
Turnberry f
Girvan f

Stranraer    Southerness

Sandyhills f

**f** = failed to meet EC standard for clean bathing
water in 1990.
Numbered beaches appear in the following chapter.

**Coastal walk**
Forth Road Bridge to Newburgh 94 miles (152km).

Shell Bay
Largo
Crail
Lower Largo f
Anstruther
Lundin Links f
Pittenweem f
Elie/Earlsferry f
Kinghorn f    Kirkcaldy    North Berwick f
3 Gullane    Milsey Bay
Burnt Island
Seacliff
Aberdour Silversands f    Pettycur    Dunbar East
Cramond    Belhaven
Silverknowes    Peffer Sands
Edinburgh    Portobello    Broad Sands f
Gosford
Seton Sands f

# The Golden List  *See page 25 for further details*

| Beach No on Map | Rating. The more stars the better. f=failed | Resort | Sewage outlets | Population discharging from outlet | Type of treatment | Discharge point relative to low water mark, unless otherwise stated. Distance given in metres | Remarks |
|---|---|---|---|---|---|---|---|
| **BORDERS** | | | | | | | |
| | ★★★ | Eyemouth | 2 | 4,500 | Other | | Rocks and sand. Bathing can be dangerous. |
| | | | | 1,000 | Raw | | |
| | ★★★ | Coldingham Bay | 1 | 200 | Raw | | Sandy. Safe bathing. |
| **1** | ★★★★ | **Pease Sands** | 1 | 1,000 | Secondary | | Red cliffs and sand. |
| **LOTHIAN** | | | | | | | |
| **2** | ★★★★ | Thorntonloch | | | | | Mostly sandy. |
| | ★★★ | Whitesands Bay | | | | | Sandy. |
| | ★★★ | **Belhaven Beach** | 1 | 4,200 | Screens/ maceration | At LWM | Sandy. |
| | ★★★ | Peffersands | | | | | Sandy. |
| | ★★★ | **Milsey Bay** | 2 | 2,100 | Raw | At LWM | Sandy and rock outcrops. |
| | f ★★ | North Berwick Bay | 2 | 2,800 | Raw | At LWM | Sandy and rock outcrops. Improvement scheme. |
| | f ★★ | **Yellowcraig (Broad Sands Bay)** | 1 | 300 | Raw | At LWM | Sandy. |
| **3** | ★★★ | **Gullane Bay** | | | | | Sand and dunes. |
| | f ★★ | Gosford Sands | | | | | Sand with rocky upper shore. |
| | f ★★ | Seton Sands | 1 | 3,700 | Primary | At LWM | Sand and rocks. |
| | ★★★ | Portobello | 1 | 4,500 | Screened | At LWM | Mostly sand. |
| **FIFE** | | | | | | | |
| | f ★★ | **Aberdour Silversands** | 1 | 2,500 | Primary | At LWM | Sandy. |
| | ★★★ | **Pettycur** | | | | | Sandy. |
| | f ★★ | Kinghom | 1 | 2,400 | Primary | 50 below | Sandy. |
| | ★★★ | Kirkcaldy Harbour | | | | | |

135

| Beach No on Map | Rating. The more stars the better. f=failed | Resort | Sewage outlets | Population discharging from outlet | Type of treatment | Discharge point relative to low water mark, unless otherwise stated. Distance given in metres | Remarks |
|---|---|---|---|---|---|---|---|
| | f ★ | Kirkcaldy Linktown | | | | | |
| | f ★★ | Leven Links | 1 | 110,000 | Screens/ maceration | 100 below | Sandy. |
| | f ★★ | Lundin Links | 1 | 1,100 | Primary | 200 below | Sandy to west. |
| | f ★★ | Lower Largo | 1 | 1,100 | Primary | At LWM | Rocky with some sand. |
| | ★★★ | Shell Bay | 1 | 100 | Primary | At LWM | Sandy. |
| | f ★★ | Elie/Earlsferry | 2 | 1,000 | Raw | At LWM | Muddy sand. |
| | f ★★ | Pittenweem | | | | | Fishing port. |
| | ★★★ | Anstruther | 7 | 4,200 | Raw | Mostly LWM | Muddy sand. |
| | ★★★ | Roome Bay Crail | 1 | 500 | Primary | Above LWM | Sandy. |
| | f ★★ ★★ | St Andrews East **St Andrews West** | 1 | 16,000 | Primary | At LWM | Sandy. |
| | f ★★ | **Carnoustie** | 1 | 10,000 | Raw | Above LWM | Sandy. |
| | f ★★ | **Arbroath** | 3 | 9,000 12,000 9,000 | Raw Screened Primary | At LWM 900 below At LWM | Red sand. |
| 4 | ★★★★/ ★★★ | Tentsmuir Point | | | | | Sand and dunes. |
| | f ★★ | Lunan Bay | | | | | Sandy. Safe bathing except at river mouth. |
| 5 | ★★★ | **Montrose** | 2 | 8,000 6,000 | Maceration Raw | At LWM At LWM | Sandy. Bathing safe except near river mouth. |

### GRAMPIAN

| | | | | | | | |
|---|---|---|---|---|---|---|---|
| | f ★★ | St Cyrus | 1 | 820 | Raw | At LWM | Sand/Saltmarsh. |
| 6 | ★★★ | **Stonehaven** | 2 | 6,500 | Macerated/ primary | 9 below LWM 1 above LWM | Long sea outfall. |
| 7 | | Muchalls | | | | | Pebbles/rock. Bathing unsafe. |

**136**

| Beach No on Map | Rating. The more stars the better. f=failed | Resort | Sewage outlets | Population discharging from outlet | Type of treatment | Discharge point relative to low water mark, unless otherwise stated. Distance given in metres | Remarks |
|---|---|---|---|---|---|---|---|
| | ★★★ | **Aberdeen Ballroom** | 2 | 269,450 | Screened/ Maceration | 2,500 below LWM | Sand. New long sea outfall under construction. |
| | ★★★ | Aberdeen Footdee | | | | | |
| | ★★★ | Balmedie | | | | | 10 miles of sand and dunes. |
| | ★★★ | Collieston | | | | | Old fishing port. |
| | f ★★ | Cruden Bay | 1 | 2,220 | Maceration | At LWM | Sand and dunes. |
| | ★★★ | Lido Peterhead | 1 | 20,450 | Screened | At LWM | Sand. Storm over flow only. |
| 8 | | Strathbeg Bay | | | | | Sand and dunes. |
| | f ★★ | St Combs | | | | | Small fishing port. |
| | ★★★ | **Fraserburgh** | 12 | 15,690 | Raw | Variable | Sand and dunes. Improvement scheme under way. |
| | ★★ | Rosehearty | | | | | Old fishing port. Golf course. |
| | f ★★ | Banff Links | 1 | 4,420 | Raw | Variable | Sand. Improvement scheme under way. |
| 9 | ★★ | Sandend Bay | 1 | 280 | Settlement | | Sandy. |
| 10 | ★★★ | **Cullen** | 2 | 1,500 | Raw | At LWM | Sandy. |
| | | Findochty | 4 | 1,050 | 2 raw 2 maceration | Above LWM 1 at LWM, 1 below LWM | Sand. 2 raw outfalls cease 1991. |
| | | Strathlene, Buckie | 12 | 15,000 | Raw | Variable | Sand. |
| | ★★★ | **Lossiemouth East** | | | | | |
| | ★★★ | **Lossiemouth Silversands** | 3 | 42,700 | Raw | 1 long/ 2 short | Sandy. |
| | | Hopeman | 1 | 1,663 | Raw | LWM | Water sports. |
| 11 | | Burghead | 1 | | Raw | Long east of harbour | Sandy. Bathing not recommended. |

## HIGHLAND

| Beach No on Map | Rating. The more stars the better. f=failed | Resort | Sewage outlets | Population discharging from outlet | Type of treatment | Discharge point relative to low water mark, unless otherwise stated. Distance given in metres | Remarks |
|---|---|---|---|---|---|---|---|
| | | Nairn | 3 | | 2 raw 1 primary | | Sandy. Improvement scheme. |
| | | Cromarty | | | Raw | | Untreated sewage discharges to beach. |
| 12 | | Dornoch | | | | | Sandy. |
| | | Sinclairs Bay Wick | 3 | 700 | 2 raw 1 primary | 2 above LWM 1 tank | Sandy. |
| 13 | | Duncansby Head | | | | | Small, sandy. |
| | | Dunnet Bay/ Murkle Bay | 2 | 200 1,000 | Maceration Primary | Above LWM Below LWM | Sand and dunes. |
| | | Thurso | 1 | 9,000 | Maceration | 450 below | Sandy. |
| 14 | | Sandside Bay | | | | | Dunes, rocky outcrops. |
| 15 | | Coldbackie | | | | | Sand/dunes. |
| 16 | | Sango Bay/ Balnakeil Bay | 1 | 200 | Primary | LWM | Sand/dunes. |
| 17 | | Sandwood Bay | | | | | Sand/dunes. |
| 18 | | Scourie | 2 | 300 | Primary | LWM | Sand. |
| 19 | | Clashnessie Bay | | | | | Sand. |
| 20 | | Clachtoll | | | | | Sand. |
| 21 | | Achmelvich | | | | | Sand. |
| 22 | | Achnahaird | | | | | Sand. |
| 23 | | Achiltibuie | | | | | Shingle. |
| 24 | | Gruinard Bay | | | | | Sand. |
| 25 | | Gairloch | 3 | | Primary | | Sandy. Safe bathing. |
| 26 | | Applecross | | | | | Sand. |
| 27 | | Coral Beaches | | | | | Sand/shells. |
| 28 | | Morar | | | | | Sand. |
| 29 | | Camusdarrach | | | | | Sand/dunes. |
| 30 | | Sanna Bay | | | | | Sand. |

| Beach No on Map | Rating. The more stars the better. **f**=failed | Resort | Sewage outlets | Population discharging from outlet | Type of treatment | Discharge point relative to low water mark, unless otherwise stated. Distance given in metres | Remarks |
|---|---|---|---|---|---|---|---|
| 31 | | Calgary Bay | | | | | Sand/dunes. |
| 32 | | Erraid | | | | | Sand/dunes. |

**STRATHCLYDE**

| Beach No on Map | Rating | Resort | Sewage outlets | Population discharging from outlet | Type of treatment | Discharge point relative to low water mark | Remarks |
|---|---|---|---|---|---|---|---|
| | | Kilchattan Bay | 1 | 170 | Raw | At LWM | |
| | | Kames Bay | se-ver-al | 550 | Raw | | Sand and pebbles. |
| | | Dunoon (West Bay) | 1 | un-known | Raw | Below LWM | Sand and pebbles. |
| | | Ganavan | 1 | 100 | Septic tank | Below LWM | Sand and rocky outcrops. |
| 33 | | Macrihanish | 1 | 200 | Raw | To LWM | Sandy. |
| | | Carradale | 2 | 480 | Raw | To LWM | |
| | | Helensburgh | 1 | 13,200 | Maceration | | Sand and pebbles. |
| | | Portkil/ Meiklecross | 2 | <100 | Raw | Above LWM | Sand and rocks. |
| | | | | <100 | Raw | Below LWM | |
| | | Gourock (West Bay) | 4 | 2,600 | Raw | Below LWM | Shingle and rocks. |
| | | Lunderston Bay | 3 | un-known | Other | Above LWM | Shingle and sand. |
| | | Wemyss Bay | 3 | 100 | Other | Above LWM | |
| | | | | 100 | Other | Above LWM | Shingle and sand. |
| | | | | 11,000 | Maceration | Below LWM | |
| | | Largs (Monument) | 1 | 12,000 | Other | Below LWM | Sand and rocks. |
| | | Fairlie | 2 | 700 | Raw | Below LWM | Sand and rocks. |
| | | | | 800 | Raw | At LWM | |
| | | Millport | 1 | 2,700 | Primary | At LWM | Sand and rocks. |
| | | Seamill | 3 | 4,500 | Raw | All at LWM | Sand and rocks. |
| | | Boydston | 1 | 4,000 | Maceration | At LWM | Sand and rocks. |
| f ★★ | | **Saltcoats** | 2 | 13,500 | Raw | Both below LWM | Sandy. Improvement scheme planned. |
| | | Stevenston | 1 | 41,000 | Screens | Below LWM | Sandy. |

| Beach No on Map | Rating. The more stars the better. f=failed | Resort | Sewage outlets | Population discharging from outlet | Type of treatment | Discharge point relative to low water mark, unless otherwise stated. Distance given in metres | Remarks |
|---|---|---|---|---|---|---|---|
| | f * | **Irvine (Beach Park)** | 3 | 25,000 | Raw | 2 below LWM 1 at LWM | Sandy. Improvement scheme for completion 1991. |
| | | Gailes | 1 | 75,000 | Screens | 1.5km beyond LWM | Sandy. |
| 34 | | Brodick Bay | 2 | 700 | Raw<br>Raw | 1 beyond LWM<br>1 above LWM | Rocks and sand. |
| | | Lamlash Bay | 4 | 950 | Raw | All at LWM | Rocks and sand. |
| | | Whiting Bay | 2 | 800 | Raw | Below LWM | Sand and shingle. |
| 35 | | Blackwaterfoot | | | | | Sand and shingle |
| | | Troon (North) | 1 | 6,300 | Raw | At LWM | Sandy. |
| 36 | *** | **Troon (South)** | | | | | Sandy. |
| | f ** | **Prestwick** | | | | | Sandy. |
| | f ** | **Ayr** | 1 | 16,200 | Screens | 140 below LWM | Sandy. |
| | | Doonfoot | 1 | 8,000 | Maceration | 220 below LWM | Sand/rocks. |
| | | Butlins (Heads of Ayr) | 1 | 8,000 | Secondary | Below LWM | Sandy. |
| | | Maidens | 1 | 600 | Primary | At LWM | Sandy and rocks. |
| | f ** | Turnberry | 1 | | Primary | Beyond LWM | Sand and rocks. |
| | f ** | **Girvan** | 3 | 4,000<br>500<br>2,500 | Screens/maceration<br>Tidal tank<br>Tidal tank | 10 below<br>At LWM<br>At LWM | Improvement scheme in preparation.<br>Sandy. |

### DUMFRIES AND GALLOWAY

| Beach No on Map | Rating | Resort | Sewage outlets | Population discharging from outlet | Type of treatment | Discharge point | Remarks |
|---|---|---|---|---|---|---|---|
| | | Southerness | 1 | 3,500 | Primary | 500 above | Sand/rock. |
| | f ** | **Sandyhills** | 1 | 200 | Secondary | Tidal watercourse | Sandy. |
| | | Brighouse Bay | 1 | 400 | Secondary | 30 below | Sandy. |
| | | Ardwell Bay | 1 | 75 | Primary | 75 below HWM | Sand/shingle. |
| | | Portlogan Bay | 1 | 75 | Primary | 200 below HWM | Sandy. |

## 1 Pease Sands, Cockburns Path, Berwickshire   OS Ref: NT7971

The deep wooded valley of Pease Burn opens out on to the sandy cove of
Pease Bay, which gained a Good Beach Guide four-star grading in 1990.
Framed by red cliffs, a shrub- and grass-covered bank fringes the landward
side of the sands beyond which is a large caravan and mobile home park.
¾ mile (1.2km) of good sandy beach is very much dominated by the
caravan site that rings the bay.

*Water quality* Beach monitored by the River Purification Board and
found to meet the EC standard for clean bathing water in 1990. One outfall
serving 1,000 people discharges secondary treated sewage.

*Bathing safety* Safe bathing.

*Access* A steep road from the A1107, just south of its junction with A1.

*Parking* Car park with 100+ spaces directly off beach.

*Toilets* At car park.

*Food* Small shop adjacent to beach.

*Seaside activities* Swimming and fishing.

*Wildlife and walks* Good walks are available in Pease Dean. A cliff path
can be followed north of the beach passing the tiny village and harbour of
Cove and leading to the Dunglass Gorge.

## 2 Thorntonloch, Lothian   OS Ref: NT752744

Shallow dunes back on to this beautiful sandy beach which is about ¼ mile
(400m) long. To the south there are beautiful views of the Berwickshire
cliffs, while to the north is the Torness nuclear power station. There is a
caravan site near the beach. The water at this beach gained a Good Beach
Guide four-star grading in 1990.

*Water quality* Not a designated EC bathing water, but the water quality
was monitored by the River Purification Board in 1990 and found to meet
the EC standard for clean bathing water.

*Bathing safety* There is a fairly strong undertow and swimmers should
use extreme caution.

*Access* The beach is a short walk from the car park.

*Parking* Car park for approximately 40 cars.

*Toilets* At the caravan site.

*Food* There is a small shop at the caravan site.

*Seaside activities* Swimming, fishing, windsurfing.

*Wet weather alternatives* None.

*Wildlife and walks* This is a good birdwatching area.

## 3 Gullane, East Lothian   OS Ref: NT4882

This is an absolutely beautiful and completely unspoilt 1½ mile (2.5km) sweeping sandy bay. The extensive flat sands exposed at low tide are backed by Gullane Bents, a series of 15 foot (5m) high dune ridges behind which scrubland slopes up 68 feet (20m) to flat grassland. Here there is parking and a picnic area, overlooked by the houses of Gullane village. The curve of sand is bounded at either end by rocky outcrops of black pillow lava. To the east there is a series of tiny sandy bays only accessible by foot along the coast path. Muirfield golf course overlooks this lovely bay and the view across the beach is frequently seen as a backdrop to televised tournaments.

**Water quality** Beach monitored by the River Purification Board and found to meet the EC standard for clean bathing water in 1990. No sewage is discharged in the vicinity of the beach.

**Litter** All litter is cleared daily in summer.

**Bathing safety** Bathing is safe from this beach.

**Access** The beach is signposted from Gullane village on the A198, there is a 110 yard (100m) walk down through the dunes to the beach.

**Parking** Car park with 500 places on grassland behind Gullane Bents.

**Toilets** Block at centre of beach signposted 110 yards (100m) from the beach.

**Food** Refreshment stand. Also in Gullane village.

**Seaside activities** Swimming and windsurfing. Riding track around the bay and three golf courses. Children's play area off path through the dunes.

**Wet weather alternatives** Golf museum adjacent to the shop owned by golf professional J. Hume. Luffness Castle and Myreton motor museum near Aberlady.

**Wildlife and walks** The beach has a large Lug Worm population as evidenced by the casts left on the sand. Rock outcrops at each end of the beach contain pools rich in marine life including mussels, crabs, anemones and numerous snails. The rocks at the west end of the beach are covered in barnacles but very little seaweed. Inland the dunes are stabilised by marram grass and the dune slacks (areas between the sand ridges) have a rich and diverse vegetation.

## 4 Tentsmuir Point, Tayport, Fife   OS Ref: NO5024

A large area of the extensive sand dunes north of the Eden Estuary dunes has been stabilised by the conifers planted in the 1920s by the Forestry Commission. The coastline can still be reached along roads cut through the forest giving access to parking and picnic areas beyond the forest. A wild and remote spot with a wide flat sandy beach backed by high sand dunes which are continually moving seawards.

**Water quality** No sewage is discharged in the vicinity of this beach.

**Bathing safety** Beware of offshore currents.

**Access** A turning off the road north-east of Leuchars leads to the forest. There are paths to the beach from the car park.

**Parking** Forestry Commission car park behind dunes.

**Toilets** At the car park.

**Food** None.

**Seaside activities** Swimming.

**Wildlife and walks** A large area of the shore, including dunes and developing scrub woodland, is a National Nature Reserve. There is a ranger service based at the car park where a nature trail commences. Wildlife is abundant. The area is a feeding ground for numerous waders and wildfowl and there is a rich vegetation. This is an excellent spot for walking with views across the offshore sand banks and away north across to the Tayside coast.

## 5 Montrose Links, Montrose, Tayside   OS Ref: NO7358

From the mouth of the South Esk 4 miles (6.5km) of magnificent beach stretch north to the mouth of the North Esk. At low tide there are 220 yards (200m) of firm clean sands backed by a 30 foot (9m) high dune ridge. Access is from the southern end of the beach where the delightful little town of Montrose is separated from the beach by two links golf courses. At the entrance a stretch of seawall edges the beach, protecting the car park and facilities above. A beach with so much space there should never be an overcrowding problem and the further north you walk along it the quieter it should be.

**Water quality** Beach monitored by the River Purification Board and found to meet the EC standard for clean bathing water in 1990. An outfall serving 8,000 people discharges macerated sewage at low water mark, another serving 6,000 people discharges untreated sewage at low water mark.

**Litter** The beach is cleaned regularly by the local authority.

**Bathing safety** Safe bathing except near the river mouths at each end of the beach. Beach wardens patrol a clearly designated area of the beach.

**Access** The beach is signposted from the A92. A road through the golf course leads to car parks at the south end of the beach. Steps lead down on to the sands.

**Parking** Two car parks adjacent to the beach with approximately 350 spaces.

**Toilets** At the car park.

**Food** Café at the car park.

**Seaside activities** Swimming, windsurfing and fishing. Children's amusement play area. Small amusement arcade.

**Wet weather alternatives** Museum, amusement arcade and indoor swimming pool.

**Wildlife and walks** The tidal basin to the west is a nature reserve. Low tide reveals extensive mud flats which are an important feeding ground for wintering birds.

## 6 Stonehaven, Grampian   OS Ref: NO8786

At a break in the rugged sandstone cliffs the waters of Cowie and Carron flow to the sea at Stonehaven. Nestling between the Downie and Garron headlands is Stonehaven itself, which retains the atmosphere of a traditional fishing village, its quaysides busy with boats. The fishing has declined but the twin basin harbour is used by pleasure craft in summer. A ⅔ mile (1km) sand and pebble beach curves away north of the harbour below the rolling farmland which rises beyond the town. The beach is not popular for swimming but is often busy with people taking advantage of the promenade facilities. Steep 200 foot (60m) cliffs rise on either side of the bay and offer excellent walking with splendid views along the cliffs and over Stonehaven bay.

**Water quality** Beach monitored by the River Purification Board and found to meet the EC standard for clean bathing water in 1990. Two outfalls serving 6,500 people discharge macerated and primary treated sewage 10 yards (9m) below and 1 yard (1m) above low water mark.

**Bathing safety** Some currents can make swimming dangerous. Inshore rescue boat and lifeboat station.

**Access** From promenade.

**Parking** Ample on sea-front and adjacent to the leisure centre.

**Toilets** On sea-front.

**Food** Café.

**Seaside activities** Swimming and windsurfing. Sailing, diving and fishing trips from the adjacent harbour. Cliff top golf course. Open air heated swimming pool and leisure centre.

**Wet weather alternatives** Dunnottar castle, Tolbooth museum of local history, indoor pool and leisure centre, amusement arcades.

**Wildlife and walks** The promenade leads north to the fishing village of Cowie. North from Cowie a grass cliff path beside the golf course provides glorious sea views across Stonehaven Bay. 2 miles (3km) along the cliff top path there is a steep valley which leads down to two secluded pebbly coves at Skatie Shore. South from Stonehaven, a mile (1.6km) walk along the cliffs leads to the War Memorial from which there are panoramic views of the coast and inland. Continuing south for 2 miles (3km), the path leads to Dunnottar

Castle. This impressive castle stands on an isolated sandstone cliff 170 feet (50m) above the sea. The connection between the castle rock and mainland was cut to allow easier defence. A further 4 miles (6.5km) south lies the Fowlsheugh Bird Reserve, one of the largest bird colonies in the UK, with 2 miles (3km) of cliff providing a home to thousands of seabirds. Parking at Crawton village provides easy access to the reserve.

## 7 Muchalls, Nr Stonehaven, Grampian   OS Ref: NO9292

This is a spectacular stretch of coastline whose rock formations include stacks, arches, and caves with an underground waterfall. There are several rock and pebble coves below the steep cliffs but take care as some are cut off at high tide with no escape routes. Swimming is out of the question due to dangerous rocks off shore but the cliff top scenery and the interesting coves with their numerous rockpools make the area worth a visit.

*Water quality* No outfalls discharge in the vicinity of the beach. Crude sewage discharges into a small stream entering the nearby beach.

*Bathing safety* There are unsafe rocks off shore.

*Access* From Muchalls village, just off the A92, there are two access routes – a very steep path and a road under the railway lead to the shore.

*Parking* In village.

*Toilets* None.

*Food* Pub and hotel in village.

*Seaside activities* Fishing.

*Wet weather alternatives* Muchalls Castle (check opening times as only open on occasional days in summer).

*Wildlife and walks* A cliff top path gives fine views of the cliff formations to the north and the numerous nesting seabirds that frequent the rocky ledges. Rock pools on the shore contain a wealth of interest for the beach walker but remember to keep an eye on the tide.

## 8 Strathbeg Bay, Grampian   OS Ref: NK0663

This little-frequented beach has 3¾ miles (6km) of sand and substantial dunes stretching from the rocky Cairnbulg Point south, past the fishing villages of Inverallochy and St Combs to Rattray Head. The beach is not particularly scenic but if you seek solitude on a remote and peaceful beach the wind-swept sands of Rattray should meet your requirements. The lighthouse off the headland indicates the presence of a reef which causes swift currents and makes swimming dangerous. South of Rattray Head a further 7 miles (11km) of deserted sandy beach stretches to Peterhead, but the shore is dominated by the St Fergus gas terminal.

*Water quality* No sewage is discharged in the vicinity of this beach.

**Litter** Marine litter is a frequent problem along these shores.

**Bathing safety** Care is required as the currents off Rattray Head are dangerous.

**Access** There is a path through the dunes at St Combs, off the B9033 south-east of Fraserburgh, and another at Rattray Head, reached via a road off the A952 south of Crimond.

**Parking** There is a car park at St Combs and very limited parking at Rattray head.

**Toilets** None.

**Food** None.

**Seaside activities** Swimming, sailing, diving and fishing.

**Wildlife and walks** The Loch of Strathbeg RSPB reserve, with its visitor centre and observation hides, lies just behind the dunes. It is the largest dune slack pool in Britain and is an important site for wintering wildfowl. Admission is by permit only, available from the warden, Jim Dunbar (Lonmay 2522).

## 9 Sandend, Grampian   OS Ref: NJ5566

From Fraserburgh to Inverness is a stretch of coast known as the Banffshire Riviera. It is characterised by towering cliffs, small sheltered sandy bays and fishing villages. Clear waters wash this most attractive sandy beach. ⅔ mile (1km) of dunes fringe the beach landwards and the bay is framed by high cliffs.

**Water quality** No sewage is discharged in the vicinity of the beach.

**Bathing safety** Heavy surf on occasions.

**Access** Sandend is signposted off the A98; it is a short walk from the car park to the beach.

**Parking** Car park with 100 spaces.

**Toilets** Public conveniences in village.

**Food** Small shop and restaurant.

**Seaside activities** Swimming, surfing, windsurfing, sailing, diving and fishing.

**Wildlife and walks** East of the bay the coast path climbs over the cliffs on to the headland which offers excellent sea and coastal views. The path continues to Portsoy, a charming fishing village with a small harbour which has won awards for its architectural restoration. West of Sandend the cliff path can be followed to the ruins of Findlater Castle with its impressive position 165 feet (50m) above the waves. Below the ruins is the lovely secluded Sunnyside beach, its sweep of golden sand nestling below the steep cliffs.

## 10 Cullen Sands, Cullen, Grampian  OS Ref: NJ5167

The dipping Cullen quartzites form a spectacular rocky coastline and create the extremely scenic Cullen Bay. From the curving quays of the harbour, sheltering below the cliffs at the eastern end of the bay, an arc of rock-studded sand sweeps west past the isolated stacks known as the Three Kings. Beyond, the Boar's Craig rises and the sands give way to rocks below the cliffs of Portknockie headland. Here there are caves, known as the Preacher's and the Whale's Mouth, to explore and numerous rockpools to investigate. Relax on the sands (but watch the tide), or stretch your legs to enjoy the wonderful scenery around the bay. The railway once passed through Cullen but all that remains is a series of graceful viaducts. They separate the narrow streets of Seatown that cluster around the harbour from the upper town with its open square and wider streets.

**Water quality** Beach monitored by the River Purification Board and found to meet the EC standard for clean bathing water in 1990. Two outfalls serving 1,500 people discharge raw sewage at low water mark.

**Bathing safety** There are strong cross tides so care is required when bathing.

**Access** From Seatown and from the road to the golf course.

**Parking** Car park close to harbour. Large car park beside beach next to golf course.

**Toilets** Public toilets at the harbour are open all year.

**Food** Tea room at beach. Two hotels in Seatown. Cafés and hotels in upper town.

**Seaside activities** Swimming, putting, bowls, tennis and a golf course. Sea-angling and boat trips from the harbour.

**Wet weather alternatives** Maritime Museum and swimming pool at Buckie, about 5 miles (9km) away.

**Wildlife and walks** From the harbour a path leads east along the shore to the excellent sandy cove of Sunnyside Bay. The path climbs to the cliff top and continues to Findlater Castle, a 15th-century ruined castle sitting on a rocky promontory 165 feet (50m) above the sea. A return journey can be made along the cliff top, giving excellent views along the coast and across to Sutherland and Caithness. Alternatively you may head east to Sandend Bay, another of the lovely coves along this coastline complete with its own small harbour. West from Cullen there is a well-marked path alongside the golf course. The path leads up from the rocky shore to Portknockie on the cliff top. There are superb views of this magnificent rocky coast; just off shore lies the Bow Fiddle rock, where erosion of the dipping rock strata has produced an arch resembling the tip of a violinist's bow. Further west from Portknockie the cliff path leads to Findochty with its sheltered sandy cove and harbour; there are superb views of the Moray Firth and Black Isle.

147

## 11 Burghead Bay, Burghead, Grampian   OS Ref: NJ1169

The solid fishing cottages that make up Burghead stand on a low rocky promontory overlooking the 6 mile (10km) curve of Burghead Bay. At the western end of these long flat sands is Findhorn, situated at the mouth of the large, tidal Findhorn Bay. The quiet but somewhat windswept beach of fine sand and pebbles is rimmed by dunes, on which there is a Forestry Commission conifer plantation. A road has been made through the mature pines at Roseisle and there are parking and picnic facilities. The beach can be reached along paths through the trees. Wartime concrete defences once stood on grassland well back from the beach but the retreating sand means that they now stand on the tidal sands.

**Water quality** No significant sewage discharges in the vicinity of the beach.

**Bathing safety** There are strong currents at the western end where the River Findhorn flows out of Findhorn Bay. Bathing is not recommended in the bay but is safe from the beach at Findhorn, Roseisle and Burghead.

**Access** At either end of the bay at Findhorn or Burghead and also by paths from Roseisle Forest.

**Parking** At Findhorn dunes and picnic site, Roseisle Forest picnic site and at Burghead.

**Toilets** At Findhorn and Roseisle picnic sites (including facilities for the disabled). Public toilets at the harbour in Burghead.

**Food** Pubs, hotels and fish and chips available in Findhorn and Burghead. Wholefood café at Findhorn Bay Caravan Park.

**Seaside activities** Swimming, diving, fishing, windsurfing and water-skiing. The bay is a sailing centre with racing throughout the summer. Rowing, sailing and motor boats are available for hire at Findhorn. Sea-angling trips from Burghead harbour.

**Wet weather alternatives** Burghead Well. Findhorn Foundation (a spiritual community based east of Findhorn village which runs a craft shop and takes conducted tours during the summer). Swimming pool at Forres.

**Wildlife and walks** There is a walk from Burghead to Findhorn along the shore, where rock and sand pools contain a variety of marine life. 2 miles (3km) south-west of Burghead is the Forestry Commission Roseisle Forest. Pathways from the beach lead to glades in the Corsican and Scots pines planted in the 1930s. Continuing along the shore the walk leads on to the Findhorn peninsula where the extensive tidal bay provides excellent birdwatching.

## 12 Dornoch, Highland   OS Ref: NH7989

The excellent Royal Dornoch links golf course attracts many visiting players but the lovely sandy beach remains quiet and uncommercialised. The approach to the beach from Dornoch is unassuming; the low-lying lands do not permit any view of the beach until you cross the dunes. To the south of the beach is the entrance to the Dornoch Firth which stretches almost 20 miles (32km) inland. The wide sands stretch 3 miles (5km) north narrowing towards Loch Fleet, a small sea-loch. There is access to the beach from the village of Dornoch, and at the northern end at Embo. Further north in Sutherland the main A9 hugs the shore which is only a ribbon of sand.

**Water quality** Sewage is treated by septic tank and discharged at Blackburn away from the beach.

**Bathing safety** There are currents at the northern and southern ends of the beach; safe bathing in the main bay at Dornoch.

**Access** From the Square in Dornoch a road leads to the shore and golf courses, another takes you to Embo; there is a short walk across dunes to the sand.

**Parking** Dornoch: Two car parks, one overlooking the sea with spaces for 20 cars, the other close by has a further 20 spaces. Embo: car park with 25 spaces.

**Toilets** New toilet block at caravan site backing beach.

**Food** None (At Embo: Grannie's Heilan Hame Café and fish and chip shop – seasonal).

**Seaside activities** Swimming. Royal Dornoch Golf Course, local pipe band parade during the summer and Highland Games during August.

**Wet weather alternatives** Dornoch Cathedral. Local social club is open for supervised games during the season.

**Wildlife and walks** Loch Fleet, a sea-loch at the northern end of the beach, is the last of the Firth indents into this coastline going north. The loch and the alderwoods behind the mound embankment are nature reserves which contain a wide variety of wildlife. The Scottish Wildlife Trust Reserve Warden runs a series of guided walks during the summer. These include an exploration of the woodland and estuary or the sand dunes and sea shore. Otherwise, access to the reserves is restricted. In the nearby Skelbo Wood, the Forestry Commission has laid out several forest trails; the walks start from the Commission's car park off the B1698.

## 13 Duncansby Head, John o'Groats, Highland   OS Ref: ND4173

Travellers taking the A9 north beyond Inverness are normally heading for John o'Groats as the most northerly point. Not to be missed is Duncansby Head, without a doubt one of the finest pieces of coastline in Britain. The road from John o'Groats takes you to the Duncansby lighthouse. From the small car park the view to the islands is hard to beat. On a clear day the panorama laid out before you can be breathtaking. Just off shore beyond the white foaming tidal races are the Pentland Skerries and Stroma, on which you can see many abandoned dwellings. Beyond, Swona, South Ronaldsay, Hoy and the mainland of Orkney complete the picture. Tucked below the headland, just off the lighthouse approach road, is a tiny beach. A mere 110 yards (100m) in length, the narrow strip of sand is shadowed by the red sandstone of the headland. A delightful spot, this may not be the beach to seek out for a day by the sea, but after enjoying a stroll on the headland, relax a while and watch the seals that bob around off shore. This is one of many little beaches along the north coast between the Duncansby and Dunnet Headlands, although most are difficult to get to and are not as attractive, lacking the backdrop of sheer red cliffs.

**Water quality** No sewage is discharged in the vicinity of this beach.

**Bathing safety** The beach shelves steeply and swimming is dangerous.

**Access** Duncansby Head is signposted from the A9 south of John o'Groats. A short walk from the parking area down the hill across turf leads on to the sands.

**Parking** Car park at Duncansby Lighthouse with approximately 25 spaces.

**Toilets** None.

**Food** None.

**Wildlife and walks** A short walk over the headland passes a narrow inlet or geo whose cliff walls rise nearly 200 feet (60m) above the waves. A short distance further and you are rewarded with the marvellous view of Duncansby Stacks, their steeple-like outlines pointing skywards. These are also known as Muckle Stack. Boat trips around this stretch of coast are available from John o'Groats.

## 14 Sandside Bay, Reay, Highland   OS Ref: NC9774

This area has some of the best rocky exposed coastline in Britain. Low cliffs, rocky outcrops and dunes bound this long flat sandy beach. At the western end of the bay is the tiny harbour of Fresgoe: a tranquil old-world air prevails around the little-used harbour. A sharp contrast to the view along the coast east to the Dounreay Fast Reactor. A remote and quiet beach.

**Water quality** No sewage is discharged in the vicinity of the beach.

**Bathing safety** Safe bathing.

**Access** The road to Fresgoe runs alongside the bay, and it is a short walk from the road down a track between dunes to the beach.

**Parking** Parking in area along the side road.

**Toilets** Toilet block on road close to the car parking area.

**Food** None. The closest shop is in Reay village 2 miles (3.5km) away.

**Seaside activities** Swimming.

**Wet weather alternatives** Dounreay Exhibition Centre.

**Wildlife and walks** There is a short cliff walk from the beach.

## 15 Coldbackie, Tongue, Highland   OS Ref: NC6160

The half-moon of Coldbackie Sands faces Tongue Bay at the mouth of the
Kyle of Tongue, one of the three deep indents into the north coast. The
undulating turf-covered moorland which dominates this corner of Scotland
slopes down to the grass-covered dunes which border the sands. Below
Meall Mor, low grass-covered cliffs flank the beach.

*Water quality* No sewage is discharged in the vicinity of this beach.

*Bathing safety* Safe bathing.

*Access* From the A836 north of Tongue, banks of dunes descend to the
beach. There is no proper footpath but it is an easy walk down to the sand.

*Parking* There is limited car parking in a layby off the main road above the
beach.

*Toilets* None.

*Food* None.

*Seaside activities* Swimming.

*Wildlife and walks* The 1000 feet (300m) peaks of Cnoc an Fhreiceadan
and Ben Tongue rise behind the beach. From the road a footpath inland
skirts the sides of the hills, passing a tiny loch to reach Tongue and the shores
of the Kyle.

## 16 Balnakiel Bay, Durness, Highland   OS Ref: NC3869

There are in fact three beaches at Durness, all worthy of note. All have clean
white sands, are unspoilt and are quiet, even at the height of the summer. To
the east of Faraid Head Peninsula, below the steep limestone cliffs on which
Durness stands, are the twin beaches of Sango Bay and Sangobeg. The best
beach, however, is Balnakiel Bay, a long curve of white sand and dunes on
the western side of the peninsula. There is easy access at the southern end of
the beach close to the ruined Balnakiel Church. The extensive wind-
sculptured dunes stretch north along the low rugged headland. The bare and
treeless landscape is dominated by wild windswept moorland in sharp
contrast to the coastline made up of warm red sandstone cliffs, folded and
faulted limestone, collapsed caverns, geos, rocky shores and sandy bays.

*Water quality* No sewage is discharged in the vicinity of the beach.

*Bathing safety* Safe bathing although in this part of the country some
might find it rather cold.

*Access* A road off the A838 from Durness village leads to a car park behind
the beach, and from here an easy path leads to the sand.

*Parking* Car park with 30 spaces.

*Toilets* Portaloo at car park.

**Food** Sango Sands Oasis Restaurant in Sango.

**Seaside activities** Swimming.

**Wet weather alternatives** Half a mile (800m) inland is a craft village in the building of a disused early warning station. The workshops are open to the public during the summer months.

**Wildlife and walks** There are walks on the cliffs surrounding the bay, and much evidence of 1000 years of human activity, including slight remains of an ancient fortress on the Faraid Headland. Steps lead down from Durness village to the beach at Sango Bay where the high arched entrance to the Smoo Cave can be found. The Allt (river) Smoo flows from the cave. The first of three chambers can be entered. The Highland Regional Ranger Service organises guided walks in the area, and further information can be obtained from the information centre in Durness. The remote north-western tip of Scotland, Cape Wrath, can be reached by a small ferry across the Kyle of Durness followed by a mini-bus service to the Cape. The bus takes you across the wild moorland to the Cape Wrath Lighthouse and there is fantastic cliff scenery along this most isolated stretch of coastline. The most spectacular cliffs are along the northern coast, where, in places, the sheer cliffs fall 800 feet (250m) to the waters below.

## 17 Sandwood Bay, Highland    OS Ref: NC2364

Sandwood Bay must be one of the most remote beaches in Britain, but equally one of the most magnificent. Lying on the west coast of Scotland between Kinlochbervie and Cape Wrath, a 4 mile (7km) walk from Blairmore brings you to this outstanding beach with its huge sand dunes and gently sloping pink sands, studded with rock outcrops. Towering sandstone cliffs extend away on either side of the bay, and to the west is a most impressive rock stack. For those who do not want to venture to such an isolated and exposed beach, there are a series of pocket-handkerchief-sized sandy beaches that surround Blairmore, the starting point for the walk to Sandwood.

**Water quality** No sewage is discharged in the vicinity of this beach.

**Bathing safety** Very dangerous.

**Access** The B801 leads along Loch Inchard to Kinlochbervie, and beyond this a steep and twisting road continues to Sheigra. Sandwood can only be reached on foot, 4 miles (7km) along the track which turns off the road between Blairmore and Sheigra.

**Parking** Limited parking at Blairmore.

**Toilets** None.

**Food** None.

**Wildlife and walks** The walk to Sandwood crosses the peat moorland of Sutherland before making a steep descent to the bay. This area is both wild and beautiful, but anyone thinking of walking here should be fully aware of the dangers of this remote and difficult terrain. Only those completely prepared should undertake the trip.

## 18 Scourie, Highland   OS Ref: NC1544

Unlike most of the crofting villages along the west coast, Scourie has some facilities to cater for the visitor. It boasts two hotels, a shop, a post office and a camp site, thus enabling the tourist to stop a while and enjoy this most picturesque district. Scourie is set at the head of a 1 mile (1.5km) rocky inlet, on the banks of a small river draining from a loch a short distance inland. There is a lovely sheltered beach on the southern flank of the bay. The wide, gently sloping sands are backed by a narrow storm beach, where small boulders and pebbles edge the sand. The irregular hummocks of this grey-green rocky landscape come down to the water's edge in the outer bay. This exposed rocky coast is coloured by bands of lichens and encrusted with barnacles and seaweed below high water mark where there are many rock-pools to explore. This is a deservedly popular spot.

*Water quality* Two outfalls, each serving 100-200 people, discharge primary treated sewage at low water mark.

*Bathing safety* Safe bathing.

*Access* There are gently sloping grass slopes down to the sand.

*Parking* Parking space available adjacent to the beach.

*Toilets* In village.

*Food* Hotel and shop in village.

*Seaside activities* Swimming.

*Wildlife and walks* A stroll around the loch, village and its quayside can be a most pleasant way to spend an afternoon. Alternatively follow the path north of the bay to Tarbet. Handa Island, lying just across the Sound of Handa, is an RSPB reserve. The numerous ledges on its vertical cliffs provide nesting sites for thousands of seabirds including guillemots, kittiwakes and fulmars. The island can be visited by boat from Tarbet daily, except Sunday, from April to August.

## 19 Clashnessie Bay, Lochinver, Highland   OS Ref: NC0631

Steep rocky cliffs, wide bays dotted with tiny islands, clean clear waters, beautiful sunsets, seabirds and seals: the perfect ingredients to make a good beach. Clashnessie is an attractive and safe beach. The 660 yards (600m) of gently sloping pink sands are framed by red sandstone cliffs. There are superb views north towards Oldany Island and east along the rugged cliffs of the Stoer Peninsula.

*Water quality* No sewage is discharged in the vicinity of the beach.

**Bathing safety** Safe bathing.

**Access** A side road from the B869 at Clashnessie leads down to the shore, and then there is a short walk down to the beach.

**Parking** Car park at beach with 10-15 spaces.

**Toilets** None.

**Food** None.

**Seaside activities** Swimming.

**Wildlife and walks** To the east there is a clifftop walk on to the Stoer Point with views of the fine cliff scenery including the Old Man of Stoer, an isolated sea stack rising 200 feet (60m) above the waves. Further along the coast stands the Stoer lighthouse. A good variety of birds can be seen on the beach and cliffs. There are also a number of walks on the wide flat moors inland.

## 20 Clachtoll, Lochinver, Highland   OS Ref: NC0427

This is one of a series of sandy coves along this stretch of coastline, north of Loch Inver, which is scenically stunning. Clachtoll is a small cove, 275 yards (250m) of beautiful white shell sand backed by machair banks and grey and red cliffs. The quiet beach is washed by clear waters and seals can often be seen close to the shore. There is a camp site behind the beach.

**Water quality** No sewage is discharged in the vicinity of this beach.

**Bathing safety** Safe bathing within the bay.

**Access** There is car parking off the B869 which runs along this stretch of coast. It is a short walk across the dunes to the beach.

**Parking** Car park with 20 spaces.

**Toilets** Toilets and showers at beach car park.

**Food** Take-away meals and snacks at the camp site.

**Seaside activities** Swimming, windsurfing, diving, sailing, canoeing and fishing. Boats can be hired for fishing. Details are available from the local Ranger.

**Wet weather alternatives** Teas and games at Stoer village hall.

**Wildlife and walks** There is a diverse range of plant and animal life around the bay, and an interesting variety of birds and mammals, including seals and whales, can be seen. Many rare plants can also be found. There is a wealth of material for those interested in conservation and the history of the area. Full details are available from the interpretative centre at the beach, and coastal walks can be arranged by the Ranger.

## 21 Achmelvich, Lochinver, Highland   OS Ref: NC0625

This is a small sandy cove at the southern end of Achmelvich Bay which can be reached fairly easily. The white sands of the bay are backed by an area of machair grassland. This sand dune type vegetation is very fragile and easily eroded, so great care must be taken not to cause damage in this area. Steep, grey, rocky cliffs rise on either side of the sands, creating a marvellous setting for the bay. Dogs are permitted on the beach under strict control but they are not allowed on the surrounding land.

**Water quality** No sewage is discharged in the vicinity of this beach.

**Litter** Litter on the beach is collected by local volunteers.

**Bathing safety** Safe bathing.

**Access** A side road off the B869 north of Lochinver leads to Achmelvich. The car park gives direct access to the turf sloping to the sand.

**Parking** Car park with 60 spaces.

**Toilets** Public toilets in car park.

**Food** None.

**Seaside activities** Swimming, surfing, windsurfing, diving, sailing and fishing.

**Wildlife and walks** There is a 1 mile (1.6km) nature trail along the coast to the small sandy bay of Alltan na Bradhan. The walk leads from the machair grassland over the sand hills and then passes through heath and bog vegetation. A leaflet describing the whole trail is available from the Countryside Ranger Centre at the rear of the car park at Achmelvich. This area also has interesting geology. There is a combination of red sandstone and grey Lewisian gneiss (pronounced 'nice') with igneous dyke intrusions – dark rock squeezed in bands up through the surrounding rock.

## 22 Achnahaird, Enard Bay, Highland   OS Ref: NC0214

Flat windswept moorland with outcrops of grey gneiss leads down to the shore of Enard Bay, a magnificent island-dotted prospect. On the western side of the Rudha Mor headland is the narrow inlet of Achnahaird Bay. The bay, in the southern corner of Enard Bay, stretches nearly a mile (1.6km) inland and low tide reveals an expanse of flat white sand. On the western side of the inlet there are extensive dunes which give way to salt marsh at the head of the bay. Irregularly layered sandstone cliffs flank the eastern side of the inlet and a stream meanders across the centre of the sands.

**Water quality** No sewage is discharged in the vicinity of this beach.

**Bathing safety** Bathe with caution as there may be some currents that could cause problems for the swimmer.

**Access** A side road from Achnahaird village leads to parking behind the

155

beach. There is access to the sands on a path down the rocks (can be difficult) or through the camp site behind the dunes.

**Parking** There is limited parking behind the dunes.

**Toilets** None.

**Food** None.

**Seaside activities** Swimming.

**Wildlife and walks** The shores of Enard Bay are part of the Inverpolly National Nature Reserve, a huge area of moorland, including the huge bulk of Suilven. There is a visitors' centre at Knockan some way inland, where there is an interpretative centre, a nature trail and a geology trail. This helps to introduce the visitor to an area that abounds in wildlife including red deer and otters. 100 bird species and 300 types of plant have been recorded within the reserve. Achnahaird Bay combines a wide variety of vegetation types: dunes, salt marsh, rocky and sandy shore. The salt marsh attracts waders and wildfowl. The rocky shore is banded with lichen and there are rock pools among the barnacle-encrusted rocks.

## 23 Achiltibuie, Badentarbat Bay, Highland    OS Ref: NC0309

Smooth heather-clad slopes descend to the crofting village of Achiltibuie which straggles 3 miles (5km) along the shore of Badentarbat Bay. The beach, which curves round the bay, lacks the sand so common on the west coast but to compensate there is a marvellous view across to the Summer Isles. A patchwork of islands and rocky skerries lies just off shore and provides the most wonderful seascape. From the pier the shingle and cobble beach stretches south to the rocky headland of Rubha Dunan.

**Water quality** No sewage is discharged in the vicinity of this beach.

**Bathing safety** Bathe with caution as there may be some currents that could cause problems for the swimmer.

**Access** The road through the village continues along the edge of the bay and the sand can be reached across the grass which slopes below the road.

**Parking** Cars park on the grass between the road and the beach.

**Toilets** None.

**Food** Shops in village.

**Seaside activities** Swimming and fishing.

**Wildlife and walks** The Summer Isles fall within the Ben More Coigach Nature Reserve (Scottish Wildlife Trust – Royal Society for Nature Conservation). 15,011 acres (6,075 hectares) include the peak which gives the reserve its name, and whose purple and red slopes dominate the views inland from Achiltibuie. There is good walking along the Coigach Peninsula west of the bay. The Summer Isles can be viewed at closer range by taking a boat trip from the pier at Achiltibuie.

## 24 Gruinard Bay, Laide, Highland   OS Ref: NG9092

There are several excellent beaches dotted around Gruinard Bay, all of which overlook the lovely Gruinard Island, centrepiece of the bay. The island was used for anthrax experiments during the last war and has been out of bounds ever since. It is now being cleaned up, so hopefully the warning signs that have prohibited landing for so long will soon disappear. The A832 skirts the southern and eastern shores of the bay, giving easy access to the three lovely cove beaches on the eastern shore. Their pink sands are set among sandstone rock outcrops. In contrast, the south-eastern shore at Little Gruinard has the bulging hummocks of Lewisian gneiss as a most attractive backdrop. Gruinard Hill provides the best views of the bay, the island, and of the Summer Isles on the horizon. Wooded slopes above the beach provide a sharp contrast to the grey rocky outcrops. At Laide, the road runs parallel with the beach behind the machair turf, which slopes to the sand of this 1 mile (1.6km) beach. This most picturesque of bays, like most of the west coast beaches, is relatively quiet and unspoilt. A holiday spent walking the coast or exploring the lochans that speckle the surrounding countryside is an ideal way to escape and relax. Facilities for the tourist are limited and there is restricted parking. In many parts of the bay parking along the back-shore causes severe erosional problems for the machair grass. It is important that the grass cover is maintained and parking should be limited accordingly.

*Water quality* No sewage is discharged in the vicinity of this beach.

*Bathing safety* Safe bathing.

*Access* The A832 follows the shore round most of the bay with easy access to the beach.

*Parking* There are two car parks in the south-eastern corner of the bay near Little Gruinard and another at Laide.

*Toilets* In Laide.

*Food* Hotel and shop in Laide.

*Seaside activities* Swimming and fishing.

*Wildlife and walks* There are trips around the bay available during the summer months which allow the visitor to take a closer look at Gruinard Island and enjoy the spectacular panoramas across the bay towards the mountains inland.

## 25 Gairloch, Highland   OS Ref: NG7679

Set among the stunning mountains of Wester Ross, Gairloch, although it is no more than a sizeable fishing village, is one of the few 'holiday resorts' on the west coast. It overlooks a fine sandy beach which curves north from the rocky promontory at Charlestown, round Strath Bay at the head of the Loch, extending west of Gairloch to Big Sand. The bay enjoys the mild climate resulting from the North Atlantic Drift, and gardens nearby are filled with plants more commonly found in more southern locations. The A832 follows the shore at the head of the beautiful Loch Gairloch, where there are rocky outcrops of gneiss. The outer section of the bay is of red sandstone with safe, sandy beaches at Sheildaig and Badachro on the southern shores, and Big Sand on the northern shore. There is a large caravan site behind the extensive beach which is sheltered by Longs Island just off shore.

**Water quality** Three outfalls discharge primary treated sewage into the River Sand. There are complaints of sewage contamination at Redpoint beach.

**Bathing safety** Safe bathing.

**Access** The A832 runs parallel with the shore between Charlestown and Gairloch. There are paths to the beach.

**Parking** Parking at Big Sand, in Gairloch and off the A832 to the south.

**Toilets** In Gairloch.

**Food** In Gairloch.

**Seaside activities** Swimming, windsurfing, sailing and fishing.

**Wet weather alternatives** Gairloch Heritage Museum.

**Wildlife and walks** From Badachro there is a footpath which leads south-west inland. It passes a small loch and leads to the cliffs of Red Point, where there are superb views across the Minch to the Hebrides. For those less able, there is road access and a car park at Red Point. A further mile to the south, there is a beautiful and remote sandy beach backed by dunes. The path continues to the south-east along the shores of Loch Torridon to Diabaig. This walk follows a spectacular length of coast which can only be reached on foot.

## 26 Applecross, Highland   OS Ref: NG7144

The dramatic and tortuous 'Pass of the Cattle' climbs over 2,000 feet (620m) as it twists its way from the A896, at the head of Loch Kishorn, across the wild mountains and moorlands to Applecross. There is a wooded approach to the cluster of white cottages which make up this remote village, on the southern shore of a wide bay. The sweeping sandy beach lies below limestone cliffs from which there are superb views across the Inner Sound to Raasay and Scalpay, with the Cuillins of Skye on the distant horizon. Having crossed desolate moorland, negotiated precipitous roads and revelled in vast panoramic views, one could be at the edge of the world. This lovely beach with its magnificent setting provides an ideal spot to rest and unwind.

**Water quality** No sewage is discharged in the vicinity of this beach.

**Bathing safety** Safe bathing.

**Access** The Pass from Loch Kishorn should not be attempted by the caravanner or the faint-hearted; the alternative route which approaches the village along the coast from Loch Torridon is an easier drive. The village stands on the shore with easy access to the sands.

**Parking** Limited at Applecross.

**Toilets** None.

**Food** Shop in village.

**Seaside activities** Swimming and fishing. Picnic site behind the beach.

**Wildlife and walks** There are good walks along this beautiful stretch of coast with eider duck, mergansers and other seabirds to be seen in the bays.

## 27 The Coral Beaches, Dunvegan, Skye  OS Ref: NG2354

A pleasant, easy, ½ mile (800m) walk across grassland takes you to two small beaches which are beautiful and totally unspoilt. Known locally as the Coral Beaches, they are in fact white sand made up of broken shells. Grass banks slope gently down to the sand. The bays, each about 220 yards (200m) in length, are separated by a low grassy promontory around which there are rocky outcrops. There are lovely views across Loch Dunvegan whose clean, clear waters wash the beach.

**Water quality** There is no sewage discharged in the vicinity of this beach.

**Bathing safety** Safe bathing.

**Access** The road north from Dunvegan becomes a narrow lane beyond Claigan. From the lane ending there is a well-defined path across the grassland to the sand.

**Parking** Limited parking along the lane.

**Toilets** None.

**Food** None.

**Seaside activities** Swimming and snorkelling.

**Wildlife and walks** There is excellent walking to the Coral Beaches and along the beautiful peninsula beyond. Numerous seals can be seen in the waters of the loch. They are often visible close inshore, and a short boat trip from Dunvegan takes you to the rocky islands where they can be seen basking on the shore.

## 28 Morar, Highland  OS Ref: NM6793

This stretch of coastline between Mallaig and Arisaig has to be one of the most memorable in Scotland. When you try to imagine the silver sands of the west coast you probably create a picture closely resembling this stretch of shore. The green crofting land, dotted with white cottages, slopes down to the white sands of the bays. South of Mallaig, with its busy harbour that links to the Islands, is the wide, sheltered Morar Bay. ⅔ mile (1km) of white sands fringes the wide Y-shaped bay which is set below undulating hills. The bay was originally the mouth of a sea-loch similar to many others that penetrate this coastline until the long finger of Loch Morar was cut off from the sea by an uplift of the land and glacial deposits. A fast-flowing river drains the freshwater lake over a weir, which is all that remains of once impressive falls which were sacrificed to a hydro-electric power scheme. The river meanders across the southern edge of the bay to the narrow sea opening.

**Water quality** There have been reports that some sewage from Morar village and the other villages along this coast ends up on the sands.

**Bathing safety** Bathing is only safe close inshore due to strong under-currents 110 yards (100m) from the shore.

**Access** The main road runs parallel with the beach and it is a short walk across the turf banks that lead down to the sand. The railway runs alongside the road and some trains will stop at Morar.

**Parking** Along the road above the beach.

**Toilets** None.

**Food** None.

**Seaside activities** Swimming and sailing.

**Wildlife and walks** At the southern end of the bay a turning off the main coast road leads along the shore of Loch Morar. Beyond the tiny hamlet of Bracora the road gives way to a path which can be followed through some spectacular scenery to Tarbet on Loch Nevis. Walking the shoreline around Morar there are stunning views east to the Inner Hebrides.

## 29 Camusdarrach Beach, Glenancross, Highland   OS Ref: NM6592

This beach was made famous in Bill Forsyth's film '*Local Hero*' (although the actual village scenes were shot over on the east coast). The mile (1.6km) of gleaming white sands backed by dunes and undulating grassland is popular, but remains beautiful and unspoilt. There is easy access to the beach, by paths from the road above the beach. A series of delightful secluded bays can be reached by walking over the hills edging the shore, forming rocky outcrops. The area is popular with tourists and in summer many caravans appear. The approach to the beach is vulnerable to erosion and visitors should use the paths to avoid damaging the dunes. Those staying late at this beach will enjoy the most breathtaking sunsets, as the sun sinks behind the rugged mountains of Skye.

**Water quality** No outfall in the vicinity of this beach.

**Bathing safety** Safe bathing but beware of some offshore currents.

**Access** Camusdarrach is situated just south of Morar Bay. The road runs parallel with the shore between Morar and Arisaig. There are paths giving access at various points across the low turf-banks that descend to the beach.

**Parking** Cars can park on the turf behind the beach.

***Toilets*** None.

***Food*** None.

***Seaside activities*** Swimming and windsurfing. Golf course.

***Wildlife and walks*** All along the western coast there is much of interest for the naturalist. Underwater there is a rich and varied marine life which can only be glimpsed from the shore. The bobbing heads of seals are common, the outline of the basking shark a rarer occurrence. On the rocks that edge these beautiful beaches cormorants, shags, gannets and terns may be seen.

## 30  Sanna Bay, Sanna, Highland   OS Ref: NM4368

On the northern side of Ardnamurchan Point, the most westerly point of mainland Britain, are the lovely white sands of Sanna Bay. This is a beautiful and unspoilt beach backed by impressive marram-covered dunes and ringed by craggy hills. There are a series of island skerries off Sanna Point at the northern end of the bay, as well as rocky outcrops along the beach, dividing the bay into three sections. The sands are washed by clean, clear seas. The south side of the bay is covered by extensive rocks encrusted with barnacles and many types of seaweeds. To the south is a second sandy cove which is shadowed by cliffs and the Ardnamurchan Lighthouse.

***Water quality*** No sewage is discharged in the vicinity of the beach.

***Bathing safety*** Offshore currents necessitate bathing with caution.

***Access*** The B8007 from Kilchoran leads to the southern end of the bay, Portuairk, and from here it is a short walk across the dunes to the beach.

***Parking*** Limited parking behind the dunes.

***Toilets*** None.

***Food*** None.

***Seaside activities*** Swimming, sailing and fishing.

***Wildlife and walks*** There is a string of small sandy bays along the north coast of Ardnamurchan, only accessible on foot. These deserted beaches offer much to interest the naturalist. Ardnamurchan Point itself is notorious in sailing circles for its unpredictable weather so do not be surprised if you see boats motoring past as quickly as possible!

## 31  Calgary Bay, Mull   OS Ref: NM3652

Calgary Bay has been described as Mull's most beautiful bay. It might best be considered as a small sea-loch with a sandy beach at its head. The gently sloping white sands are backed by small dunes and flat machair grassland. Rocky shores extend at right angles from both sides of the beach. There are areas of both flat rock and boulders amongst which there are numerous rock-pools rich in animal and plant life. Steep cliffs and grassy slopes rising behind the rocky shore enclose the bay. This lovely beach is understandably popular with visitors in the summer. Emigrants from this area may well have founded the Canadian city which bears the same name.

**Water quality** No sewage is discharged in the vicinity of this beach.

**Bathing safety** Safe bathing.

**Access** The B8073 from Tobermory leads south to Calgary. The road skirts the grassland behind the beach and continues along the southern shore.

**Parking** There is a car park at the northern end of the beach and a small parking area at the southern end.

**Toilets** At the southern end of the beach, on the road behind the dunes.

**Food** None.

**Seaside activities** Swimming and fishing.

**Wildlife and walks** From the car park at the northern end of the beach a track leads to an old pier. This continues for a short distance as a footpath above the rocky shore where a series of lava dykes can be seen as grey bands where the molten lava has pushed up between the surrounding rocks.

## 32 Erraid, Fionnphort, Mull   OS Ref: NM3120

Mull has 300 miles (500km) of breathtaking coastline including sheer cliffs, stacks and arches. There are also tiny bays nestling below the cliffs with a backdrop of brooding mountains. The Ross of Mull, a long, low peninsula to the south of the island, has some of the best coastal features. There are cliffs of basalt columns, the Carsaig Arches at Malcolm's Point, numerous caves and secluded sandy bays which can only be approached on foot. The extensive sands at the western tip of the Ross are much more accessible. A road from Fionnphort, point of departure for the ferries to Iona, proceeds south along the Sound of Iona to extensive sandy beaches sheltered by Erraid Island. Between the island and the mainland, the Sound of Erraid is a sandy beach at low tide backed by sand dunes and machair grassland. At either end of the Sound there are rocky outcrops, and a host of islets and skerries lie just offshore. The grassland behind the beach is used for camping and as a result the beach can be quite crowded in summer. Those wanting to get away from the busier beaches should seek out the bays along the southern coast. There is easy access to Ardchiavaig, with limited parking.

**Water quality** No sewage is discharged in the vicinity of this beach.

**Bathing safety** Bathing can be dangerous due to the skerries and currents.

**Access** A side road from the A849 at Fionnphort leads south to Fidden skirting the dunes south to Knockvolgan.

**Parking** Parking space is available behind the dunes.

**Toilets** None.

**Food** None.

*Seaside activities* Swimming.

*Wildlife and walks* The lovely island of Iona is well worth a visit; boat trips leave from Fionnphort. There are sites of great historical interest including the St Oran Chapel and the Iona Cathedral. Scenically also, the island has much to offer with its beautiful shoreline, clear blue seas, and white sands.

## 33 Machrihanish, Campbeltown, Strathclyde   OS Ref: NR6521

A ribbon of pale sand edges the undeveloped west coast of the Mull of Kintyre, from West Loch Tarbert to Machrihanish. All along this western shore there are sea views north to the mountains of Jura and the low lying Islay. Ireland, only 20 miles (32km) away, is clearly visible on a good day. 4 miles (6km) of sandy beach studded with rocky outcrops sweep north from the headland at Machrihanish. Pounding surf washes the gently sloping sands which are backed by mountainous dunes. There is a championship golf course at the southern end of the beach and an airfield on the flat grassland stretching inland from the dunes. This delightful beach is popular in summer.

*Water quality* One outfall serving 200 people discharges untreated sewage at low water mark.

*Bathing safety* Dangerous undertows just off shore can cause problems for bathers.

*Access* There is access from either end of the beach with a short walk to the sands. The B483 from Campbeltown leads to Machrihanish at the southern end of the beach. The A83 hugs the western shore from Tarbert to Machrihanish Bay where it swings inland crossing the Mull towards Campbeltown.

*Parking* There is off-the-road parking at Machrihanish and at Westport off the A83 at the north end of the beach.

*Toilets* None.

*Food* None.

*Seaside activities* Swimming, surfing and fishing.

*Wildlife and walks* The plain that spans the peninsula from Campbeltown on the east coast to Machrihanish is in contrast to the tree-clad slopes to the north and the windswept Mull to the south. The Mull coast has cliffs dotted with caves, and most of its length cannot be reached except on foot. It is well worth the effort. There are often seals, basking sharks or porpoises to be seen offshore.

## 34 Brodick Bay, Brodick, Isle of Arran   OS Ref: NS0237

Below the bare granite summit of the majestic Goat Fell, wooded slopes descend to the water's edge of Brodick Bay north shore. The busy pier on the rocky southern shore is the main landing point for the island. The rocky shore gives way to a 1 mile (1.6km) arc of sand and pebble beach extending around the head of the bay. The beach is bisected by a river which meanders across flat grassland behind the beach before crossing the sands. The beach has a most beautiful setting, overlooked by the impressive Brodick Castle. The bay enjoys a particularly mild climate which is reflected in the Castle Gardens where thriving semi-tropical plants can be found.

**Water quality** Two outfalls serving 700 people discharge untreated sewage, one below and one above low water mark. There have been reports of sewage solids and litter washing on to the beach.

**Bathing safety** Safe bathing.

**Access** The car park at Brodick is adjacent to the beach. A few steps from the car park take you to the sands.

**Parking** Parking for 100 cars at Brodick and Claddach.

**Toilets** At Brodick and Brodick Country park.

**Food** Several small cafés.

**Seaside activities** Swimming, windsurfing, canoeing and fishing. Canoes, rowing boats, windsurf boards and fishing tackle are all available for hire. Golf course.

**Wet weather alternatives** Brodick Castle, Heritage Museum and Transport Museum.

**Wildlife and walks** On the northern side of the bay is the Brodick Country Park. Its 173 acres (70 hectares) include the formal gardens and woodland of Brodick Castle which have a notable rhododendron collection. There is a self-guided nature trail and access to a path climbing Goat Fell. There is a permanent Ranger Naturalist Service and a series of guided walks are organised during the summer months, which include a seashore life walk. A walled Victorian garden has been restored and in addition there is an ice house, Bavarian summer house and a children's adventure play area.

## 35 Blackwaterfoot, Arran   OS Ref: NR8928

The northern half of Arran is scenically outstanding, with lush glens cutting deep into the massive granite mountains. This area has been classed as a National Scenic Area. Beaches attractive to the tourist predominate around the south of the island and include Lamlash Bay, sheltered by Holy Island, Whiting Bay and Blackwaterfoot. The latter, on the western shore of the island, has 1 mile (1.6km) of sand and shingle with rocky outcrops containing rockpools that are worth exploring. Sand dunes and a links golf course stretch south round the bay.

**Water quality** No sewage is discharged in the vicinity of this beach.

**Bathing safety** Safe bathing.

**Access** There is a short walk from car park to the beach.

**Parking** There is a car park next to the golf club and Kinloch Hotel has 200 spaces.

**Toilets** At Blackwater harbour.

**Food** Kinloch Hotel.

**Seaside activities** Swimming.

**Wet weather alternatives** Kinloch Hotel has a swimming pool, squash court, sauna and solarium.

**Wildlife and walks** The lane past the golf course leads towards Drumadoon Head where there is a most impressive sill, produced when molten rock is forced upwards through other rocks. The path continues north along the line of a raised beach to the Kings Cave; can be followed along the wooded slopes to Tormore and Machrie Bay. There is much evidence of man's past activities in the area with standing stones, and hut circles on the hillside.

## 36 Troon, Ayrshire   OS Ref: NS3230

Troon is Old Welsh for nose, and describes the promontory which divides the town's shore into two distinct halves. A lighthouse stands at the end of the rocky promontory overlooking the traditional harbour and the modern marina which make this a popular spot with sailing enthusiasts. Gently sloping sands extend both north and south of the harbour. Victorian red sandstone houses and a low sea wall overlook the wide sweep of sands. Here the amusements of the holiday resort are to be found: the children's paddling pool, putting and a funfair. Troon is also a golfer's paradise, with five courses on the dunes north and south of the town. These include Royal Troon and three municipal courses.

**Water quality** South beach monitored by the River Purification Board and found to meet the EC standard for clean bathing water in 1990. One outfall serving 6,300 people discharges raw sewage at low water mark on the north beach.

**Bathing safety** Safe bathing.

**Access** Direct from promenade.

**Parking** Two car parks with 230 spaces.

**Toilets** Two blocks on promenade.

**Food** Hotels and cafés close to beach.

**Seaside activities** Swimming, surfing, windsurfing, sailing and fishing. Windsurfing school and marina for sailing. Paddling pool and children's funfair on the South beach.

**Wet weather alternatives** None.

**Wildlife and walks** From the South beach there are views across Ayr Bay to Lady Isle, a Scottish Wildlife Trust Nature Reserve, but access is by permit only. Fullerton estate on the edge of town has woods, parks and gardens.

# Wales

Sand dunes of Anglesey, pounding surf on the Lleyn, miles of sand, cliffs and secluded coves of West Wales and the beautiful Gower – this is the coast of Wales. There are numerous lovely beaches which are comparable with the best anywhere in the country and they have the added advantage of not being too crowded. Unfortunately there are individual beaches throughout the region that have failed to meet the minimum EC standard for clean bathing water due to the inadequate disposal of sewage from their shores. The north and south coasts suffer from the close proximity of large industrial centres. The large conurbations of South Wales – Swansea, Cardiff, Port Talbot and Newport – all contribute to the pollution of the south coast with discharges of domestic and industrial waste. The north coast is affected by pollution from Merseyside and the Wirral. Milford Haven has suffered from oil pollution problems from the terminals and refineries that line its shore. Further west, away from centres of population, beaches remain on the whole clean and unspoilt; definitely worth exploring.

**Beaches receiving the European Blue Flag in 1990:**

Pembrey (Cefn Sidan).

Benllech-Craig Dullan
**1** Traeth Lligwy (Moelfre)
Llandudno North Shore **f**
Cemaes Bay **f**
Llandudno West Shore **f**
Kinmel Bay **f**
Church Bay
Rhyl **f**
Beaumaris **f**
Trearddur Bay
Benllech **f**
Rhosneigr Beach Road
Bangor
Rhosneigr Porth
Prestatyn **f**
**2** Aberffraw
Prestatyn Barkby
**3** Llanddwyn
Penrhyn Bay **f**
Abergele Towyn **f**
Morfa Dinlle
**4** Dinas Dinlle
Colwyn Bay
Pontllyfni
Criccieth **f**
Porth Nefyn
Trefor
Morfa Bychan
Porth Dinllaen **f**
Pwllheli
**5** Traeth Penllech
**8** Harlech
**6** Porthoer
Llandanwg
**7** Aberdaron
**9** Tal-y-bont
Llanbedrog **f**
Barmouth
Abersoch
**10** Fairbourne
Morfa Aberech
Afon Wen
Tywyn
Aberdovey **f**
**11** Borth
Aberystwyth North
Aberystwyth South **f**
Clarach **f**
**12** New Quay
Aberystwyth
New Quay South
**13** Cwmtudu
Aberporth
Little Quay
**15** Mwnt
**14** Penbryn
Poppit Sands
Tresaith
Newport
Newport South
**16** Abereiddy
Whitesand Bay
Saundersfoot West
Newgale
Llanreath Bay
Saundersfoot Harbour **f**
Broadhaven
Saundersfoot East
**8** Marloes Sands
**21** Pembrey (Cefn Sidan)
Dale
Pendine
Swansea
West Angle Bay
Sands
Amroth
Newport
**Pembroke**
Burry Port
Aberavon **f**
Rest Bay **f**
Cardiff
**19** Broad Haven
Tenby North
Trecco Bay
**20** Barafundle
Lifeboat
Swansea Bay **f**
**Penarth f**
Tenby North
Sandy Bay **f**
Manorbier Beach **f**
Tenby South
Ogmore by Sea **f**
Jackson's Bay **f**
Tenby South Opp.
Southerndown
Kiln Park
**27** Nash Point
Cold Knap **f**
Whitmore Bay **f**

**22** Rhossili Bay
Bracelet Bay
**23** Port Eynon
Limeslade Bay
**24** Oxwich Bay
Langland Bay
**25** Three Cliffs Bay
**26** Caswell Bay

Chester

Newport

**f** = failed to meet EC standard for clean bathing water in 1990.
Numbered beaches appear in the following chapter.

**Coastal walk**
Pembrokeshire Coast Path
Cardigan to Tenby 180 miles (290km) mostly in the
Pembrokeshire National Park.

## The Golden List
See page 26 for further details

| Beach No on Map | Rating. The more stars the better. **f**=failed | Resort | Sewage outlets | Population discharging from outlet | Type of treatment | Discharge point relative to low water mark, unless otherwise stated. Distance given in metres | Remarks |
|---|---|---|---|---|---|---|---|
| **CLWYD** | | | | | | | |
| | f ★★ | **Prestatyn** | 1 | 16,246 | Screens/ maceration | 1000 below | Sandy. Safety patrols. Linked to Rhyl scheme. |
| | f ★★ f ★★ | **Rhyl** | 1 | 22,600 | Maceration/ tidal tank | 400 below | Sandy. Safety patrols. Bathing safe inshore except near river mouth. £8 million LSO scheme. |
| | f ★ | **Kinmel Bay (Sandy Cove)** | | | | | Sandy. Bathing safe except near river mouth. Linked to Rhyl scheme. |
| | f ★★ | Abergele (Towyn) | 1 | 4,237 | Screens/ maceration/ tidal tank | 100 above | Sand/shingle. Safe bathing. Linked to Rhyl scheme. |
| | | Abergele (Pensam) | 1 | 7,487 | Screens/ maceration/ tidal tank | 100 above | Sand at low tide. Safe bathing. Linked to Rhyl scheme. |
| | ★★★ | Llandulas | 1 | 1,550 | Screens/ maceration/ tidal tank | 75 below | Sand/shingle. Storm overflow on beach. LSO improvement scheme. |
| | ★★★ | **Colwyn Bay** | 1 | 25,800 | Screens/ maceration/ tidal tank | 1000 below | Some complaints. Improvements planned. |
| **GWYNEDD** | | | | | | | |
| | f ★★ | Penrhyn Bay | | 3,500 | Screens/ maceration/ tidal tank | 100 above | Sand/shingle. |
| | f ★★ | **Llandudno (North)** | | | | | Sandy. |
| | f ★ | **Llandudno (West Shore)** | 1 | 34,000 | Screens/ maceration/ tidal tank | LWM | Sand/shingle. Bathing safe at high tide only. Some complaints due to unsatisfactory discharges in Conwy Estuary. £7.8 million improvement scheme. |
| | f ★★ ★★ | **Penmaenmawr** **(Conwy Bay)** | 1 2 | 3,700 160 | Maceration Raw | 200 above 200 above | Sand/shingle. Improvements planned. |

| Beach No on Map | Rating. The more stars the better. f=failed | Resort | Sewage outlets | Population discharging from outlet | Type of treatment | Discharge point relative to low water mark, unless otherwise stated. Distance given in metres | Remarks |
|---|---|---|---|---|---|---|---|
| | | **ANGLESEY** | | | | | |
| | f ★★ ★★ | Beaumaris | | | | | Shingle/sand. Bathing safe on incoming tide, dangerous on the ebb. |
| | | Red Wharf Bay | | | | | Bathing safe except at ebb tide. |
| | f ★★ | **Benllech** | 1 | 2,284 | Raw | 200 below | Sandy. |
| 1 | ★★★ | Moelfre (Treath Lligwy) | 1 | 894 | Raw | 100 below | Shingle. Safe bathing. |
| | | Amlwch (Bull Bay) | 1 | 4,200 | Raw | 50 below | Outfall half mile east of bay. Storm overflow below LWM. |
| | f ★★ | Cemaes Bay | 1 | 1,000 | Maceration/ tidal tank | 70 below | Sandy. |
| | | Holyhead | 5 | 11,000 | Raw | All above LWM | Docks area. |
| | ★★★ | **Trearddur Bay** | | | | | Sand and rocks. Good swimming. |
| | ★★★ | **Rhosneigr** | 1 | 1,532 | Raw | 150 below | Outfall discharges from rocks. |
| 2 | ★★★ | Aberffraw Bay | 1 | 534 | Screens/ maceration | At HWM | Sandy. |
| 3 | | Llanddwyn | | | | | Sandy. |
| | | **GWYNEDD cont.** | | | | | |
| 4 | ★★ | **Dinas Dinlle** | | | | | Sandy. |
| | ★★★ | Trefor | 1 | 582 | Secondary | At LWM | Sand/shingle. |
| | | Nefyn | 1 | 2,800 | Maceration | At HWM | Sand. Surfing. |
| | ★★ | Morfa Nefyn | 1 | 2,100 | Maceration | At LWM | Sand/rocks. |
| | f ★★ | Porth Dinllaen | | | | | Sand/rocks. |
| | | Rhos-y-Llan | 1 | 420 | Primary | Off rocks | Sandy. |
| 5 | | Traeth Penllech | | | | | Sand/rocks. |
| | ★★★ | Porth Iago | | | | | Sand. Surfing. |
| 6 | ★★★ | Porthor | | | | | Sand. |

| Beach No on Map | Rating. The more stars the better. **f**=failed | Resort | Sewage outlets | Population discharging from outlet | Type of treatment | Discharge point relative to low water mark, unless otherwise stated. Distance given in metres | Remarks |
|---|---|---|---|---|---|---|---|
| **7** | ★★ | Aberdaron | | | | | Sandy. Surfing. |
| | ★★★ | *Abersoch* | 1 | 1,356 | Secondary | 100 below | Sandy. |
| | **f** ★★ | Llanbedrog | 1 | 672 | Maceration/ tidal tank | 50 below | Sandy. |
| | ★★★ | *Pwllheli* | 1 | 4,107 | Maceration/ tidal tank | At harbour mouth | Sandy. LSO planned. |
| | ★★★ | Morfa Aberech | | | | | Sandy. |
| | | Afon Wen | 1 | 46 | Maceration/ tidal tank | At LWM | Sand/shingle. |
| | **f** ★★ | *Criccieth* | 1 | 800 | Tidal tank | 50 below | Sand/shingle. New LSO proposed. |
| | ★★★ | *Morfa Bychan* | 1 | 800 | Tidal tank | 50 below | Sandy beach. Contaminated by local streams. Safe bathing except SE end. |
| **8** | ★★ | *Harlech* | 1 | 1,291 | Primary | At LWM | Sandy beach. Bathing unsafe. |
| | ★★ | *Llandanwg* | 1 | 258 | Primary | At LWM | Sand/rock. Bathing safe at high tide. |
| **9** | | Tal-y-Bont | | | | | Sand, dunes. |
| | ★★★ | *Barmouth* | 2 | 800 1,400 | Raw Maceration | At LWM At HWM | Sandy. Estuary unsafe for swimming. New outfall near to completion. |
| **10** | ★★★ | *Fairbourne* | 1 | 474 | Primary/ tidal tank | 400 below | Sandy. |
| | **f** ★★ | Llwyngwril | 1 | 370 | Raw | At LWM | Sand/shingle. |
| | ★★★ | *Tywyn* | 1 | 2,811 | Maceration/ tidal tank | At LWM | Sandy. Surfing. Scheme under investigation. |
| | **f** ★★ | *Aberdovey* | 1 | 6,000 | Primary/ tidal tank | At LWM | Bathing safe from beach north of village. Sewage outfall in estuary. |

**DYFED**

| **11** | ★★★ | **Borth** | | | | | Bathing dangerous near mouth of the estuary. Good elsewhere. |

| Beach No on Map | Rating. The more stars the better. f=failed | Resort | Sewage outlets | Population discharging from outlet | Type of treatment | Discharge point relative to low water mark, unless otherwise stated. Distance given in metres | Remarks |
|---|---|---|---|---|---|---|---|
| | f ★ | **Clarach Bay** | | | | | Bathing safe close inshore. |
| | f ★  ★★★ | Aberystwyth Harbour Aberystwyth South **Aberystwyth North** | 1 | 9,100 | Screened | | Bathing safe centre of prom and south of harbour in calm seas. New LSO planned. |
| | | Llanrhystud | 1 | 500 | Primary | | Shingle. Sand at low tide. |
| | | Llansantffraid | 1 | 1,160 | Primary | At LWM | Sand and shingle. |
| | | Aberarth | 1 | 470 | Primary | At LWM | Shingle beach. |
| | ★★★ f ★★ | Aberaeron | 1 | 5,000 | Raw | At LWM | Sand and shingle. Under investigation. |
| | ★★★ | Little Quay Bay | | | | | Sand. Safe bathing. |
| 12 | ★★★ ★★ | **New Quay** (South) | 1 | 6,000 | Maceration | 1300 below | Long sea outfall off Llanina Point. |
| 13 | | Cwmtudu | | | | | Shingle and sand. |
| | f ★★ | Llangranog | 1 | 400 | Primary | 75 below | Sand/shingle. |
| 14 | | Penbryn | | | | | Sand. |
| | f ★★ | Tresaith | 1 | 180 | Maceration | 75 below | Sand and shingle. Safe bathing. Lifeguards. |
| 15 | | Mwnt | | | | | Sand. |
| | f ★★ | Aberporth | 1 | 1,842 | Maceration | 75 below | Sandy. Bathing safe except when strong north winds blow. |
| | ★★★ | Poppit Sands | | | Secondary | | Sand and shingle. Estuary polluted by outfalls at Cardigan. Bathing safe only at slack water. |
| | ★★★ | Newport | 1 | 1,400 | Maceration | At LWM | Bathing safe in centre of beach except on ebb tide or when rough. Sand/shingle. |
| | | Pwllgwaelod | 1 | 880 | Secondary | At LWM | Grey sand. |
| | | Fishguard | 1 | 2,480 | Screens/ maceration | At LWM | |
| | ★★★ | Goodwick | 1 | 2,710 | Raw | At LWM | Ferry terminal. |

| Beach No on Map | Rating. The more stars the better. f=failed | Resort | Sewage outlets | Population discharging from outlet | Type of treatment | Discharge point relative to low water mark, unless otherwise stated. Distance given in metres | Remarks |
|---|---|---|---|---|---|---|---|
| 16 | *** | Abereiddy Bay | | | | | |
| 17 | *** | **Whitesand Bay** | | | | | Surf bathing. Strong currents. |
| | *** | **Newgale** | | | | | Shingle and sand. Surfing. |
| | *** | **Broadhaven** | 1 | 2,200 | Secondary | At HWM | Sandy. Surfing. |
| 18 | | Marloes | | | | | Sand and rock. |
| | *** | Dale | 1 | 600 | Maceration/ tidal tank | Above LWM | Shingle and sand. |
| | | Sandy Haven | 1 | 1,360 | Secondary | At LWM | Red sand. |
| | *** | Angle Bay | 1 | 500 | Secondary | At LWM | Shingle and muddy sand. |
| 19 | | Broad Haven | | | | | Sand, dunes. |
| 20 | | Barafundle Bay | | | | | Sand, good bathing. |
| | *** | Freshwater East | 1 | 600 | Raw | At LWM | Sandy. |
| | f ** *** | Manorbier Beach Manorbier West | 1 | 520 | Secondary | At LWM | Sand and shingle. |
| | *** | **Tenby** | 1 | 25,000 | Screened/ maceration | 2.7km below | Sandy. |
| | *** ** f ** f * | **Saundersfoot:** **West** **East** **Beach** Harbour | 1 | 11,000 | Primary | 50 below | Sand and shingle. |
| | *** | **Amroth** | | | | | Sand and shingle. |
| | *** | **Pendine Sands** | | | | | Sand and dunes. Part of beach often closed for MOD firing range. |
| 21 | *** | **Pembrey Sands** | 1 | 2,500 | Secondary | Above HWM | Sand and dunes. Bathing safe except on spring high water. |
| | *** | Burry Port | 1 | 6,000 | Primary | Below LWM | Industrial and muddy. Bathing unsafe. |

| Beach No on Map | Rating. The more stars the better. f=failed | Resort | Sewage outlets | Population discharging from outlet | Type of treatment | Discharge point relative to low water mark, unless otherwise stated. Distance given in metres | Remarks |
|---|---|---|---|---|---|---|---|
| **WEST GLAMORGAN** | | | | | | | |
| | ★★★ | Broughton Bay | | | | | Sandy, bathing unsafe. |
| **22** | ★★ | **Rhossili Bay** | | | | | Sandy. |
| | | Mewslade Bay | 1 | 270 | Primary | Below LWM | Sandy. |
| **23** | ★★★ | **Port Eynon Bay** | 1 | 1,208 | Secondary | At LWM | Sand and dunes. |
| **24** | ★★★ | **Oxwich Bay** | | | | | Sand and dunes. |
| **25** | ★★★ | Three Cliffs Bay | | | | | Sandy. |
| | | Southgate | 1 | 500 | Secondary | Below LWM | Rocky. |
| | | Brandy Cove | 1 | 2,000 | Secondary | Below LWM | Rocky. |
| **26** | ★★★ | **Caswell Bay** | | | | | Sandy. Surfing safe except on ebb tide. |
| | ★★★ | **Langland Bay** | | | | | Sandy. |
| | ★★ | **Limeslade Bay** | | | | | Sandy. |
| | ★★★ | **Bracelet Bay** | | | | | Sandy. |
| | f ★★<br>f ★ | **Swansea Bay:**<br>The Mumbles | 1 | 170,000 | Screened/ tidal tank | Below LWM | Subject of many complaints. New projects totalling over £50 million for whole bay area. |
| | | Baglan (Neath) | 1 | 60,000 | Screened | 3.1km below | Improvements planned as above. |
| | ★★ | Afan (Port Talbot) | 1 | 60,000 | Screened | 2.4km below | Improvements planned as above. |
| | f ★★ | Aberafan West | | | | | |
| **MID GLAMORGAN** | | | | | | | |
| | ★★★ | **Rest Bay** | | | | | Sand and rocks. STW in operation. |
| | | Porthcawl | 1 | 19,000 | Raw | Below LWM | Sand and rocks. |
| | f ★★ | **Sandy Bay** | | | | | Sand and rocks. |
| | ★★ | **Trecco Bay** | | | | | Sand and rocks. |

| Beach No on Map | Rating. The more stars the better. f=failed | Resort | Sewage outlets | Population discharging from outlet | Type of treatment | Discharge point relative to low water mark, unless otherwise stated. Distance given in metres | Remarks |
|---|---|---|---|---|---|---|---|
| f ★ | | Ogmore by Sea | 1 | 140,000 | Secondary/ other | Into river Ogmore approx 1.6km from sea | Sand and rocks. Lifeguards. |
| ★★★ | | **Southerndown** | | | | | Sand and rocks. Strong currents off Trwyn y Witch headland. Lifeguards. Surfing except at high tide. |

## SOUTH GLAMORGAN

| Beach No on Map | Rating | Resort | Sewage outlets | Population discharging from outlet | Type of treatment | Discharge point | Remarks |
|---|---|---|---|---|---|---|---|
| 27 | | Nash Point | | | | | Rocky. Bathing unsafe. |
| | | Tresilian Bay | 1 | 8,000 | Maceration | At LWM | Rocky. Bathing unsafe. |
| | | Limpert Bay | 1 | 4,500 | Maceration | At LWM | Rocky. Overlooked by power station. |
| | ★★ | Font-y-Gary Bay | 2 | 3,045 936 | Raw Raw | At LWM At LWM | Rocky. Lifeguards. |
| | f ★★ | **Cold Knap Beach** | | | | | New scheme proposed for completion in 1995, with Whitmore and Jacksons Bay. |
| | f ★★ | **Whitmore Bay** | 2 | 21,000 23,000 | Maceration Raw | At LWM At LWM | Sand, shingle and mud. |
| | f ★★ | **Jacksons Bay** | | | | | |
| | f ★★ | St Mary's Well | | | | | Shingle and rocks. |
| | f ★ | Penarth | 4 | | | | Shingle and rocks. Bathing dangerous. |

## 1 Traeth Lligwy, Moelfre, Anglesey   OS Ref: SH4987

A hard, flat, sandy beach ⅔ mile (1km) wide is revealed at low tide, ideal for sand castles and ball games. There are some areas of mud on the sand surface but signs indicate the areas to avoid. Gently sloping, grass-covered cliffs ring the bay to the south of the dunes that back the centre of the beach. A cliff path along the low rugged cliffs that rise to the north of the beach leads to the adjacent Dulas Bay. This more secluded bay has a fine sandy beach which can only be reached on foot.

**Water quality** Beach monitored by the NRA and found to meet the EC standard for clean bathing water in 1990. One outfall serving 894 people discharges raw sewage 110 yards (100m) below low water mark at Moelfre south of the bay. The stream which crosses the beach may well be polluted; presence of solids and an unpleasant smell at times.

**Bathing safety** Safe bathing but beware of offshore winds.

**Access** Three lanes off the A5025, one at the Moelfre roundabout and two slightly further north, lead to the bay. The car park is adjacent to the sand.

**Parking** Two privately run car parks with 500 spaces, rough surfaced.

**Toilets** One block at car park.

**Food** Refreshment caravan.

**Seaside activities** Swimming.

**Wildlife and walks** Cliff top paths can be followed in both directions from the beach. Walking south, the path over the headland provides excellent views of the rocky coastline. It leads to the picturesque little fishing village of Moelfre. Above the beach, in the rolling green field which slopes down to the shore, there are the remains of a 4th-century fortified village, Din Lligwy, and also a megalithic burial chamber.

## 2 Aberffraw, Anglesey   OS Ref: SH3568

A wide, flat, sandy beach is bounded landwards by a series of sand dune ridges, behind which flat grassland extends inland. This makes the dunes a prominent feature in a landscape that seems to be dominated by the sky. Aberffraw village is set back from the beach on the higher ground that rises to the west. The beach extends about ⅔ mile (1km) from low cliffs at the western end, below which the river flows.

**Water quality** Beach monitored by the NRA and found to meet the EC standard for clean bathing water in 1990. One outfall serving 534 people discharges screened and macerated sewage at high water mark west of the beach.

**Litter** The beach is cleaned during the summer.

**Bathing safety** Safe bathing, although the estuary area should be avoided on the ebb tide.

175

**Access** A lane off the A4080 just south of Aberffraw village leads to car parking behind the dunes. Easy walk through the dunes to beach.

**Parking** Parking for several hundred cars between ½ and 1 mile (0.75km–1.6km) from beach, on grassed common land.

**Toilets** In village and at Llywelyn.

**Food** In village and at Llywelyn.

**Seaside activities** Swimming.

**Wildlife and walks** The marram grass-covered dunes are well developed; depressions between the ridges (wet slacks) abound with wild flowers and low scrub, for example creeping willow. There is a 2 mile (3km) walk along the cliffs from Aberffraw leading to the church of Llangwfan. This area was the site of Llewelyn the Great, Prince of Gwynedd's Summer Palace although no trace remains.

## 3 Llanddwyn, Newborough, Anglesey OS Ref: SH4163

From the rocky Llanddwyn Island a lovely sand beach curves 3 miles (5km) east to Abermenai point, the end of a sand spit at the mouth of the Menai Straits. The beach is backed by the extensive sand dunes of Newborough Warren. At the western end there is a conifer wood planted by the Forestry Commission. This remote, gently shelving beach is usually quiet and has superb views of Snowdonia and the Lleyn Peninsula.

**Water quality** No sewage is discharged in the vicinity of this beach.

**Bathing safety** Safe bathing except at the eastern end; currents at the entrance to the Menai Straits can cause problems.

**Access** Road from Newborough village leads to a Forestry Commission car park within their plantation, and a path leads to the beach.

**Parking** Car park with space for several hundred cars in cleared forest areas behind beach.

**Toilets** At car park.

**Food** None.

**Seaside activities** Swimming and sailing.

**Wildlife and walks** There is a forest trail starting from the car park. The dunes of Newborough Warren behind the beach and Llanddwyn Island are both nature reserves; access to the dunes is restricted to prevent damage. Access to the island is by a causeway, and you get good views back along the beach and to the mountains in the distance. There is a ruined church and navigation beacon on the island. There are extensive cockle beds on the Straits side of Abermenai Point. Across the sand flats, a footpath leads through the Warren to Newborough Village.

## 4 Dinas Dinlle, Gwynedd    OS Ref: SH4456

Three miles (5km) of wide open beach stretches from Dinas Dinlle, a 100 foot (30m) hill which dominates the surrounding flat coastal plain, north to the mouth of the Menai Straits. The hill shadows the small village of the same name, with its string of bungalows, cafés and shops facing the beach. A moderately steep bank of large pebbles gives way to sand at low tide. The adjacent grassland on which stands the Caernarfon airport is protected by a low sea-wall. Good surfing conditions frequently prevail.

*Water quality* No sewage discharged in the vicinity of this beach.

*Litter* The beach is cleaned regularly throughout the summer.

*Bathing safety* Safe bathing except at the northern end.

*Access* Dinas Dinlle is signposted from the A499 south of Caernarfon. The road runs along adjacent to the beach, with easy level access from or through gaps in the low sea wall.

*Parking* Parking along the whole length of the road, with about 1 mile (1.6km) of pebbled parking areas.

*Toilets* Blocks at either end of the beach and one at the centre.

*Food* Several shops and cafés at the southern end of the beach.

*Seaside activities* Swimming, surfing and fishing.

*Wet weather alternatives* Airport viewing pavilion.

*Wildlife and walks* Good for a bracing winter walk.

## 5 Treath Penllech, Tudweiliog, Gwynedd    OS Ref: SH2034

A super beach; a wide sandy arc stretches over ⅔ mile (1km) below the rocky, grass-topped cliffs that fall steeply to the shore. A long strip of soft sand remains at high water and the wide flat sands studded with rocks towards the southern end are exposed at low tide. Treath Penllech forms part of a larger indented bay on this northern coast of the Lleyn Peninsula. There are good views from the cliff top to the headlands in either direction. By following the clifftop path, small sand and shingle coves can be reached. The relentless waves that wash this coast make for excellent surfing conditions.

*Water quality* No sewage is discharged in the vicinity of this beach.

*Bathing safety* Safe bathing.

*Access* From the B4417 take the road through Penllech, turning left at the T-junction. There is parking off this road, above the beach. A steep path down a narrow valley leads to the shore ⅔ mile (1km) away.

*Parking* Summer parking on a private field off road north east of Pen-y-graig.

*Toilets* None.

**177**

**Food** None.

**Seaside activities** Swimming, surfing, windsurfing, diving and fishing.

**Wildlife and walks** The area is popular with divers because of its rich marine life; the rockpools give a hint of what can be seen below the waves. A path along the cliff top, above which choughs may be seen, leads to other delightful little sandy coves.

## 6 Porthor, Gwynedd   OS Ref: SH1630

This is the last and the most accessible in a series of long secluded bays along the north coast of the Lleyn Peninsula. This small cove is ringed by steep grass-covered cliffs, typical of this whole coastline. It is also called 'Whistling Sands' because the white sands seem to whistle or squeak as they are walked on. To really get away from it all try Porth Iago and Porth Colmon further north.

**Water quality** No sewage is discharged in the vicinity of this beach.

**Bathing safety** Safe bathing.

**Access** From the B4413 south of Pen-y-groeslon lanes lead down to car park just before Carreg. Steep path down from cliff top.

**Parking** Car park on cliff top 220 yards (200m) from beach.

**Toilets** At car park.

**Food** Café on beach.

**Seaside activities** Swimming and fishing.

**Wildlife and walks** Low tide reveals rockpools at the western end.

## 7 Aberdaron, Gwynedd   OS Ref: SH1726

A sheltered bay except when a south or south-west wind blows and the waves come crashing in. The mile (1.6km) long sandy beach below the cluster of housing that makes up the fishing village of Aberdaron completely disappears at high tide. Take care not to get caught below the rocky cliffs that fringe the bay and extend south to the toe of the Lleyn.

**Water quality** Beach monitored by the NRA and found to meet the EC standard for clean bathing water in 1990. No sewage is discharged in the vicinity of the beach.

**Bathing safety** Safe bathing.

**Access** Ramp to beach.

**Parking** Adjacent to ramp.

**Toilets** Adjacent to ramp.

**Food** Cafés and two pubs in village.

*Seaside activities* Swimming, windsurfing, diving, fishing and sailing.

*Wildlife and walks* Cliff-top walks lead south to the 500 foot (150m) hill Mynydd Mawr that rises above the end of the Peninsula. There are spectacular views of the rocky coast and of Bardsey Island, 2 miles (3km) off shore. Westwards, the cliff paths lead to the cove of Porth Ysgo not accessible by road. Boat trips to Bardsey Island leave from Aberdaron.

## 8 Harlech, Gwynedd   OS Ref: SH5831

From Harlech, with its castle perched on a rocky cliff 60 yards (55m) above the coastal plain, there are superb views over the dunes and golf links below and across Tremadoc Bay to the Lleyn Peninsula. 4 miles (6km) of soft sands, edged by a wide belt of dunes, extend from Harlech Point south to Llandanwg. There is masses of room on the extensive, flat, rather windswept sands. The fragile dunes have suffered from erosion and restoration work is being undertaken to help them recover; please assist this work by avoiding any further damage. There is access to the beach at Llandanwg, where board walks lead across the dunes to the beach. The church of old Llandanwg village can be seen half buried in sand.

*Water quality* Harlech and Llandanwg are monitored by the NRA and were found to meet the EC standard for clean bathing water in 1990. One outfall at Harlech serving 1,291 people discharges primary treated sewage at low water mark. One outfall at Llandanwg serving 258 people discharges macerated and primary treated sewage at low water mark. A new sewage treatment works is planned for operation in 1995.

*Litter* Some marine debris is washed on to the shore.

*Bathing safety* The estuary and the area around Harlech Point is unsafe for bathing due to strong currents. Further south, the beach is safe for bathing. HM Coastguard search unit post at the car park. Emergency phone on path to beach and lifebuoys.

*Access* The beach is signposted from the A496 at Harlech. The road leads to car parking behind the dunes. A path leads through dunes.

*Parking* Car park with 300 spaces behind the dunes.

*Toilets* At the car park.

*Food* None.

*Seaside activities* Swimming, surfing, windsurfing, sailing, canoeing and fishing. St David's Golf Course.

*Wet weather alternatives* Harlech Castle, sports hall with indoor swimming pool, galleries and craft shop in Harlech.

*Wildlife and walks* The northern end of this beach and the shore of the estuary fall within the Morfa Harlech Nature Reserve; access is by permit only. The Snowdonia National Park Information Centre is in the town.

## 9 Tal-y-Bont, Gwynedd  OS Ref: SH5921

A first-class beach; miles and miles of golden sand backed by high dunes – 15 miles (24km) in all, unspoilt and set against the magnificent scenery of North Wales. The beach stretches from Shell Island Peninsula in the north, so called because of the variety of shells to be found there, towards Barmouth in the south. A road just north of Tal-y-bont leads to car parking behind the dunes. There are a lot of caravan parks along this section of coastline; at Tal-y-bont they remain hidden behind the dunes, but it does mean that the sands can be popular in summer. However, the wide flat sands revealed at low tide provide plenty of space.

**Water quality** No sewage is discharged in the vicinity of this beach.

**Litter** Beach cleaned by the local authority.

**Bathing safety** Safe bathing. Emergency phone at the car park.

**Access** Beach signposted off the A496 north of Tal-y-bont, road leads to a car park behind the dunes. Good paths through the dunes lead to the beach.

**Parking** National Park car park behind the dunes has 120 spaces.

**Toilets** At the car park.

**Food** None, cafés in village.

**Seaside activities** Swimming, surfing, windsurfing, canoeing and fishing.

**Wildlife and walks** The dunes at the north end of the beach form the Morfa Dyffryn Nature Reserve; access is by permit only.

## 10 Fairbourne, Gwynedd  OS Ref: SH6116

Fairbourne has a magnificent setting at the mouth of the beautiful Mawddach estuary with the backdrop of the Welsh mountains. 2 miles (3km) of sandy beach stretch north from the small resort of Fairbourne to the mouth of the estuary. The promenade gives way to the dunes of Morfa Mawddach, a sand spit. A narrow gauge railway runs from Fairbourne along the beach to the point, where a ferry will take the visitor across the estuary to the old quay of Barmouth on the opposite shore. There are lots of shells to be found on this beach.

**Water quality** Beach monitored by the NRA and found to meet the EC standard for clean bathing water in 1990. One outfall discharges macerated and primary treated sewage through a tidal tank 440 yards (400m) below low water mark. A £1.7 million scheme will extend this outfall further out to sea.

**Bathing safety** Safe bathing except near the estuary mouth.

**Access** Beach signposted from the A493 through the town. Direct access from the promenade. Access for the disabled.

**Parking** Extensive car parking near the beach.

*Toilets* Near main access to beach.

*Food* Refreshment kiosks and cafés on the sea front. Restaurant at the point.

*Seaside activities* Swimming, windsurfing, sailing and fishing. Amusements. Narrow gauge railway. Windsurfing boards available for hire.

*Wet weather alternatives* Fairbourne railway and Butterfly Safari.

*Wildlife and walks* There is excellent walking country within easy reach of Fairbourne; footpaths lead along the estuary. The panorama walk above Barmouth provides superb views of mountains, river and sea.

## 11 Borth, Dyfed   OS Ref: SN6190

A former fishing village, Borth is a major centre for caravan and camping holidays. The sandy beach extends for some 2 miles (3km) north around the dunes of the National Nature Reserve at Ynyslas and to the Dyfi estuary. The Ceredigion Heritage Coast Path, southbound towards Aberystwyth, starts at Borth.

*Water quality* Beach monitored by the NRA and found to meet the EC standard for clean bathing water in 1990. No sewage is discharged in the vicinity of the beach, but there is an outfall serving 6,000 people discharging primary treated sewage in the estuary.

*Bathing safety* Waters in the Dyfi estuary are dangerous, otherwise Borth and Ynyslas beaches are safe for responsible use.

*Access* Direct from the promenade in Borth or via footpaths through the dunes at Ynyslas.

*Parking* Parking for 200-300 at Borth and similar numbers at Ynyslas.

*Toilets* On the promenade (with facilities for the disabled).

*Food* Hotels, restaurants, cafés.

*Seaside activities* Swimming, surfing, windsurfing, sailing and sea angling. Golf course.

*Wet weather alternatives* Borth Livestock Centre, Tre'r Ddol Museum. A full list of all attractions and leisure facilities in the district is available from the Borth Tourist Information Centre.

*Wildlife and walks* Ceredigion Heritage Coast Path leads south through Clarach to Aberystwyth. Ynyslas Nature Reserve offers conducted tours and guided nature trails. Walks in the RSPB Reserve at Ynys Hir.

## 12 New Quay, Dyfed   OS Ref: SN3959

This traditional fishing town perched on the steep slopes above the harbour has three beaches. Treath-y-Dolau, to the south of the harbour, is backed by contorted shale cliffs. The harbour beach, bounded by the stone pier,

181

and Traethgwyn stretching around the curve of New Quay Bay are both gently sloping sandy beaches. At low tide Llanina Point to the north can be rounded to reach Cei Bach beach, a quiet ½ mile (800m) of sandy beach, backed by a shingle ridge and shrub-covered slopes.

**Water quality** Beach monitored by the NRA and found to meet the EC standard for clean bathing water in 1990. One outfall serving 6,000 people discharges macerated sewage from a tidal tank at low water mark off New Quay head.

**Bathing safety** Safe from all beaches.

**Access** Short walk down road which slopes down from town to the beach.

**Parking** Car parks in town.

**Toilets** Close to the beach.

**Food** Hotels, motels, and cafés.

**Seaside activities** Swimming, surfing, windsurfing, sailing and fishing. Boats and surf boards for hire.

**Wet weather alternatives** Bird hospital and lifeboat station. Guide to attractions and leisure facilities available from Information Centre.

**Wildlife and walks** Ceredigion Heritage Coast Path provides walks with views of dramatic cliff scenery. Ceredigion District Council produces leaflets which describe each of the many beaches from Borth in the north to Gwbert-on-Sea in the south.

## 13  Cwmtudu, New Quay, Dyfed   OS Ref: SN3558

A small secluded cove among the rugged cliffs south-west of New Quay, Cwmtudu lies at the mouth of the wooded Afon Fynnon Ddewi valley. A group of houses nestles in the valley. The shingle beach has a small amount of sand at low tide and is edged by cliffs with striking rock formations. Caves among the folds and faults were once used by smugglers.

**Water quality** No sewage is discharged in the vicinity of this beach.

**Bathing safety** Safe.

**Access** Signposted from the A487 south of New Quay. Several miles' drive along lanes leading to the cliff-top car park. Steep path down to the cove.

**Parking** Car park with 30 spaces.

**Toilets** None.

**Food** Café.

**Seaside activities** Swimming.

**Wildlife and walks** The Ceredigion Heritage Coast Path, 110 yards (100m) up the road from the beach, leads around the headland to the north and gives views over the bay. Earth banks above the craggy inlet are the remains of an Iron Age fort. From here the path continues along the coast for 3 miles (4.8km) to New Quay Headland and Birds Rock.

## 14 Penbryn, Dyfed   OS Ref: SN2953

A wooded valley cuts through the steep cliffs to reach the beach: ⅔ mile (1km) of golden sand with small dunes on either side of the River Hoffnant. The headland to the east is blue-grey shale and mudstone smoothed at its base by the waves. Access to the sandy bay beyond the headland is possible at low tide; beware of the rising tide as there is no escape from the cove at high tide. Dogs are banned from the beach from May to September north of the stream, which is the area owned by the National Trust.

*Water quality* No sewage is discharged in the vicinity of the beach.

*Bathing safety* Safe bathing.

*Access* Penbryn is signposted from the A487. Short downhill walk from the car park to the beach.

*Parking* National Trust car park with 150 spaces.

*Toilets* In the car park (facilities for the disabled).

*Food* Farmhouse café and shop in National Trust car park.

*Seaside activities* Swimming.

*Wildlife and walks* Footpath to the west of the sand dunes leads to St Michael's Church which commands good views of the Hoffnant valley. A track from Llanborth car park leads up between hedges and banks to give excellent coastal views westwards. Dogs on leads are welcome on the footpaths.

## 15 Mwnt, Cardigan, Dyfed   OS Ref: SN1952

A natural suntrap and surrounded by National Trust land, this beautiful undeveloped sandy beach is quite easily accessible and can be very popular in summer. The 330 yards (300m) of gently sloping sands are fringed by folded and faulted shale and mudstone cliffs. The beach is shadowed by the imposing form of Foel-y-Mwnt, a conical hill on the headland. The tiny whitewashed church of The Holy Cross nestles in a hollow at its foot. The only other obvious sign of man is the remnant of a limekiln adjacent to the path down to the beach; limestone was landed in the bay and fired ready for use by the local farmers. Dogs are banned from May to September.

*Water quality* No sewage is discharged in the vicinity of this beach.

*Bathing safety* Safe bathing inshore; care is required as surface currents, due to waves breaking on the headland, deflect across the bay. Emergency phone on cliff path.

*Access* Mwnt is signposted from the B4548 north of Cardigan. Lanes lead to car park above the beach. Steps and a steep path down the cliff to the beach.

*Parking* National Trust car park with 250 spaces.

*Toilets* At the head of the steps to the beach (facilities for the disabled).

*Food* Refreshments available from Easter to October.

*Seaside activities* Swimming.

*Wildlife and walks* National Trust cliff-top walks. A pack detailing walks in the Cardigan area is available from local tourist information centres. Foel-y-Mwnt hill on the headland provides good views of the bay south to Cardigan Island and the narrow rocky inlet to the north. On the cliff tops above the beach there is a small remnant dune system where marram grass covers the wind-blown sand. Dogs on leads are welcome on the footpaths.

## 16 Abereiddy Bay, Abereiddy, Preseli, Dyfed   OS Ref: SM8031

One of many small bays that have known a very different and more active past. The slate that gives the small beach its dark grey sand was quarried and the remains of the workings can still be seen at the northern end of the beach. A small harbour on the north side of the headland where the rock has been cut away forms a deep blue pool.

*Water quality* No sewage is discharged in the vicinity of this beach.

*Bathing safety* Dangerous undercurrents and undertows off parts of the beach; life saving equipment and an emergency telephone are available.

*Access* Lanes from the A487 north of St David's lead to the hamlet of Abereiddy.

*Parking* Large car park for 200 cars.

*Toilets* At rear of car park.

*Food* Ice-cream van and teas on beach.

*Seaside activities* Swimming, diving, canoeing, surfing and fishing.

*Wildlife and walks* The Pembrokeshire Coast Path leads in both directions along this most impressive and unspoilt stretch of rocky coastline, several stretches of which are owned by the National Trust.

## 17 Whitesand Bay, St David's, Preseli, Dyfed   OS Ref: SM7327

Gorgeous sunsets framed in the wide arc of Whitesand Bay, from the remote rocky headland of St David's to St John Point, are an added attraction of this lovely beach. There are splendid views away to Ramsey Island and the Bishops and Clerks; the South Bishop can be identified on the far horizon by its lighthouse. The wide white sands stretch for ⅔ mile (1km). Large pebbles are thrown to the top of the beach by the waves that frequently crash on to this beach, much to the delight of many surfers. Open fields slope down to the shore from the imposing craggy hill Carn Llidi, which provides good walking with excellent sea views. St David's Head is owned by the National Trust.

**Water quality** Beach monitored by the NRA and found to meet the EC standard for clean bathing water in 1990. No sewage is discharged in the vicinity of this beach.

**Bathing safety** Dangerous and unpredictable currents off parts of the beach and at some states of the tide; warning signs indicate where to bathe. Flags indicate when it is safe to bathe. Lifeguards patrol the beach during the summer. Weever fish.

**Access** Road off A487 north of St David's, signposted to Whitesand, leads directly to car park adjoining the sand.

**Parking** Car park behind beach, with approximately 400 spaces.

**Toilets** At car park.

**Food** Café/shop at car park.

**Seaside activities** Swimming, surfing, canoeing, diving, windsurfing and fishing.

**Wildlife and walks** The coast path north provides an interesting circular walk, taking in St David's Head with the remains of a fort and a burial chamber, and returning round Carn Llidi Hill. A guide describing the route is published by the Pembrokeshire Coast National Park and can be obtained at information offices locally. Ramsey Island lies just south of the bay, and boat trips from Whitesand (12-person inflatables, May-September) take you round the island to view the seabird breeding colonies.

## 18 Marloes Sands, Marloes, Preseli, Dyfed   OS Ref: SM7908

'Magnificent Marloes', a mile (1.6km) of wide flat golden sands, stretches from the imposing bulk of Gateholm Island in the north-west to Red Cliff and Hoopers Point to the south-east. Beds of rock laid flat on a sea bed long ago are tilted and seem to be pushing up through the sands. Their jagged outlines point skywards along the length of this glorious bay. The steep cliffs that bound the beach reflect these dipping strata; do not attempt to climb them as they are dangerous. The barnacle- and seaweed-covered rocky outcrops testify to the fact that the whole beach disappears at high water. There is only one access point to the beach where a tiny stream flows through a narrow valley, so take care not to get cut off at the extremities of the beach by the incoming tide.

**Water quality** No sewage is discharged in the vicinity of this beach.

**Bathing safety** Beware of currents and rocks. Life-saving equipment is available. Take care as some areas of the beach are quickly cut off by the rising tide. The cliffs are dangerous; do not climb.

**Access** From Marloes village a lane, signposted Marloes Sands, takes you to the National Trust car park.

**Parking** National Trust car park with about 50 spaces.

**Toilets** None.

**Food** None.

**Seaside activities** Swimming and fishing.

**Wildlife and walks** The coast path that follows the cliff top round the bay provides excellent views of the sands. There is a 2 mile (3km) nature trail starting from the National Trust car park. Walkers using the trail are guided by a leaflet produced by the Dyfed Wildlife Trust (DWT). To the south-west, the coast path leads to West Dale Bay and a series of secluded sandy beaches around the Dale Peninsula that can only be reached on foot. To the north-east, the path heads to Albion Reach and Martin's Haven. A National Park guide, available from the DWT Information Centre, describes a walk around the headland. Boat trips run from Martin's Haven to Skomer Island, renowned for its seabirds, wild flowers and seal colonies, and a marine area now designated a Marine Nature Reserve.

## 19 Broad Haven South, Bosherston, Dyfed    OS Ref: SR9893

A classic golden beach with a clear stream meandering across a wide flat 'V' of golden sands, backed by dunes and with rocky cliffs rising at either side. A distinct rocky outcrop lies just off shore. This unspoilt beach is only accessible by foot across the dunes but still gets busy in summer. It is perfect for relaxation or for exploration. There are lily ponds in the nature reserve behind the dunes and surprises round every headland: tiny rocky inlets, deep crevices, stacks and blow holes, not to mention the wildlife.

**Water quality** No sewage is discharged in the vicinity of this beach.

**Litter** Beach cleaned regularly by the National Trust.

**Bathing safety** Safe bathing. Life saving equipment available.

**Access** A lane from Bosherston leads to the National Trust car park; a path leads to the beach, and there is also a steep path to the beach from Bosherston a mile (1.6km) inland.

**Parking** National Trust car park on headland above beach, National Park car park in Bosherston.

**Toilets** At car park in summer.

**Food** None.

**Seaside activities** Swimming.

**Wildlife and walks** Separated from the beach by the dune ridge are the Bosherston Lily pools, three lakes created in the late 18th century by damming three narrow valleys behind the beach. Water lilies and freshwater wildlife abound. Paths and causeways form circular walks around the area, starting at the car park in Bosherston. South of the bay the coast path proceeds along the cliff top to the tiny rocky inlet where St Govan chapel stands at the foot of a long flight of steep steps down the cliffs. Further south there is a 130 foot (40m) deep cleft in the cliff known as the Huntsman's Leap: a local huntsman is supposed to have died of fright after realising what his horse had just leapt! The path continues along this most beautiful rocky coastline towards the Elegug Stacks, a series of impressive limestone stacks, about 3 miles (5km) away. A large arch carved by the waves from the limestone cliffs is known as 'The Green Bridge of Wales'.

## 20 Barafundle Bay, Stackpole, Dyfed   OS Ref: SR9995

The National Trust owns an 8 mile (13km) section of the coast around Stackpole, including the beautiful Barafundle Bay. The beach can only be reached by foot with a mile (1.6km) walk along the cliff top from Stackpole Quay. One of many tiny harbours that once proliferated in West Wales, the stone quay in this tiny inlet has been restored by the National Trust. From the clifftop path you get your first glimpse of the bay, an impressive view of soft golden sands backed by high dunes, with steep limestone cliffs rising on either side. The cliffs, with distinctive dark bands at their base due to the encrusting seaweeds, barnacles and lichens, extend to Stackpole Head which shelters the bay.

**Water quality** No sewage is discharged in the vicinity of this beach.

**Litter** Clean; a small amount of litter is washed up. In summer the beach is cleaned daily by the National Trust.

**Bathing safety** Safe bathing. Life saving equipment at top of steps down cliff.

**Access** A lane east of Stackpole, signposted to Stackpole Quay and Barafundle, leads to the car park at Stackpole Quay. A 10-minute walk along the coast path, signposted from the car park, leads to the bay; follow the steps down the cliff to reach the sands.

**Parking** National Trust car park at Stackpole Quay with about 230 spaces.

**Toilets** At car park.

**Food** None.

**Seaside activities** Swimming.

**Wildlife and walks** The coast path from Stackpole Quay crosses the beach and, climbing through the trees, the path tracks around Stackpole headland, passes Rame Blow Hole, and continues on to Broadhaven Bay. There are excellent views of the rocky coastline, and north-east the ranks of red sandstone headlands extend to the horizon. Walking south-east there are views down on to tiny sandy coves which cannot be reached because of the steep limestone cliffs that tower above.

## 21 Pembrey Sands, Llanelli, Dyfed    OS Ref: SN3802

A marvellous beach with 7 miles (11km) of sand edged by a belt of sand dunes, known locally as Cefn Sidan. A 1990 Blue Flag winner, the beach falls within the Pembrey Country Park which also covers the extensive grassland and forest behind the dunes. The middle of the beach near the visitors' centre can be very busy on a warm sunny afternoon, but the extremities remain relatively quiet although they are often used for marine sports. Land yachting by the local club is well worth watching. Whether you want to relax on the sand and enjoy the clear views to the Gower on the horizon, or be more active, the country park has lots of facilities, both natural and man-made, to keep the whole family happy. Dogs are not permitted in the central ¾ mile (1.2km) section of the beach.

**Water quality** Beach monitored by the NRA and found to meet the EC standard for clean bathing water in 1990. One outfall serving 2,500 people discharges secondary treated sewage above high water mark.

**Litter** Flotsam and jetsam are washed up on this beach, but it is cleaned regularly.

**Bathing safety** Safe bathing. Lifeguards patrol the beach near the main access point from June to September.

**Access** Country park signposted from the A484. Board walks from the car parks lead through the dunes to the beach.

**Parking** Several car parks behind dunes with about 1,000 spaces.

**Toilets** One toilet block with facilities for the disabled.

**Food** Permanent kiosk with outdoor seating provides snacks and drinks.

**Seaside activities** Swimming, windsurfing, sailing and fishing. Pitch and putt golf, miniature and narrow gauge railways, adventure play area and dry ski slope. Events are regularly staged on the beach, for example sand sculpture competitions and treasure hunts.

**Wet weather alternatives** Kidwelly Castle and Industrial Museum, Pembrey Motor Sports centre. The Country Park Information Centre presents displays and exhibitions about the beach and country park (open all year).

**Wildlife and walks** There are four self-guided nature trails around the country park: woodland walk, floral trail, the yellow post walk (which includes the beach, dunes, forest and grassland), and the leisure route, suitable for wheelchairs and pushchairs. There is a permanent orienteering course, a programme of guided walks by the Ranger service and a nature quiz for children. Full information is available from the visitors' centre.

## 22 Rhossili Bay, Rhossili, West Glamorgan    OS Ref: SS4287

A spectacular 3 mile (5km) sweep of golden sands edges Rhossili Bay, stretching from Worms Head north to Burry Holms. The sands are shadowed by Rhossili Down; its grass slopes rise 600 feet (200m) above the beach and are popular with hang gliders. The southern end of the beach is ringed by steep cliffs which fall away northwards, where the Down is replaced by sand dunes. Worms Head, contrary to its name, is in fact an island, only linked to the mainland at low tide. The remains of a wreck can sometimes be seen at low tide. This lovely beach and the adjacent Down are owned by the National Trust.

**Water quality** Beach monitored by the NRA and found to meet the EC standard for clean bathing water in 1990. No sewage is discharged from this beach. Complaints of visible sewage have been received.

**Bathing safety** Safe bathing.

**Access** The B4247 leads to Rhossili village. There is a good path down the cliffs to the beach.

**Parking** Car park in village.

**Toilets** At the car park.

**Food** In the village.

**Seaside activities** Swimming, surfing and fishing.

**Wildlife and walks** Worms Head island and the adjacent stretch of coast are a National Nature Reserve. The limestone cliffs are rich in flora, and nesting birds can be seen on the nature trail. The limestone rocky shore of the Gower is one of the best examples in Britain. There is a network of paths on the headland and the adjoining Down where superb views can be obtained.

## 23 Port Eynon, West Glamorgan    OS Ref: SS4685

The rocky headland, Port Eynon Point, to the south shelters this sandy cove. The road from the Post Office leads down to the shore where a short section of newly built promenade gives access to the beach. On either side, high dunes back the wide, flat sands. High cliffs rise on either side of the bay with rocky outcrops at their base. On the eastern side of the bay stand the newly excavated remains of a salt house and workings. The wide, gently sloping sands are safe for bathing, and an ideal spot for building sand castles or playing cricket. A dog restriction bye-law is being considered.

**Water quality** Beach monitored by the NRA and found to meet the EC standard for clean bathing water in 1990. One outfall serving 1,200 people discharges primary and secondary treated sewage at low water mark off Overton Mere, east of Port Eynon Point.

**Litter** The beach is cleaned daily in summer and twice weekly in winter.

**Bathing safety** Warning notices indicate where it is safe to bathe. The beach is patrolled by lifeguards from May until September.

**Access** From the village a road leads to main access point where there is direct level access to the sands. Board walks and marked paths through dunes.

**Parking**  Car park behind dunes with 500+ spaces.

**Toilets**  At beach entry point.

**Food**  Shop and café at beach entrance.

**Seaside activities**  Swimming, surfing, windsurfing, diving, canoeing and fishing. A boat ramp leads from the car park to the tidal sand, providing easy access to the beach for boats.

**Wildlife and walks**  The South Gower Coast Nature Reserve stretches from Port Eynon to Worms Head at Rhossili, comprising 6 miles (10km) of rocky shore with faulted and folded grey limestone cliffs. There is a most interesting limestone flora, and nesting birds can be seen on some ledges. The limestone rocky shore of the Gower is one of the best examples in Britain. There is a footpath on to Port Eynon Point which climbs the cliff from the eastern end of the beach. The path leads to the Culver Hole, a deep cleft in the cliff which has been sealed off with a wall. There is a nature trail from the Rhossili Bay car park at the opposite end of the Nature Reserve.

## 24  Oxwich Bay, Oxwich, West Glamorgan    OS Ref: SS4986

A superb beach; from the steep tree-clad slopes of Oxwich Point a sweep of very fine soft sand backed by high dunes curves 2 miles (3km) round the bay to Great Tor – a stretch of towering rocky limestone cliffs. At low tide wide, flat sands are revealed. There is only one indentation into the crescent of sand, where the dunes are interrupted by the river Nicholaston Pill which meanders through marshland before crossing the beach. The main access is from Oxwich village where there are full facilities. The North Devon Coast can be seen on the horizon and in the evening it appears as a string of lights. At low tide Oxwich Bay links with Three Cliffs Bay to the east, giving 3 miles (5km) of continuous south-facing sands.

**Water quality**  Beach monitored by the NRA and found to meet the EC standard for clean bathing water in 1990. No sewage is discharged in the vicinity of this beach.

**Bathing safety**  Safe bathing; lifeguards from May to September.

**Access**  Narrow lanes lead to Oxwich village at the western end of the bay, and a car park next to the dunes faces directly on to the beach. There is a ramp for launching boats that could be used for easier access to the hard tidal sand. There is also access to the other end of the beach: a 15-minute walk from Penmaen along the footpath marked Tor Bay leads to a steep path down the cliff.

**Parking**  Large car park at Oxwich village, plus limited parking at Penmaen. In summer, National Trust car park (a farmer's field) at Penmaen.

**Toilets**  Two blocks at Oxwich car park.

**Food**  The Oxwich Bay Hotel which stands at the eastern end of the beach provides meals and bar snacks. There is a kiosk for refreshments at the car park, and cafés and a shop within the village.

***Seaside activities*** Swimming, windsurfing, sailing, diving, canoeing and fishing. A slipway across the sand enables boats to be launched and makes the bay popular with waterskiers. There is a windsurfing school on the beach.

***Wildlife and walks*** The Oxwich National Nature Reserve covers most of the beach, backshore and the Oxwich Point headland. The reserve includes a wide variety of habitats: sandy beach, dunes, salt- and freshwater marshes, cliffs, woods and grassland. There are marked footpaths throughout the reserve, and board walks give access to the dunes. A path west of the hotel leads through the trees past St Illtyd's Church to steps which climb to the headland and along the coast to Horton. There is an interpretative centre at the car park at Oxwich. At the western end there are barnacle- and mussel-encrusted rocks below the cliffs, and low tide reveals pools full of life.

## 25 Three Cliffs, Parkmill, Glamorgan   OS Ref: SS5488

The ruins of the Pennard Castle stand above the river valley which opens out to the eastern corner of this lovely sandy bay, ringed by steep cliffs. A three-pointed outcrop of rock curving out from the cliffs on the eastern side gives the bay its name. Wind-blown sand has built a series of burrows at the back of the beach. At low tide the river Pennard Pill completes a wide oxbow meander behind the burrows and then flows across the beach. Beyond the three cliffs there are wide, flat sands at low tide that merge with the sands of Oxwich Bay to the east.

***Water quality*** No sewage is discharged in the vicinity of this beach.

***Bathing safety*** It is dangerous to swim at middle tide near the three cliffs due to severe tidal conditions; notices at the entrance to the beach indicate where it is safe to bathe.

***Access*** From Penmaen a lane leads to a steep path from the cliff top down to the beach. Another path leads from Parkmill. Also reached from Oxwich Bay.

***Parking*** Car park at Penmaen, limited spaces at the post office, and a National Trust seasonal car park (a field) close by for summer use.

***Toilets*** None.

***Food*** None.

***Seaside activities*** Swimming, diving, surfing, fishing, windsurfing and canoeing from the beach.

***Wildlife and walks*** Footpaths criss-cross the bracken- and heather-covered headlands. They offer good views of the bay and adjacent Oxwich Bay.

## 26 Caswell Bay, Mumbles, West Glamorgan   OS Ref: SS5987

Another of the lovely bays to be found on the Gower. High rocky cliffs shadow this ⅔ mile (1km) of golden sand. There are only 55 yards (50m) of soft sand remaining at high tide but low tide reveals wide flat sands with rocky wave-cut platforms bounding either side of the beach. Beyond the rocks there is the small Brandy Cove which can only be reached down a very steep cliff path or over the rocky shore. There is easy access to the main beach: the road runs adjacent to the beach and a few steps lead down to the sand from a neat paved area with shop and refreshment facilities.

**Water quality** Beach monitored by the NRA and found to meet the EC standard for clean bathing water in 1990. One outfall serving 2,000 people discharges secondary treated sewage below low water mark in Brandy Cove. Both beaches will benefit from a proposed scheme for a long sea outfall in the vicinity.

**Bathing safety** Bathing requires care due to severe tidal conditions; the beach is patrolled by lifeguards from May to September.

**Access** From the road there are steps down on to the sand.

**Parking** Car park on the landward side of the access road with 500 spaces.

**Toilets** In the car park. Facilities for the disabled.

**Food** Shop, and refreshments available at the beach entrance.

**Seaside activities** Swimming, surfing, windsurfing, diving, canoeing and fishing.

**Wildlife and walks** A network of paths cover the wooded headlands above the beach and follow the Bishopston Valley inland from Pwlldu Bay.

## 27 Nash Point, Marcross, S. Glamorgan    OS Ref: SS9263

From the headland at Nash Point with its two lighthouses (one now disused) there are good views of the North Devon coast across the Bristol Channel and north-west to Swansea and the Gower. Paths lead down into a deep valley which opens out on to the beach. Impressive layered limestone cliffs, typical of this area of Heritage Coast, extend away in both directions. The sheer walls are very unstable so do not sit too close to them or attempt to climb on them. There is one small area of sand; otherwise the beach is composed of large flat rocks where the cliffs have been eroded. Although the main beach area has continuous access, the extremes of the beach can become tide traps as the beach becomes covered at high tide.

**Water quality** No sewage is discharged in the vicinity of this beach.

**Bathing safety** Bathing is very dangerous because of submerged rocks and tidal races. Do not climb on the cliffs.

**Access** There are steep paths from the headland car park.

**Parking** Parking in private field on headland adjacent to lighthouse.

**Toilets** None.

**Food** Car park kiosk sells ice cream.

**Seaside activities** Fishing.

**Wildlife and walks** There is a nature trail through the wooded valley.

# Northern Ireland

The coast of Northern Ireland remains largely undiscovered to those outside the province although its most famous feature, the Giant's Causeway, is one of the natural wonders of the world. It consists of huge basalt columns that disappear below the waves like a stairway to the depths. Rich in geology, the coastline is made up of a succession of bays and rugged headlands. There are the strands of County Londonderry with their popular holiday resorts, and the nine glens of County Antrim, each with a little beach nestling at its mouth. There are also the magnificent sea loughs of County Down: Belfast, Strangford and Carlingford, all rich in wildlife. Unfortunately, undiscovered does not necessarily mean unthreatened, and Strangford Lough in particular has been suffering from the effects of the scallop dredge in recent years. While this may not necessarily affect the quality of its beaches, the rape of such a beautiful and unique habitat should concern anyone who cares for our coasts and coastal life.

***Beaches receiving the European Blue Flag in 1990:***

Magilligan (Benone).

## Northern Ireland

1 Magilligan
(Benone)

Castlerock

3 Portrush

2 Portstewart

4 White Park Bay

Ballycastle

■ Coleraine

■ Londonderry

Ballygally

5 Brown's Bay

6 Helen's Bay

7 Crawfordsburn

Groomsport

Ballyholme

Millisle

Belfast ■

**f** = failed to meet EC standard for clean bathing water in 1990.
Numbered beaches appear in the following chapter.

### Coastal paths
The Ulster Way 450 miles (725km) in total; a series of paths,
many of which are coastal, circling the Province.

8 Tyrella

Newscastle **f**

9 Murlough

Warren Point

10 Cranfield

## The Golden List  *See page 25 for further details*

| Beach No on Map | Rating. The more stars the better. f=failed | Resort | Sewage outlets | Population discharging from outlet | Type of treatment | Discharge point relative to low water mark, unless otherwise stated. Distance given in metres | Remarks |
|---|---|---|---|---|---|---|---|
| 1 | **** | **Benone** | | | | | Miles of sandy beach. |
| | ** | **Castlerock** | 1 | 2,000 | Primary | At LWM | Sandy. |
| 2 | *** | **Portstewart** | 1 | 4,000+ | Raw | At LWM | Miles of sandy beach. |
| 3 | | **Portrush:** | 1 | 5,000 | Maceration | At LWM | Sandy. |
| | ** | **Curran Strand** | | | | | |
| | *** | **Mill Strand** | | | | | |
| | ** | **Ballycastle** | 1 | 3,700+ | Primary | At LWM | Sandy. Safe swimming. |
| 4 | | White Park Bay | | | | | Sandy, dunes. |
| 5 | ** | **Browns Bay** | | | | | Sandy. Safe swimming. |
| 6 | *** | **Helen's Bay** | 1 | 1,600 | Tidal tank | At LWM | Sandy. Safe swimming. |
| 7 | *** | **Crawfordsburn** | 1 | 200+ | Secondary | Discharges to stream | Sandy. |
| | ** | **Ballyholme** | | | | | Sandy. |
| | *** | **Groomsport** | 1 | 40,000+ | Screened | At LWM | Sandy. |
| | *** | **Millisle** | 1 | 1,000+ | Primary | At LWM | Sandy. |
| 8 | **** | **Tyrella** | | | | | Sandy and very safe beach. |
| 9 | | Murlough | | | | | Sandy. |
| | f ** | **Newcastle** | 2 | 5,000+ | Raw | At LWM | Sandy. New STW now in operation. |
| 10 | **** *** | **Cranfield** | | | | | Long sandy south-facing beach. |

## 1 Benone, Limavady, Co. Londonderry   OS Ref: C7037

From Magilligan Point at the entrance to Lough Foyle, 7 miles (11km) of firm flat golden sand stretch east to the cliffs at Down Hill. Dunes fringe the wide curving beach, with sand hills covering the peninsula. The eastern end of the beach is backed by 750 foot (225m) cliffs, which are themselves shadowed by a heather-clad land plateau and the Binevenagh Mountains. This beautiful beach was awarded the Blue Flag for the first time in 1990. The new leisure complex provides excellent facilities close to the beach. If you prefer to get away from the sand castles and games, the miles of sand offer solitude with only the sea and sky for company. The 110 yards (100m) of sand virtually disappear at high tide, covered by waters which were only one of a handful to achieve a four-star Good Beach Guide grade. Dogs must be under supervision and on a lead.

**Water quality** Beach monitored by the DoE and found to meet the EC standard for clean bathing water in 1990. No sewage is discharged in the vicinity of the beach.

**Litter** The beach is cleaned regularly.

**Bathing safety** Bathing from some areas of the beach is unsafe due to currents; notices indicate where not to bathe. The beach is patrolled by lifeguards from June to September.

**Access** It is a short walk from the car park on to the beach at Benone.

**Parking** There is a car park behind the dunes with 300 spaces. Car parking is also permitted on the sands but should be avoided on any beach.

**Toilets** Public toilets at beach and also facilities at the leisure complex.

**Food** Refreshments are available at the leisure complex.

**Seaside activities** Swimming, surfing, windsurfing, sailing and fishing from the beach. Golf course, tennis and children's activity area are available at the leisure complex. A concrete ramp to the beach allows access to launch boats.

**Wet weather alternatives** Benone Tourist Complex.

**Wildlife and walks** It is claimed that up to 120 different species of shell have been found on Benone beach in one day, and an outdoor field studies recreation centre at Magilligan reflects the fact that the whole area is excellent for those interested in flora and fauna. 140 acres (56.6 hectares) of the sand dune system around the Martello Tower on Magilligan Point form a Nature Reserve and there is restricted access to protect this fragile environment. The coastline is the limit of the North Derry Area of Outstanding Natural Beauty. Inland, the Binevenagh mountains are good for hill walking and afford good views of the coast.

## 2 The Strand, Portstewart, Co. Londonderry   OS Ref: C8338

This is a small, quiet resort compared to its near neighbour, Portrush. The town, set around its harbour, is located on a promontory. To the west are 2 miles (3km) of beautiful sandy beach, backed by 185 acres (75 hectares) of dunes owned by the National Trust. The flat sands are safe for swimming and good for fishing. There is good cliff scenery extending east towards Portrush, and the North Antrim Coast Path follows the cliff top.

*Water quality* Beach monitored by the DoE and found to meet the EC standard for clean bathing water in 1990. One outfall serving over 4000 people discharges untreated raw sewage at the low water mark.

*Litter* The beach is cleaned regularly.

*Bathing safety* Beware of currents that may affect bathing safety; the beach is patrolled by lifeguards during July and August.

*Parking* On the beach at low tide, but motorcycles are not permitted.

*Toilets* One for men and one for women.

*Food* One confectionery shop at the beach entrance.

*Seaside activities* Swimming, surfing, windsurfing, sailing, diving and fishing. Two golf courses. Boat trips from the harbour along the Causeway.

*Wildlife and walks* The dunes support a wide variety of fauna and flora, and offer attractive walks through the dunes from the beach to the estuarine shore of the river Bann. Bar Mouth, on the Castlerock shore at the mouth of the Bann, is a good birdwatching area noted for unusual passage migrants. The hide will accommodate wheelchair-users.

## 3 West Bay Strand, Portrush, Co. Antrim   OS Ref: C8740

Portrush is the largest seaside holiday centre in Northern Ireland. This Victorian and Edwardian resort is located on rocky Ramore Head and has all the facilities and amusements that might be expected of a traditional holiday town. From its elevated position there are excellent views along the coast to Donegal in the west and Rathlin Island in the east. A low sea wall bounds the soft sands of the west bay which curves gently south from the small harbour. The promenade which runs along the sea wall is on two levels separated by grassy banks. The larger East or Curran Strand is also backed by a sea wall but this gives way to dunes and a links golf course.

*Water quality* Beach monitored by the DoE and found to meet the EC standard for clean bathing water in 1990. One outfall serving 5,000 people discharges macerated sewage at low water mark.

*Bathing safety* Beware of currents that may affect bathing safety. The beach is patrolled by lifeguards during July and August.

*Access* Steps and a ramp from the promenade.

*Parking* 150-200 spaces at West Strand, 250-300 at East Strand.

**Toilets** For men and women at each end of West Strand and on East Strand.

**Food** Promenade café.

**Seaside activities** Swimming, surfing, windsurfing, sailing, diving and fishing. Boat trips from the harbour.

**Wet weather alternatives** 'Water World' alongside the old harbour has a swimming pool complete with flumes and jacuzzis. Its facilities include an aquarium and light entertainments. Amusements.

**Wildlife and walks** A section of the rocky shore on the eastern side of Ramore Head between the Portandoo Harbour and Bath road is a Nature Reserve noted for its fossil ammonites. Adjacent to the reserve is the Portrush Countryside Centre, an interpretative centre which can provide further information about the reserve and surrounding area. East of Portrush there is superb cliff scenery, including towering limestone cliffs eroded by the waves to form arches and caves. The white cliffs are replaced by the brown basalt which forms the famous Giant's Causeway further east. The coastal path follows the clifftop to the picturesque ruin of Dunluce Castle which offers superb views along the coastline (the castle is closed on Sunday mornings and on Mondays during the winter).

## 4 White Park Bay, Portbradden, Co. Antrim  OS Ref: D0245

Stacks and rocky outcrops stud this magnificent bay owned and managed by the National Trust. The long curve of flat white sand is backed by dunes and circled by white chalk cliffs. On the western shore of the bay the whitewashed houses of Portbradden sit below the cliffs. The village's tiny church, St Gothan's, is the smallest in Ireland, a mere 11 feet by 6 feet (3.3m by 1.8m). Portbradden marks the junction between the chalk cliffs and the brown basalt of the Dunseverick and Causeway coast. The stretch of coast from Gid Point, the western boundary of White Park Bay, to Benbane Head is the Dunseverick Coast. The dipping rocks and basalt columns are less well-defined than those of the Giant's Causeway beyond Benbane Head. However, the series of rugged headlands and small indented bays, with the cliff top ruins of Dunseverick Castle and the numerous offshore stacks, make this section of quieter coastline extremely attractive. The bay is popular with naturalists, for nearly every type of maritime vegetation can be found along this section of coastline, including strand line, salt marsh, cliff grassland, maritime scrub and heath. There is a wide variety of bird and marine life to be seen.

**Water quality** No sewage is discharged in the vicinity of this beach.

**Litter** The beach is cleaned regularly.

**Bathing safety** Strong currents make bathing dangerous.

**Access** There is car parking to the east of Templastragh on the A2 and on a minor road to Portbradden on the eastern shore of the bay. There is also a path from Ballintoy, 1½ miles (2.4km) east of the bay. During July and August an open-topped bus makes the journey between Coleraine and Bushmills with stops at Portstewart, Portrush, Portballintrae and the Causeway.

**Parking** Car park near the youth hostel east of Templastragh and on the cliff top near Dunseverick Harbour.

**Toilets** Near car park.

**Food** In village.

**Seaside activities** Swimming and fishing.

**Wildlife and walks** There is a 1 mile (1.6km) nature trail at White Park Bay, and a leaflet guide is available from the National Trust shop at the Giant's Causeway. The North Antrim Coast Path follows the cliffs west of the bay. It skirts Dunseverick harbour and castle and continues beyond Benbane Head to the Giant's Causeway. 40,000 basalt columns, formed by cooling lava, create the unique features of the Causeway. It has been estimated that somewhere in the region of 500,000 people view the Causeway each year. The main access point for those not wanting to walk the 5 miles (8km) to Benbane Head from White Park Bay is at Causeway Head off the B146 north of Bushmills. There is parking and a National Trust Information Centre. The centre houses an exhibition of the history, geology, fauna and flora of the area. During the summer a bus will take visitors from the centre to the top of the Grand Causeway. To appreciate this magnificent scenery to the full, a walk to Benbane Head is recommended. There is a path along the base of the cliffs passing the Grand Causeway, and other features include the Organ, the Amphitheatre, the Wishing Well and Lovers' Leap. The return journey can be made along the cliff top. 2½ miles (4km) along the coast path east of White Park Bay is the Carrick-a-rede rope bridge. The fragile swinging bridge spans a 60 foot (18m) wide by 80 foot (24m) deep ravine which separates Carrick-a-rede island from the mainland. The bridge is constructed each May by fishermen to provide access to their salmon fisheries. The walk across and back is not for the faint-hearted! A National Trust car park at Larrybane gives closer access.

## 5 Brown's Bay, Islandmagee, Whitehead, Co. Antrim    OS Ref. D4303

Brown's Bay is at the northern end of Island Magee, a long peninsula which bounds Lough Larne. At the northern end of the peninsula two headlands, Barrs Point and Skernaghan Point, frame a deeply indented bay. A ⅔ mile (1km) crescent of sandy beach with rocky outcrops, containing numerous rockpools, is revealed by the falling tide. The beach is easily accessible and is a good amenity beach, suitable for a family day by the sea.

**Water quality** Beach monitored by the DoE and found to meet the EC standard for clean bathing water in 1990. No sewage is discharged in the vicinity of the beach.

**Litter** The beach is cleaned regularly by the local council.

**Bathing safety** Safe bathing.

**Access** The B90 circles the northern half of Island Magee and runs parallel with the bay. A sea wall and promenade edge the sand.

**Parking** Council car park with 124 spaces.

**Toilets** Public toilets at car park.

**Food** Nearby shop for confectionery and ice cream.

**Seaside activities** Swimming, windsurfing, diving and fishing. Golf course.

**Wildlife and walks** There are local walks on the headlands at either side of the bay.

## 6 Helen's Bay, Bangor, Co. Down   OS Ref: J4683

This small sandy beach is sheltered by headlands at either end. From the Horse Rock below Grey Point the beach stretches to Quarry Point in the east and is backed by a stone promenade and a golf course on the grassland which slopes up from the promenade. Grey Point with its disused fort commands an excellent view of Belfast Lough and the Antrim coast. A wooded avenue leads from Grey Point 2½ miles (4km) inland. It was once a private carriageway built by the first Marquis of Dufferin and Ava, after whose mother, Helen Sheridan, the bay is named.

**Water quality** Beach monitored by the DoE and found to meet the EC standard for clean bathing water in 1990. One outfall serving 1,600 people discharges sewage through a tidal tank at low water mark.

**Litter** The beach is cleaned regularly.

**Bathing safety** Safe bathing.

**Access** Helen's Bay Halt is ⅔ mile (1km) away and the car park is only 55 yards (50m) from the beach.

**Parking** There is a car park at the west end of the bay.

**Toilets** In the car park, including facilities for the disabled.

**Food** None.

**Seaside activities** Swimming and golf course.

**Wildlife and walks** The beach lies on the North Down Coastal Path. To the east is Crawfordsburn beach and country park. Seals and a variety of seabirds are just some of the wildlife of interest in this area.

## 7 Crawfordsburn, Bangor, Co. Down   OS Ref: J4783

Crawfordsburn and Helen's Bay are both within very easy reach of Belfast, by road along the A2 and also by train. As a result they can be very popular in summer. The 550 yard (500m) sandy beach at Crawfordsburn is divided in two by the stream that flows from the glen behind the sands. The beach and the glen fall within the Crawfordsburn Country Park. On the right bank of the stream stands the house of the Scottish family who settled here in the 17th century and gave the bay their name. The house is now a hospital and its extensive lawns are a caravan park. For those wishing to escape from the busy part of the beach, Swinerley Bay to the east is more secluded.

**Water quality** Beach monitored by the DoE and found to meet the EC standard for clean bathing water in 1990. One outfall serving 200+ people discharges macerated and secondary treated sewage to the stream flowing across the beach.

**Bathing safety** Safe bathing.

**Access** Crawfordsburn Halt is ¾ mile (1.2km) from the beach along the road through the country park. The country park car park is 440 yards (400m) from the beach.

**Parking** Large car park in country park.

**Toilets** In the car park (with facilities for the disabled).

**Food** Café.

**Seaside activities** Swimming, golf course. Orienteering courses held in the country park.

**Wildlife and walks** The stream from Crawfordsburn village flows through a steep-sided valley, wooded with some exotic species. Below the village, it descends to a waterfall and flows under one of the railway viaduct's 80 foot (24m) high arches. Marked footpaths provide circular walks of varying lengths. Information about the park, including its walks and wildlife, is available from the interpretative centre. The beach is part of the North Down Coastal Path and also forms part of the Ulster Way. It follows the coast from Hollywood, passes through the glen to the Clandeboyne Estate and on to Newtownards.

## 8 Tyrella Beach, Clough, Co. Down    OS Ref: J4535

Situated in Dundrum Bay, Tyrella is a 3 mile (5km) stretch of unspoilt sandy beach facing south and backed by dunes. The clean, shallow water and safe bathing make this a very popular beach on sunny Sundays in the holiday season: at other times it is blissfully quiet. There are six golf courses within a 12 mile (20km) radius of the beach, including the excellent Royal County Down. This beach gained a four-star Good Beach Guide grading for the second time in 1990.

**Water quality** Beach monitored by the DoE and found to meet the EC standard for clean bathing water in 1990. No sewage is discharged in the vicinity of this beach.

**Bathing safety** Safe bathing.

201

**Access** The A2 between Clough and Killough passes directly behind the beach.

**Parking** At present, some cars do park on the beach: this is a practice that the Marine Conservation Society strongly disapproves of. Alternative parking should be found.

**Toilets** On the beach.

**Food** Snack vans visit the site.

**Seaside activities** Swimming.

**Wet weather alternatives** Leisure centres at Newcastle and Downpatrick, each about 6½ miles (10km) away.

**Wildlife and walks** The Murlough Nature Reserve is close by – a dune system with plenty of wildlife and vegetation. There are signs of man's early habitation of the area: castles, dolmens (ancient cairns) and some of the earliest Christian remains (a result of St Patrick landing in the area). The Ulster Way goes past the beach.

### 9 Murlough, Dundrum Bay, Co. Down    OS Ref: J4033

A long, broad, sandy bay lying at the foot of impressive 3,000 foot (1,000m) mountains, 'where the mountains of Mourne sweep down to the sea'. The beach and dunes extend over 4 miles (6km) northwards from the coastal resort of Newcastle to the Dundrum channel which connects Dundrum Inner Bay with the open sea. At the northernmost end some 2½ miles (4km) of beach and 700 acres (283 hectares) of sand dunes are owned and managed by the National Trust as a National Nature Reserve. The southern dunes are owned by the Royal County Down Golf Club. A narrow shingle beach lies between the wide sandy bay and the ⅔ mile (1km) wide sand dunes. The beach has long been popular with the holiday maker, walker and naturalist. The flat sands are safe for swimming.

**Water quality** No sewage is discharged in the vicinity of this beach.

**Litter** The beach is cleaned regularly.

**Bathing safety** Safe bathing.

**Access** Access from the main A24 Belfast to Newcastle road, 2 miles (3km) from Newcastle. Car parking available at Dundrum and Slidderyford Bridge, where there are two entrances. Access to the beach is on foot across the dunes by board walks. Tracks are suitable for wheelchair-users.

**Parking** A small car park for eight cars at Dundrum. At Slidderyford there are some 600 car spaces on the road side, using the hard shoulder, or 350 spaces in an off-road car park signposted Murlough Nature Reserve.

**Toilets** Toilets (with facilities for the disabled) at the car park, and at the Slidderyford entrance.

**Food** None.

*Seaside activities* Swimming, fishing, windsurfing. Other facilities at Newcastle, 2 miles (3km) away.

*Wet weather alternatives* Various facilities at Newcastle.

*Wildlife and walks* The beach lies on the Ulster Way, which continues through Newcastle and the Mournes to the south, and through Dundrum village and along a National Trust coastal path around Dundrum Inner Bay to the north. There are extensive paths through the nature reserve. Guided walks are organised by National Trust staff in the summer. The reserve is noted for its geographical development, its archaeological history and its rich variety of fauna and flora. The vegetation of the dunes includes strand line, dune grasslands, dune heath, scrub and woodland. Seals may be seen in summer months. Both Dundrum Inner and Outer bays are noted for their wintering sea duck, waterfowl and waders. A birdwatching hide is situated on the Inner Bay shore near Dundrum. There is a small interpretative centre situated in the car park. The imposing Norman castle at Dundrum gives magnificent views over the area.

## 10 Cranfield, Kilkeel, Co. Down   OS Ref: J2611

An Area of Outstanding Natural Beauty and adjoining an area of Special Scientific Interest, Cranfield Bay is situated at the entrance to Carlingford Lough. The south-facing sand and shingle beach is backed by dunes and has the magnificent Mourne mountains as a backdrop. The beach stretches from the rocky outcrops at Greencastle Point to the boulders at Cranfield Point. There are good views across the Lough to Ballagan Point and away down the coast beyond Dundalk Bay. The water is some of the cleanest you will find in the UK – in 1990 it achieved Good Beach Guide four-star status at one of the monitoring sites.

*Water quality* Beach monitored by the DoE and found to meet the EC standard for clean bathing water in 1990. No sewage is discharged in the vicinity of the beach.

*Bathing safety* Safe bathing.

*Access* A road leads from Cranfield to the car park, from which there is a short walk across the grass to the beach.

*Parking* Car park with 150 spaces.

*Toilets* Public conveniences.

*Food* Hotel, two cafés and three shops.

*Seaside activities* Swimming, windsurfing, diving, waterskiing and fishing. Beach entertainment and band concerts. Golf course.

*Wet weather alternatives* Analong cornmill and marine park.

*Wildlife and walks* Mourne mountains are excellent for walking, with the Silent Valley Reserve just north of Kilkeel. A 3,000 million gallon (14,000 million litre) reservoir is set among the peaks and there is some fine parkland on the approaches to the dam.

# *Index*

# *Join the Fight to Save our Seas*

Yes, I want to join the Marine Conservation Society.
Please enrol me as a (tick box)

Annual Member £12☐    Family Member £16 ☐    Life Member £200 ☐
   (Overseas members add £4 a year postage. Institutions may join for £30 a year.)

NAME _____

ADDRESS _____

_____

I enclose a cheque for Membership fee        £
                       Donation (if you wish)  £
                       Total                   £

☐  Please send me details of how to make my subscription worth nearly £3
    more with a Deed of Covenant and how to pay by banker's order.
(please tick)
Send this form to:    **Marine Conservation Society**
                      9 Gloucester Road
                      Ross-on-Wye HR9 5BU

# *Keep the Good Beach Guide Up to Date*

Use of a guide such as this relies on the Marine Conservation Society being
   made aware of any changes at the beaches listed. If you come across a
   change or discrepancy at a site, or disagree with any of our comments, please
   let us know.

I have a potential alteration for the next edition of the Good Beach Guide:

Page number:

Name of beach:

Alteration/comment:

☐  Beach survey forms are also available for any interested volunteers who
   wish to help expand our beach database. Please tick the box if you would like
   to be sent copies of the survey forms.

S.S CHEEMA

3 cleeve way
wellingborough
0483361649K

S 374 X AL.

Virtual Vision.

AMBECARS
9/10N